The Greatest Raid of All

'Peter' Lucas Phillips was born in 1897 and educated at St Lawrence College and King's College, London University. In the First World War he served in the Royal Artillery in France and Flanders, becoming a Major before he was twenty-one. During the Second World War he fought in the campaigns of Dunkirk, the Western Desert and Italy. He became a Brigadier and was awarded the MC, the OBE and the Croix de Guerre. He was the author of several successful war books, including *Cockleshell Heroes*, *The Greatest Raid of All*, *Escape of the Amethyst*, *Alamein* and *Springboard to Victory*.

Lucas Phillips was a passionate gardener and also wrote several books on gardening. He died in 1984.

D1114308

C. E. LUCAS PHILLIPS
OBE MC
Foreword by The Earl Mountbatten of Burma, KG

THE GREATEST RAID OF ALL

PAN GRAND STRATEGY SERIES

PAN BOOKS

First published 1958 by William Heinemann Ltd

This edition published 2000 by Pan Books
an imprint of Pan Macmillan Ltd
Pan Macmillan, 20 New Wharf Road, London N1 9RR
Basingstoke and Oxford
Associated companies throughout the world
www.panmacmillan.com

ISBN 0 330 48070 7

3 5 7 9 8 6 4 2

A CIP catalogue record for this book is available from
the British Library.

Typeset by SX Composing DTP, Rayleigh, Essex
Printed and bound in Great Britain by
Mackays of Chatham plc, Chatham, Kent

CONTENTS

List of Photographs

Photographs by permission of the Imperial War Museum

List of Figures in the Text

Symbols Used

- ⚓ 20 millimetre gun
- ⚓⁴ Quadruple 20 millimetre
- ○— 40 millimetre gun
- ○— Heavy anti-aircraft battery (four guns)
- □— Coast defence battery (four guns)
- ○< Searchlight

Author's Note

'Having been associated with practically all combined operations, from two-man raids to the planning for Normandy, I have no hesitation in saying that the finest and most profitable of the lot was your raid on St Nazaire.'

Thus Lord Louis Mountbatten, as he then was, wrote to Lieutenant-Colonel Charles Newman after Newman's release from captivity in 1945. Yet, of the many exploits of the war, of which this was perhaps the most daring and brilliant of all, few have received so little attention from the investigator. Indeed, no account, official or otherwise, has yet been published which is complete and wholly accurate, even the official casualty numbers being at fault. Captain Robert Ryder's little book, *The Attack on St Nazaire*, gives an excellent short narrative and still better appreciation, but it is surprising that no full-dress account has yet been written.

The book now presented, accordingly, is an attempt to fill the gap and it will have failed in its purpose if it does not now show that the St Nazaire Raid shines with a lustre equal to that of the most brilliant of any small exploit of warfare. Small in numbers, but large in achievement. For the gallant 600 who sailed up the Loire on that cloudy March night in 1942, with guns to right and left and ahead of them, achieved a purpose out of all proportion to their small number and of an extent that was not fully realized until after the war was over. It would be inappropriate to repeat here the comparison made with Zeebrugge in the main text, but it is very apt to quote the verdict of Admiral of the Fleet Sir Charles Forbes in his introduction to Captain Ryder's book.

'Without in any way wishing to belittle Zeebrugge,' wrote Sir Charles, 'one should now talk of St Nazaire instead.'

These things will appear. On the other hand, no attempt has been made to minimize the less satisfactory features, such as the reluctance of the Admiralty to provide the essential ships, the unhappy collapse of the bombing support programme, the loss of command of the battle through failure of wireless communications and the severe, indeed the heart-breaking, losses among the vulnerable motor launches.

As far as possible, this book has been written entirely from original evidence, British, German and French. No existing account has been taken for granted. In this pursuit I have received generous help from Amphibious Warfare Headquarters and from Lieutenant-Commander P. K. Kemp and Commander M. G. Saunders (particularly for German records) of the Historical Section of the Admiralty. The French Embassy has also courteously assisted and the Librarian of the Imperial War Museum has expertly excavated in her rich soil. In addition to a large store of original documents, I have received personal narratives from fifty-three British and eleven German officers and men who participated in the planning or execution of the Raid, and in most instances these informants have seen and concurred in those portions of the manuscript that concerned them.

To all these informants, many of whom have put up with much cross-examination, I am very much indebted. For reasons of length, I have been most regretfully obliged to omit a large wealth of detail, particularly regarding the River Battle, the escapes and the preliminary planning, with which they have so generously supplied me.

I cannot possible enumerate, as I should like, all these contributors to the store of information, but for specially valuable or continuous help at many stages I owe particular thanks to Admiral of the Fleet the Earl Mountbatten of Burma, Lieutenant-Colonel S. W. Chant, OBE, MC (who has been a particularly valuable and resourceful aide in the hunt for information), Captain S. H. Beattie, RC, RN, Major R. K. Montgomery, MC, RN, Dr P. J. C. Dark, Major W. O. Copland, DSO, Mr R. O. C. Swayne, MC, Commander E. A. Burt, DSC, Mr R. C. M. V. Wynn, DSC, Commander D. M. C. Curtis, DSC, Mr T. W. Boyd, DSO, Mr G. R. Wheeler, MM, Major Anthony Terry, MC, Mr John Coste, DSC, and Mr I. L. Maclagan. For the planning and preparation I have been critically guided by Vice-Admiral J. Hughes-Hallett, CB, DSO, MP, Major-General J. C. Haydon, CB, OBE, DSO, Colonel R. D. Q. Henriques, CBE, and Wing Commander The Marquess de Casa Maury, as well as by Earl Mountbatten himself. Mr H. E. Hewett, Secretary of the St Nazaire Society, aptly described by Earl Mountbatten as 'the most exclusive society in the world', has helped me to make contact with a great number of the gallant 'Charioteers' in many parts of the world.

Among German informants, I am chiefly indebted to Kapitän zur See C. C. Mecke, Herr Edo Dieckmann, Dr Lothar Burhenne, Fregattenkapitän F. K. Paul, Kapitän zur See Moritz Schmidt and Dr Herbert Sohler.

Above all, however, I am in debt to Captain R. E. D. Ryder, VC, and Lieutenant-Colonel A. C. Newman, VC, OBE, TD, DL, for their continuous guidance at all stages and for their constructive criticisms of my draft manuscript throughout. Without their help the story of St Nazaire could not have been told.

From this mass of detailed evidence, official and personal, often contradictory, often incomplete or uncertain, I have done my best to give a true representation of the facts, weighing the evidence in the scales of judgment as best one can. In personal and minor detail, however, some points still remain indecisive, for in all the crowded and stirring events of a close action it is not always easy for the participants themselves to be entirely certain of what has occurred. If some small errors have crept in from such causes, this narrative will nonetheless, I hope, stand as witness to an aggregation of deeds of individual heroism that has seldom been excelled.

The title of the book is taken from Hilary St George Saunders, historian of the Commandos, in his book *The Green Beret*.

The ranks throughout are those appropriate to the time.

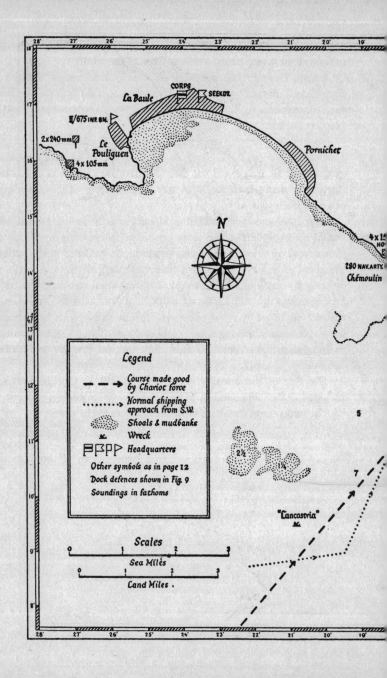

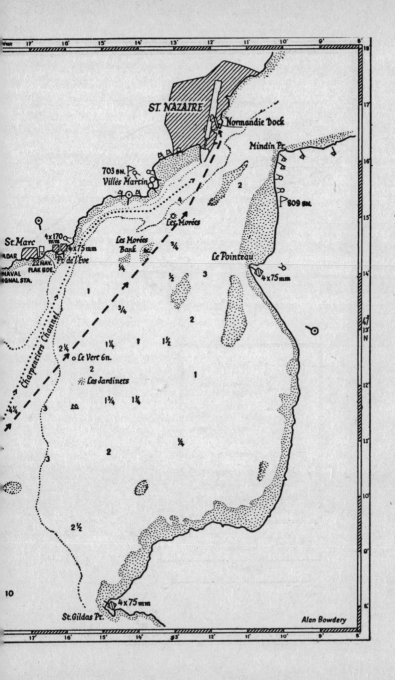

ST. NAZAIRE

Normandie Dock

Mindin Pt.

703 BN.
Villès Martin

809 BN.

Les Morées

St. Marc
4 x 170 mm
4 x 75 mm
Pt. de l'Eve
22 NAV.
FLAK BDE.
RADAR
NAVAL
SIGNAL STA.

Les Morées
Bank
¾

Le Pointeau

¼

4 x 75 mm

Charpentiers Channel

2¼
o Le Vert 6n.

2
Les Jardinets

4½

½

2½

10

4 x 75 mm
St. Gildas Pt.

Alan Bowdery

Foreword

By Admiral of the Fleet the Earl Mountbatten of Burma, KG

Of all the operations with which I was concerned in the late war, the successful raid on the battleship dock at St Nazaire is perhaps the one I am most proud to have been associated with. It was one of those actions which can only be attempted precisely because it must appear, to the enemy, to be absolutely impossible to undertake; and for this reason alone it required courage and determination of a quite unusual order to carry out. What is more, this complicated operation had been planned in greatest detail; and once the forces were committed each individual small ship and each little group of soldiers had to fight it out, guided by orders received at home, but entirely in the light of their own initiative.

I know of no other case in naval or military annals of such effective damage being inflicted so swiftly with such economy of force. For in less than half an hour from the moment the *Campbeltown* rammed, all the commando's chief demolition objectives were successfully achieved. This brilliant attack was carried out at night, under a vicious enemy fire, by a mere handful of men, who achieved, with certainty and precision, what the heaviest bombing raid or naval bombardment might well have failed to do. The great Normandie Dock was put out of action and was made useless to every kind of ship – and, indeed, was to remain unusable for the next ten years or so. The Germans were prevented from being able to use the only dock on the Atlantic seaboard to which their great battleship *Tirpitz* could go, to repair damage sustained in raiding the Atlantic; in fact, this effectively prevented them from operating her against our convoy routes altogether. Thus the main object of the raid was brilliantly achieved.

No fewer than five VCs were won at St Nazaire, out of a total force of

611 – surely by far the highest proportion of VCs ever awarded for a single operation; and this is the measure of the heroism of all who took part in that magnificent enterprise.

1. WHAT THE FRENCHMEN SAW

Forty minutes before midnight on 27 March 1942, while a thunderstorm was sounding to the north and east and lightning flashed upon a clouded sky, the cry of the air-raid sirens roused from their sleep the citizens of the French port of St Nazaire. They roused also the German garrison who held so tight a grip on a port vital to the Nazi purpose. The crews of anti-aircraft guns and searchlights took post. Another RAF raid was imminent.

A few minutes later, as the German radar station at Le Croisie picked up the leading bombers, the long, chill fingers of the searchlights began to probe the sky. Very soon every window in the town was shaking as the German guns opened fire in a cannonade more violent than any heard before and fountains of red and green tracer were shooting up into the vault, silencing the distant thunder and outshining the lightning of the sky.

The same spectacle, vivid as distant fireworks in the wide night, was seen from far out to sea by a flotilla of little British ships which, unknown to either French or Germans, was moving steadily in upon a mission that was soon to shake the enemy defences to their foundation and to bring to the patriot French a surge of hope and a bitter trial.

To the ears of the French and Germans, as well as to those of the little force at sea, there came from above the clouds, mingled with the hum of German fighter aircraft, the deep drone of heavy bombers from the island fortress of Britain 250 miles away. They came mainly from the north-west, but some from the east, dipping into the clouds as their rear gunners detected the German fighters, climbing out again when ice formed upon their wings. Yet no hurricane of bombs resulted. Indeed, only four aircraft released their missiles, one at a time and at long intervals;

but a fire was started in the Forge de l'Ouest, hard by the great dock.

On the ground men listened in some puzzlement as the Whitleys circled and manoeuvred, without bombing. Kapitän zur See Mecke, commanding the German 22nd Naval Flak Brigade, which manned the anti-aircraft guns, listening at his headquarters at St Marc and noting the extraordinary manoeuvres of the British aircraft on his radar screen, became more and more suspicious that these manoeuvres were merely a blind for 'some devilry' not yet apparent, and he communicated his suspicions to all command posts of the German army, navy and air force.

Shortly, however, the raiding aircraft one by one turned away, their engines fading to a whisper in the night, though from time to time others could faintly be heard very high up above the clouds. No object whatever seemed to have been achieved; except that the fire in the Forge de l'Ouest continued to burn fiercely. The guns ceased fire, the searchlights were switched off and an uneasy quiet settled upon the town and the broad estuary.

Neither French nor Germans knew that this strange behaviour of the British was mainly due to humanitarian reasons. For the thunderclouds so obscured the pilots' vision that they were unable to make out with certainty the German-occupied docks, which were their objective, and, rather than bring avoidable peril to French civilians, they abandoned their mission, as they had been told to do, with results of which we shall presently be the spectators.

Thus Frenchmen and Germans alike listened expectantly for the All Clear to permit them to relax and sleep again. The darkened town, the docks and the railway yards lay still and silent under the quilted clouds. Yet no All Clear sounded. Gradually, with an irony that none could see, the clouds that had impeded the bombers cleared away at their lower levels and a full moon – the moon that would have guided them surely to their mark – shone through the higher nimbus, but shone too late, upon the naked roofs, upon the false peacefulness of the wide estuary and upon the monstrous concrete kennels where lurked the U-boats of the German 7th and 6th Submarine Flotillas. Still no All Clear. No one saw a German patrol boat winking an urgent signal of alarm away at the mouth of the river.

The patient Nazairiens in their cellars and shelters looked inquiringly at each other. Those who had their beds below turned back to sleep. The Germans who had no action stations and the hands from the German ships in harbour, in their separate shelters, fidgeted to return to their bunks and billets. The maintenance hands of the submarines loitered secure within the massive protection of their concrete roof. But the men who manned the guns and searchlights remained at their posts, maintaining, in accordance with new orders that they had received from Mecke, a posture of readiness to react instantly to the totally unexpected events that were to follow.

At 1.30 in the morning of the 28th, some dwellers in the moonlit Boulevard Wilson, which runs along the sea front south-westwards from the docks, and in which the German Hafen-kommandant had his headquarters, beheld to their astonishment what appeared to be two torpedo boats and a dozen motor launches riding up the estuary, illuminated from both banks of the river by a concentration of searchlights that flung their beams, not upwards as they were accustomed to do, but horizontally upon the sea. They saw a German *Sperrbrecher*, moored in the roads, wink an urgent signal lamp to the advancing flotilla and, apparently receiving no answer, let fly the strikers of her quick-firing guns. They saw the German naval troops who were in their air-raid shelters run out from them to fetch their weapons, lie down in the boulevard and open fire with small arms and machine-guns upon the flotilla, which vigorously replied.

Thus, without warning of sirens, the Nazairiens heard the artillery break out again on all hands – at first intermittently, hesitantly and with uncertain note; then, after a few minutes, in a violent crescendo. 'A sudden tumult burst.' The blast of guns was now accompanied by the new, more menacing, sound of shells bursting, bursting at ground level very close at hand. To this was quickly added the sharp rattle of machine-guns. Frenchmen who had served their time with the colours could not fail to interpret the notes of this violent orchestra. No air-raid this; St Nazaire was being assaulted from the sea.

The listening French, excitement beginning to mount in their hearts, then heard great explosions, as of mines or very heavy charges, shake the house. Débris of all sorts spattered down in the streets and on the roofs. Those who could look safely from their windows, or come cautiously to their doors, saw to their astonishment the flotilla of motor launches, in double column of line-ahead, great fins of water splaying out from their bows as they moved at speed, swing into a dazzling concentration of search-lights in the harbour mouth, through which the streams of coloured tracer, like shuttles in an infernal loom, darted in all directions. To this concentration of light under the dim, cold moon was added a series of fierce yellow-tongued conflagrations as, one after another, the motor launches, their naked petrol tanks hit, burst into flames, with violent explosions. The sea itself was on fire as the spilled petrol spread across the surface and clouds of black smoke drifted across the pool of light. 'The very sky was alight with these conflagrations, and that of the Forge de l'Ouest continued to rage.'

For about an hour the Nazairiens listened to this violent clamour. 'The confusion was total.' It then gradually assumed a somewhat different note, as, one by one, a few of the launches – so very few – turned their bows to the open sea and, at full speed, once more ran the gauntlet of the German batteries. Last scene of all, to those who could watch, was that of a lone gunboat, every gun and light concentrated upon her in a tumult of gun flashes, darting tracers, and shellfire bursting into fountains of water, miraculously escaping, surely under the hand of Providence, through a cloud of her own white smoke.

The gunfire slackened, limited to that of small quick-firing pieces. German lorries were heard driving at speed through the streets of the town, laden with troops, and presently the dominant sounds were those of machine-guns and rifles and the sharp bursts of hand grenades. Armoured cars tore through the streets. An infantry battle was plainly being fought. Was this, Frenchmen asked one another, the beginning at last of the counter-invasion by their Allies? There were many whose hearts beat high. There were several, it is said, whose thoughts turned to the few hidden arms they possessed, ready to join in the fight for deliverance.

Before daylight all gunfire ceased, but desultory rifle fire was heard in the streets of the town itself. It must, then, be the Tommies. A German motorcycle combination, its machine-gunner spitting fire at random, was bowled over by counter-fire from an unseen hand. Two figures in the old familiar khaki hammered at the front door of a little house and said in garbled French: 'Show us the way through to the back.' They passed through, climbed a wall and were gone. Elsewhere the poultry were wakened to a frightened clamour as men dropped astonishingly into their run. At another house a tall, moustached figure in the kilt asked for water for the wounded. Other shadowy figures moved from house to house. Men bleeding from wounds sought shelter in cellars and outhouses.

The morning brought confusion and an atmosphere of terror. There was still a little spasmodic shooting and the Germans, their garrison heavily reinforced, were in a state of high nervous tension. They, too, thought that an invasion was being attempted and suspected that the patriot French would rise in support of it. They picketed every road junction in the town, firing at shadows and at each other. A smell as of exhausted fires came from the docks. A convoy of German ambulances swept in and took away a stream of wounded. The Nazairiens, of course, were completely in the dark – and the Germans themselves, angry, bewildered and their nervousness soon to be amply justified, almost as much so. Was this really the prelude to invasion? If not, what had been the objective of the British?

Sadly the French, as they attempted to go out about their business, saw small parties of British soldiers and sailors, many of them very severely wounded, being rounded up one by one and bundled into lorries – dishevelled, bleeding, limping, supporting one another, their badges and rank marks torn from them by the Germans, but still looking proud, even gay. From other points along the coast more parties of British sailors and soldiers, escaping by miracles from the petrol flames of their sunken craft, were brought in, barefoot and, except only for a blanket, naked. The bodies of others, dead from gunshots, or drowned, or charred from the fierce flames of petrol fires, were gathered up from the beaches or from the sullen waters of the Loire.

But French workmen who went back to their tasks in the docks saw also another picture. They saw a British destroyer rammed firm and deep in the gate of the enormous dry dock, that dock which was the largest in the world and which would accommodate any battleship of the world's navies. They saw power-houses wrecked and burning. And in the forenoon a mighty explosion shook the town as the destroyer blew up.

For the British commandos of the Special Service Brigade and for their naval comrades in arms this was the end of Operation Chariot and the end of the war, save for those few who astonishingly made good their escapes. But for the French of St Nazaire, as one mysterious explosion followed another long after the raid was over, it was the beginning of three days of terror and of death, when the delayed-action results of this most daring of raids stampeded the angry and bewildered Germans, contrary to their disciplined habits, into a paroxysm of indiscriminate shooting, in which they shot down, not only innocent Frenchmen and women, but also their own comrades.

Of all these things we shall hear in due place, and hear also how, in this welter of blood and flames, a blow was struck for the Allied cause that immediately altered the course of naval strategy to its advantage. It was a blow far more difficult to deliver, at least equally dangerous, far more successful and deserving even more renown than the famous Zeebrugge Raid in 1918, so closely comparable in purpose. For the Zeebrugge Raid, carried out against a port only eighty miles away, and on the open seaboard, with three times the number of men, was tactically less difficult and strategically not a success, in spite of all its lustrous heroism; since the submarine base was blocked for only twenty-four hours, whereas the Normandie Dock at St Nazaire was blocked for ten years. Gradually as the facts disclosed themselves in the next few days to the eyes of the RAF cameras and to the ears of the keenest of Intelligence Services, the gallant exploit of Ryder and Newman and their companions stood revealed, not as a mere nuisance raid, not as just another sally by a beleaguered garrison, but, in the words of Sir Winston Churchill, as 'a deed of glory intimately involved in high strategy'.

Not less memorable were the words spoken to the survivors of the gallant band of Operation Chariot by the French Prime Minister five years later, with that warm and generous eloquence for which Frenchmen have such a gift.

'You,' said M. Ramadier, 'were the first to bring us hope.'*

---

* Except when otherwise stated, the quotations in this chapter are from an official report from the Mayor of St Nazaire to the Minister of Justice in November 1944.

2. THE BLACK HOUR

Except that it is French, St Nazaire does not differ greatly from other dockyard towns. The cooking is better than on Tyneside or the Clyde, but not the sanitation. Unlike La Baule, the fashionable watering-place eight miles to the westward, it is a town garbed for the greater part in tones of sombre grey. No fashionable hotels here earn multiple stars in the traveller's guidebook. No smart shops tempt the wealthy client. Trams jangle along its streets and of its fifty thousand inhabitants the most important element is that which works daily in the great docks. The maps and photographs show that there are in fact two towns. There is the Old Town, of narrow streets and mainly small houses, lying within the compass of the dockland itself and constituting a serious threat to the advance of Newman's men; here was the original St Nazaire, when it was no more than a little fishing village before the coming of the big ships.

To the westward of the Old Town lies the much larger, relatively modern town, of formal, rectangular layout, built from the prosperity of the docks, where we shall see the combined commandos making their bold attempt to break through the gathering German forces. Along the river front stretch the great docks and shipbuilding yards, products of the nineteenth century, when the old inland port of Nantes, some thirty-five miles up the Loire, became unsuitable for the bigger and still bigger ships of the age of steam. All around lies a scene of flat monotony and utilitarian uses and inland of the town there stretches a great marsh of some thirty square miles, along the fringes of which Corporal Wheeler and Lance-Corporal Sims were to wander in the darkness and bewilderment at the start of their astonishing escape from German clutches.

As we open the files of the sombre days of January 1942 and read the records of events that governed the lives of nearly all the world, it is to this busy but unpretentious town that we first turn our gaze. Here there was no whisper or omen of this great event to come. An alien discipline imposed order and obedience. No patriot movement had yet shown its head. For to St Nazaire, as a seaport town, the fall of France in 1940 had brought the bitterness of enemy occupation. The Germans held it firmly in their grasp and the great docks were conscripted to their warlike needs under the Admiral Superintendent of the Dockyard.* At the various headquarters the swastika flew for all to see and from the jackstaff of every German ship in harbour hung the emblem of the black cross. The stamping sentries, the guns along the sea's fringe and the edicts in public places bore witness to a conqueror's hold.

For to Germany, still at war with the British peoples, the only combatants of those involved in the hurricane of events of 1940 whom she had failed to conquer, but now freshly at war with America also, the port of St Nazaire was of great importance, not only in a material sense, but also strategically. Standing on the north bank of the estuary of the great river Loire, which at this point is about a mile wide, St Nazaire lies six miles back from the open waters of the Bay of Biscay. This wide expanse of water is throughout of shallow depth and patterned with an archipelago of dangerous mud banks, except for a single deep-water channel, known as the Charpentiers Channel, which runs close to its westward shore and immediately under the muzzles of a belt of guns, as may be seen from the map on pages xii and xiii. Thus the estuary vividly resembles a pair of wide-open jaws, toothed with guns above and below, into the throat of which the 611 souls of the seaborne light brigade that sailed with Ryder and Newman were to charge with the same fearlessness as the 'noble six hundred' of Lord Cardigan's light cavalry at Balaclava.

Nature and the hand of man had therefore made of St Nazaire an ideal lair for German submarines; and here the Todt Organisation, that paramilitary body of constructional engineers

* V-Ad. von Trotha according to most accounts; Mecke thinks it was then V-Ad. Rother.

who were moulding Hitler's Fortress Europe in unnumbered tons of concrete, were building, in the lock known as the St Nazaire Basin, but which we, for greater convenience, shall call the Submarine Basin, one of their fabulous series of massive, bomb-proof submarine shelters. At the time when Ryder and Newman paid their brusque visit in 1942, they had completed nine, with five more still to be done.

Besides these concrete submarine kennels, the docks generally, with their excellent repair facilities, were of great value to the German warships, their tankers and such merchant shipping as managed to elude the British grasp. Above all, and the object to which our attention is to be most closely riveted, was the special dock built for the construction of the great French transatlantic liner *Normandie*. She was the largest ship in the world, and the dock, which to the French was known as the Forme Ecluse Joubert, but which we shall more conveniently call the Normandie Dock, was also of its kind the largest in the world, capable of accommodating a ship of 85,000 tons or more. We shall be looking more closely at this great and significant structure presently and shall note that its unique facilities gave it strategic status.

Because of the importance to them of these naval facilities, the Germans had taken care to fortify the town and docks heavily, adding to the existing French defences. It was, indeed, the most strongly fortified German base along the whole of the western seaboard of Europe, except Brest. Coast defence guns of medium and heavy calibres, manned by 280 Naval Artillery Battalion, threatened the entrance to the estuary, searchlights were sited to sweep both sky and sea and the whole area bristled with the small calibre guns of dual purpose of 22 Naval Flak Brigade, capable of engaging both aerial and surface targets. All these things we shall look at more closely when the time comes to examine the strength of the opposition that Ryder's and Newman's 600 were called upon to face.

These spectacles of German domination the Nazairiens witnessed daily, enforced onlookers of the enemy's purpose and activity. They saw the German warships come and go. They had seen the *Scharnhorst* in the big dry dock. They looked out upon the submarines of the 7th Flotilla stealing out shark-like upon their murderous missions. They watched the great kennels being built and in the docks they laboured under German orders to repair and maintain the ships of the enemy. Daily Germans of the naval artillery regiments, the crews of the submarines, destroyers, minesweepers and tankers strode in their midst. The women of the German auxiliary services, who were also to be numbered among the unforeseen victims of the Raid, were there too; and only a few hours before the charioteers rode in upon them, Admiral Doenitz himself had visited St Nazaire to inspect the submarine base and had put some pertinent questions.

From time to time the people of St Nazaire were also visited by senior officers from General Dollmann's 7th Army headquarters in Angers, and more often by others from the fashionable hotels and villas of La Baule, where were to be found the Corps headquarters of General Ritter von Prager and those of the Seekommandant Loire, Kapitän zur See Zuckschwerdt; and where also we shall see the wounded British prisoners lying in hospital. Thus on every hand Frenchmen could see the evidence of the German effort against the one nation that had so long defied them – Britain.

They could not see clearly, however, what lay beyond, nor could they hear the truth of things in the world outside, save for those who, in the quiet of their homes, listened to the voice of the BBC. And what the BBC had to say in those first days of 1942 was melancholy enough to lovers of liberty throughout the globe. Everywhere the fortunes of the Allies were at their lowest ebb. The United States had scarcely begun to collect herself for the unexpected struggle imposed on her by the recent affront on Pearl Harbor. The Russians, formerly the fellow-conspirators of Germany, but forced into the war against her in the previous June, were being driven back inexorably as Hitler's armies bit deep into their territory. Greece had been overrun by the enemy, and, with the exceptions of Switzerland, Sweden and the Peninsula, the whole of Europe was now in the grip of Hitler and his 'Italian jackal'.

Britain, having for so long maintained the struggle alone and with her forces stretched to the uttermost over the seas of the world, had suffered grievous and heartbreaking reverses by land and sea since the sudden aggression of Japan had added a still further strain on her resources. In the Western Desert, after

driving Rommel pell-mell back for some 350 miles, our Eighth
Army, whose valiance in the face of odds had so often stirred the
nation, had in January been forced to retreat in their own turn for
half that distance. A much bombed and sorely tried people at
home read with rising consternation the daily tale of the sweeping
Japanese successes in the Far East, which, on 15 February, while
the Operation Chariot was being actively planned, was to
culminate in that most galling of all our reverses – the surrender
of our great citadel of Singapore. 'The crash of external disaster,'
wrote the Prime Minister, 'fell heavily upon us.' This month we
touched the very nadir of our fortunes.

But if the imminent fall of Singapore was an humiliation,
strategically the greatest menace to the nation and to the Allied
cause lay at sea. The Battle of the Atlantic was the most vital and
the most critically poised of all our campaigns. The Germans had
long since given up the immediate hope of being able to invade
Britain, and their air forces had failed to subjugate the RAF. The
German effort against this country therefore became essentially a
naval one. Hitler in his famous Directive No 21, when he ordered
the German general staff to make preparations for war against
Russia, prescribed that the weight of army and air forces should
be massed primarily on this purpose, but that 'the main force of
the Navy will remain unequivocally directed against England'.

In pursuit of this directive, the efforts of the German navy,
avoiding carefully any pitched battle with the British fleet, were
concentrated upon the denial to us of all supplies by sea, supplies
without which the nation could not for long pursue hostilities nor its
citizens sustain their daily life. For this piratical war against merchant
ships they had two main weapons – the submarine and the heavy
warship. It was with the submarine that at that time they made their
main effort and by the end of 1941 Admiral Doenitz had nearly 250
U-boats at his command, their total being added to at the rate of
fifteen a month. For the first time in history they began raiding across
to the American coast and before the end of February they had sunk
more than half a million tons of shipping off the American coast.

Besides the submarine, the Germans had weapons of tremendous destructibility in their powerful, modern battleships and
battle cruisers – fast, heavily armed and very difficult to sink. The

Scheer, the *Hipper*, the *Scharnhorst*, the *Gneisenau*, the *Graf Spee*, shrewdly handled, had already shown what damage they could do when loosed into the Atlantic. The giant *Bismarck*, 45,500 tons, threatening a far more violent massacre, had been brought to book only just in time. The Admiralty, therefore, naturally viewed with the greatest anxiety any prospect that the German navy would attempt to repeat their exploits, and were concerned to do anything that would deny to enemy ships the ports and docks on the Biscay seaboard, where they were on the doorstep of the Atlantic and much more dangerous than when in northern waters. Whatever else was lost, the Battle of the Atlantic must at all costs be won. Therefore, so long as the doors of these asylums remained open to the enemy, we were obliged to hold back powerful naval forces which might more positively have been employed to augment our strained resources in the waters of the world.

Among these several asylums along the Biscay seaboard, St Nazaire was of a very special significance because of that great dock, the Normandie Dock, that has already been briefly mentioned. To the Germans the special importance of this dock was that it was the only one on their whole western seaboard that would accommodate the new battleship *Tirpitz*, most modern and most powerful warship of the world's navies. To the British, and now to the Americans also, the import of this menacing fact had been seen all too clearly the year before when the *Bismarck*, sister ship of the *Tirpitz*, had broken out into the Atlantic and had presented a fearful risk to our merchant shipping before she was brought to bay and sunk on 27 May. It was precisely for St Nazaire that she had then been making for repairs and the port had been specially made ready for her reception. Should the *Tirpitz* sally out on a similar mission, and sustain damage, she stood virtually no chance at all of returning to her home waters by the far northern route, as we should be waiting for her. This Hitler well knew. St Nazaire was the only port in the world open to her.

Let us see, therefore, in the very simplest light, what was now, late in January 1942, the strategic threat to our existence with which our naval planning staff, and Mr Churchill himself, were brought face to face.

Away in Norwegian waters, the great *Tirpitz*, having completed her trials, was now beginning to shift restlessly. In company with her were the pocket battleships *Scheer* and *Lutzow*, together with a number of heavy cruisers. The notorious *Scharnhorst*, *Gneisenau* and *Prinz Eugen*, subjected to frequent but successful bombing raids, lay uncomfortably at Brest, whence they were expected at any moment to sally out (as they in fact did on 12 February) to join forces with the Norwegian squadron, either in the Atlantic or in northern waters, preparatory to a sortie against our shipping. If they made such a sortie, the Iceland-Faroes gap and the Denmark Strait would be barred against their return, but the Biscay ports lay open to them as ready sanctuaries. Of these St Nazaire was the only one for the *Tirpitz*. Destroy the Normandie Dock, and the *Tirpitz* would almost certainly not venture out into the Atlantic.

Thus the existence of the Normandie Dock, and its availability to the *Tirpitz*, elevated St Nazaire, in the eyes of those responsible for directing our naval policy, from being only one of a number of enemy submarine and destroyer bases into a major strategic factor directly governing the dispositions of our ships of war and the whole of our policy for the protection of Allied shipping in the Atlantic.

Indeed the Prime Minister himself, in a minute to the Chiefs of Staff on 25 January, had written: 'No other target is comparable to it (the *Tirpitz*). . . . The whole strategy of the war turns at this period on this ship, which is holding four times the number of British capital ships paralysed, not to speak of two new American battleships retained in the Atlantic.'

It was in this dark hour, when the very arteries of our existence westward and southward through the Atlantic were being menaced, and when the forces of liberty were being pressed back by land and sea in four continents, that a lamp was lit in the sombre town of St Nazaire which was to warm the spirit of a nation sorely tried with reverses and to illumine the darkened hopes of our allies across the narrow seas.

3. 'BE OFFENSIVE'

An army, or any other military force, that lacks the resources for a sustained offensive is driven to adopt various stratagems if it is not to lose its fighting spirit by sitting down in a passive attitude. In defence, everyone knows today, the offensive spirit must somehow be asserted and maintained. Thus a besieged force sallies from its gates to damage and unnerve the enemy as much as possible. Thus in the Western Desert the Eighth Army developed its 'Jock columns', to harass and unbalance the Germans and Italians. Such raids and minor exploits, unless related to the commander's main purpose, are apt to be frowned upon by orthodox military authority. They were never once attempted against our own shores by the Germans, to whose doctrine of concentration on the main purpose such exploits did not conform. They dissipate one's forces, distract one's attention from the main design, cause unnecessary losses and, if they fail in their purpose, are liable to do more harm than good to morale. They are essentially guerrilla tactics and are typically the methods of a force of inferior numbers that has been obliged to adopt a prolonged defensive.

From 1940 onwards, for some years, Britain was in just that position. We were menaced by an enemy of superior strength who, having failed to defeat our arms or frighten us into surrender, was trying now to destroy our means of life and to reduce our homes to heaps of rubble. By sea and air, Britain, aided by the forces of the Commonwealth and Empire and by contingents of Free French, Poles and others who had escaped from the Nazi-occupied countries, fought a bitter fight for survival. Our towns were being frequently bombed by night. Parachute mines were dropped in the ports. Innumerable homes lay in ruins. Great heaps of rubble and brittle lakes of broken glass confronted the early morning traveller emerging from his shelter of the night. In London the platforms and passages of the Underground railways had become the sleeping places for many thousands of people. Telephone lines were down. Gas, electric and water mains were cut. A rigorous blackout flung its mantle of obscurity over towns and country, hampering all movement by night. Trains were few and crowded to the doors. Food and petrol and clothes were short, all strictly rationed. But the whole country was united in a wonderful comradeship of all classes. The factories were working round the clock. There was a sense of relief at being on our own and there was on all hands the cry: 'Let's get on with it.'

There was, however, no hope for a long time to come of launching a grand offensive on the Continent. Except for local theatres overseas, our posture, while we built up our forces, was bound to be one of defence. No one was more determined that that defence should be an offensive one than Mr Churchill. Partly with these purposes in view, and also for the purpose of training, planning and experimenting for the great day when we should be ready to assault Hitler's Fortress Europe, the Prime Minister had given increasing emphasis to the new inter-Services organization that had become known as Combined Operations; and in October 1941 he astonished everyone by appointing as its head a relatively junior naval officer, but one already distinguished for his initiative and courage – Captain the Lord Louis Mountbatten.

Even in that dark hour, when we were at the bottom of the pit, Mr Churchill was looking ahead to the offensive. Mountbatten, summoned to Chequers, listened deeply stirred by this embodiment of an unconquerable spirit as Mr Churchill expounded his purpose: 'Your job,' the Prime Minister concluded, 'is to be offensive. Train for the offensive – work out the craft, the equipment, the tactics, the administration and everything else needed to initiate and sustain the offensive.'

With this inspiration to sustain him, Mountbatten was now installed at Combined Operations Headquarters (COHQ) in Richmond Terrace, which lies between Whitehall and the Thames. His appointment was as Director of Combined Operations, with the rank of Commodore; but as the title was very shortly altered to

'Chief' we shall call him that, or CCO, throughout. It was not until after the St Nazaire operation had been put in train, and just before its execution, that Lord Louis was given his fullest power and authority and that his organization was developed on the elaborate scale that was to characterize it.

The main purpose of Combined Operations at that time was to carry out raids along the long enemy coastline that stretched from the Pyrenees far away to North Cape in the Arctic Ocean. 'One operation a fortnight' was the order that Mountbatten gave soon after his arrival. Sometimes these raids resulted from requests made from one of the Services, or even from a civil ministry, but more often they were of COHQ's own devising. Thus the probing minds of the eager enthusiasts on the planning and operational staff ranged daily over that far-stretched line, examining the maps and photographs of every beach, creek and harbour, studying the Intelligence collated by Wing Commander the Marquess de Casa Maury, bound by few orthodoxies, admitting few impossibilities, but often baffled by the lack of men or ships or gear to fulfil their purposes.

For an inherent problem for 'Combined Ops', and one that Sir Roger Keyes (Mountbatten's predecessor) had striven without avail to overcome, was the fact that it was not in itself a Service and hence commanded no forces except such as might be specially apportioned to it. These comprised only a few army commandos – those units of picked men formed specially for raiding purposes – and the landing craft that carried them to their objectives, and even the crews of these landing craft were not under CCO's command administratively. There never was, and never could be, an air element that CCO would call his own. When an operation required assistance from one of the three Services in their separate capacities, as frequently occurred, Combined Ops might find themselves confronted, as they did in planning for the St Nazaire Raid, with a reluctance on the part of that Service to divert to subsidiary purposes men and materials from its already over-strained resources. For COHQ could not, of course, overrule any of the Service ministries in matters of their own responsibility.

That part of Mountbatten's headquarters with which we shall be most closely concerned in this ambiguous but inevitable situation occupied itself with operational planning; and the aspect of it that most clearly impresses itself on our minds was the complete and intimate integration, 'at all levels', of the representatives of the three Services, working as one combined team. As soon as their busy and questing minds had sighted a promising target, meriting serious examination, an inter-Service committee, under a chairman, was formed, who proceeded to assess all the factors in detail and to prepare a preliminary plan. If Mountbatten approved it, the project, perhaps after further study and elaboration, was formulated into an Outline Plan and sent forward to the Chiefs of Staff, that august committee of the chiefs of the three Services whose approval was required for any operation.* The plan then left the paper stage, theory became translated into performance and there remained the task of finding the men, ships, aircraft and equipment to carry out the enterprise by methods that we shall shortly observe.

This inter-Service planning staff at COHQ, was, by normal British standards, a very peculiar one, since it was, to a large extent, making plans to be carried out by forces not wholly at its disposal. When, as occurred in the St Nazaire Raid, the enterprise required ships or forces outside CCO's own limited resources, the command of it passed to one or other of the Commanders-in-Chief of the Naval Commands – 'our patrons', as Mountbatten called them. Being in command of the operation, the patron obviously had considerable licence to amend the plan. The safeguard against any ruination of it was to be found in the Chiefs of Staff Committee, to whom Mountbatten could always refer for a ruling and whose ruling became an order.

The staff for all this busy hatching of plots at COHQ was headed by officers who at that time bore the somewhat pallid title of 'Adviser' for each Service. As Naval Adviser, and becoming chairman of the St Nazaire committee, was Captain John Hughes-Hallett, an officer of an alert manner, an incisive mind, an

---

* Admiral of the Fleet Sir Dudley Pound (First Sea Lord), General Sir Alan Brooke (Chief of the Imperial General Staff), and Air Chief Marshal Sir Charles Portal (Chief of the Air Staff). Later Mountbatten himself became a member of this committee.

impatience with conventional staff methods, tenacious in maintaining a decision once made. He was a qualified air pilot and had also a passion for bicycling. His principal staff planning assistants were Commander David Luce, and the gay and charming Lieutenant-Commander A. N. F. de Costobadie.

The Military Adviser was Brigadier J. C. Haydon, DSO, OBE, an Irish Guardsman, of small stature and charming manners, beneath which, however, lay a keen mind and a firm purpose. He was Mountbatten's deputy. In addition, pending the return of Brigadier Robert Laycock from the Middle East, he commanded the Special Service Brigade, that formation of the twelve Commandos of which we shall soon be seeing a great deal. The 'two hats' that he wore were thus useful on the St Nazaire committee, for he knew very well the men who would have to attack the targets on shore and was responsible for their training. The Assistant Military Adviser was Lieutenant-Colonel D. W. Price, and in the St Nazaire planning and preparation a leading part was also taken by Major R. D. Q. Henriques, Royal Artillery. Lean and tall, later a celebrated novelist and successful farmer, Robert Henriques contributed to the common effort a part that was at once imaginative and factual. He was Charles Haydon's brigade major in the Special Service Brigade and thus also personally knew the Commandos who were to take part.

The Air Adviser was Group Captain A. H. Willetts, an officer of rather slight stature, fair and somewhat reserved manner, but of ability and charm. All of these, we must remember, at their equivalent levels, worked entirely as an inter-Service team concerned with the common interest.

Despite this exemplary co-partnership at COHQ as a whole, these plans and preparations had to be obscured in a night of secrecy. The curtain of security was obliged to be drawn tightly against all eyes and ears. One's most trusted friends must not be admitted behind it. The need to be on one's guard was ever present, and no man must be told more of any affair than he need know for his own part in it. To the staff of COHQ and to the commander appointed for an expedition, necessarily seeking co-operation on many hands, this need not to disclose one's purpose was only too often an obstruction and embarrassment, as Ryder and Newman were to find. Only by persistence, or sometimes by craft, were some such difficulties overcome.

This, in broad outline, was the manner in which COHQ handled all these matters at that time; and of all the projects that they devised, none was bolder in conception, none was more heroic in execution and none appealed so much to the heart of Mountbatten himself as Operation Chariot.

4. A PLOT IS HATCHED

An abortive attempt to devise a means of attacking St Nazaire had begun as early as 10 August 1941, when Admiral of the Fleet Sir Roger Keyes, of Zeebrugge fame, was head of Combined Operations, with the title of Director. On that date the Admiralty requested the Commander-in-Chief Plymouth (Admiral of the Fleet Sir Charles Forbes) to investigate the possibility of an operation, 'in consultation with the DCO'. Two objectives were suggested for destruction – the lock gates and the U-boats. Sir Charles was a distinguished officer of an old school, of a slight figure, concealing a very shrewd brain beneath a quiet manner, often sitting long hunched up and silent at conferences and then suddenly shooting a penetrating question. He replied to the Admiralty enquiry with a long and highly critical appreciation. The dangerous shoal waters, the risk of detection and attack by superior forces on the long sea passage, the lack of suitable craft that could carry enough fuel for the round voyage, the difficulties of achieving surprise, which was essential – these and other points were emphasized.

Keyes commented shortly a few days later, suggesting the usual technique hitherto employed on commando raids, by which converted cross-Channel steamers (predecessors of the Landing Ships Infantry) proceeded to a point near the enemy coast and there launched the troops in small assault landing craft of the sort known as Eurekas. But the objection to this method, of course, was that it could scarcely avoid detection from the air or sea patrols, and thus give the show away by its very characteristic appearance. Throughout this stage the operation was considered purely in terms of a commando exploit, all the demolitions to be carried out by troops landed from the assault craft.

Shortly afterwards Forbes reviewed the problem in another
memorandum and a meeting was held at the Admiralty on 19
September. Ways and means could not be found. The meeting
was advised by Keyes' military representative that the commando
force for the shore destructions alone would have to be at least
three hundred strong, plus the demolition parties. No further
positive action was taken and on 29 October the Chief of Staff at
COHQ minuted: 'C-in-C Plymouth has turned this down again.'
But a further minute of the same date adds, with a significance for
our story which, as will appear before long, was almost prophetic:

'The only known change in circumstances since that estimate
was made [19 September] is the availability of a lock gate
destruction expert in the person of Captain Pritchard.'

Even Mountbatten after his arrival at COHQ seems to have
regarded the adventure as impracticable; and in November he
asked Special Operations Executive if they could undertake the
demolitions by means of their secret 'cloak and dagger' agents.
For SOE, however, though their study of it is reflected in a very
long document, it was far too big a task.

There the embryo of this exploit lay, apparently inert and
lifeless, but the great dock continued to weigh heavily in the
calculations of the naval staff, vitally affecting the strategy of
the Atlantic.

*

One day late in January 1942 (apparently on the 27th),
Mountbatten had luncheon with his friend Captain Charles
Lambe, who was Deputy Director of Plans at the Admiralty and
about to become Director. During the meal Lambe brought up
the matter of St Nazaire; he was a good deal worried by the
problem and disappointed that the project had been turned down.
Could Combined Operations examine it in a fresh and unconventional light?

It so happened that at Richmond Terrace on that same
morning Hughes-Hallett had been 'running my eye down the
French coast' in the course of the search for targets, together with
Dick Costobadie. St Nazaire, Bayonne and a smaller target had
caught their attention as worth examining. What had appealed to

Hughes-Hallett in St Nazaire, he said, was 'the flaw in the defences that permitted vessels of light draught to approach over the mud flats at high water of extraordinary spring tides'.

This Mountbatten heard when he returned from lunching with Lambe and summoned his staff. He sent also for the half forgotten file that had originated in August, but it could not immediately be found, for someone was 'sitting' on it. To his staff he said: 'I think this is worth going into again. Let us get out something unconventional.'

Thus what might have been approached as a mere raiding objective was now revealed to be an operation 'intimately involved in high strategy'. It was by far the most important task that Combined Operations had yet tackled. From its inception and ever afterwards Mountbatten, amid all his other preoccupations, took the closest personal interest in it, for its high purpose and its daring conception appealed at once both to his imagination and to his strategical sense. His eyes were wide open – more so than those of some other men – to the multiple perils that threatened those who were to carry it out. If he did not think of Balaclava, nonetheless that wide, gun-fringed mouth of the Loire only too obviously resembled the jaws of death into which an amphibious Light Brigade was to be ordered to charge. Paradoxically, however, he saw that not the least chance of success was, in his own words, the very fact that to the enemy the exploit must appear 'absolutely impossible to undertake'.

From then onwards things moved with speed. Haydon, Hughes-Hallett, Willets and their subordinate staff officers proceeded to a joint examination in detail. Technical specialists were called in and of these the most important for our story was Captain W. H. Pritchard, the RE officer already mentioned, whose consuming purpose was the destruction of dockyards. Casa Maury was asked if he had any Intelligence material and replied:

'St Nazaire! Yes, heaps!'

He produced a very fat file of exceptional value, collated for the greater part from various sources when he had been Intelligence Officer of 19 Group, Coastal Command, at Plymouth. It contained not only air photographs and such other material as one might expect, but also exact technical information, photographs and detailed engineer drawings of the great Normandie Dock gates which were the very kernel of the nut to be cracked. There were also complete details and drawings, originating from our secret agents, of the submarine pens. In addition to this paper information, Casa Maury also produced a very fine model of the docks constructed by the modelling section of the RAF Photographic Reconnaissance Unit. This was to prove of incalculable value not only to the planners but also to the commandos who, on that coming night in March, would have to move about the docks with even more confidence and certainly with more speed than those who worked in them daily.

In the study of this file and this model the planners' chief attention was directed early to the Normandie Dock and it will pay us as spectators of this drama to observe at this stage some of the salient factors about this great structure that were now revealed to the planners.

They learnt that, as we ourselves have already seen, the Normandie Dock was the largest structure of its kind in the world, serving as a lock when filled with water or as a dry dock for the repair of ships when empty. Begun by the French Government in 1928, it had taken four years to build, measured 1148 feet long by 164 feet wide and could accommodate a ship of more than 85,000 tons. It lay roughly north and south. To control the flow of water in or out of the dock there were at each end of it, north and south, two enormous sliding steel gates, measuring 167 feet long, 54 feet high and no less than 35 feet thick, each built in the form of a great sectional steel box with compartments that could be filled with water to any extent necessary to withstand various pressures. Lock gates of this description, which slide in and out rather than swing, are technically known as 'caissons', and this term we shall adopt to distinguish them from other lock gates in this dockyard.

To move these massive portals, either for the passage of ships or for the emptying or filling of the dock, powerful gear was obviously necessary. The method of operation was to wind the great caissons laterally on rollers in or out of deep sockets, technically called 'cambers', situated on the west side of the dock. Each of the two caissons was wound in and out of its camber by means of large twin wheels, which, with the motors that actuated

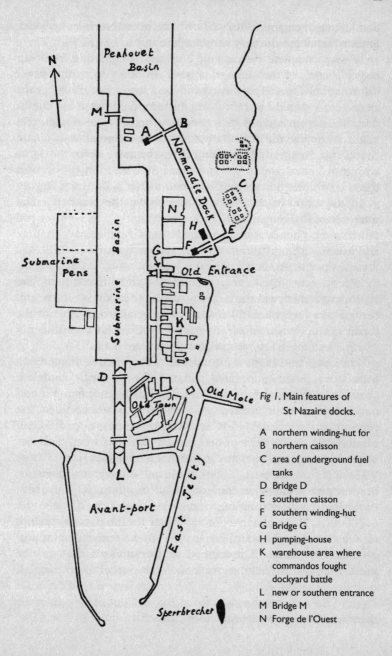

Fig 1. Main features of St Nazaire docks.

A northern winding-hut for
B northern caisson
C area of underground fuel tanks
D Bridge D
E southern caisson
F southern winding-hut
G Bridge G
H pumping-house
K warehouse area where commandos fought dockyard battle
L new or southern entrance
M Bridge M
N Forge de l'Ouest

them, were housed at the extremity of each camber. We shall refer to these small buildings as winding-houses.

When it was desired to use the Normandie Dock as a dry dock, instead of as a lock, it was, of course, necessary to pump out all the water and for this purpose there was a large pump house, with its motors at ground level but with its pumps, of massive strength, deep in a cavern some forty feet directly below; safe enough, one might have thought, even from a commando – but not safe enough for Stuart Chant, limping down the dark, steep stairs with a wounded knee, and his gallant sergeants. This pump house and the two winding-houses are illustrated in Fig 2, on the following page, and the planners noted with interest that they were all on the west side of the Normandie Dock.

From air photographs in Casa Maury's Intelligence file they also noted with satisfaction that the southern caisson, which was the one open to attack from the sea, was not protected by a boom, though an anti-torpedo net, suspended from its floats, hung like an underwater curtain some fifty yards outside. Nor was there any barbed wire anywhere to be seen. In the shallows of the estuary there was no evidence of any mines, 'so,' in Hughes-Hallett's words, 'we decided to assume that there were none.'

The caisson was a most formidable nut to crack. It might never have been possible to have planned the job with complete confidence, in spite of the very detailed Intelligence file, if it had not been for one very fortunate circumstance. It so happened, the committee were delighted to learn from the encyclopedic Casa Maury, that the caissons of the Normandie Dock were of almost identical design and construction to that of the great King George V Dock at Southampton.* Thus it was not long before, in answer to an urgent request, an engineer of the Southern Railway, who were the owners of the King George V Dock, arrived within the doors of COHQ, causing some little flutter because, in the middle of a battle-dress London, he arrived silk-hatted and morning-coated, *en route* to an investiture at Buckingham Palace. The silk-hatted visitor, bearing plans and specifications, revealed all

---

* It had been built by the Furness Shipbuilding Company after study of the Normandie Dock with the Southern Railway engineers.

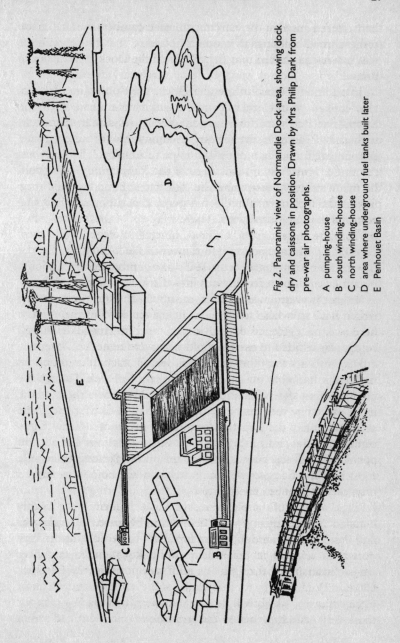

Fig 2. Panoramic view of Normandie Dock area, showing dock dry and caissons in position. Drawn by Mrs Philip Dark from pre-war air photographs.

A pumping-house
B south winding-house
C north winding-house
D area where underground fuel tanks built later
E Penhouet Basin

and offered his help for any technical calculations; if he made
some shrewd guess that it was St Nazaire that the committee
was interested in, and not the 'K G V', he kept his thoughts to
himself.

In addition to the Normandie Dock, the St Nazaire planners
also looked at the great concrete submarine kennels in the
Submarine Basin, but these, so fabulously solid that they could
withstand a direct hit by the largest known bomb, were a target
that no small raiding force could hope to destroy. The dock was
the thing. However, if the waters of the Submarine Basin could
be made tidal, by destroying the lock gates that controlled their
flow, then the use of the U-boat pens, it was hoped, would be
considerably interfered with. There were six of these gates – two
on its eastern side in the original, nineteenth-century entrance,
called the Old Entrance, and four more in the long channel of the
new or Southern Entrance of 1907 date, embraced within long,
clasping arms that stretched out into the waters of the Loire.

These, however, were by no means all the destructions that
would have to be tackled by a raiding force, for they would also
have to assault gun positions that threatened them and destroy all
bridges by which the enemy could bring up forces for a counterattack. Another tempting target was seen in the underground oil
fuel tanks that lay to the east of the Normandie Dock. Though the
planners kept the Normandie Dock steadily before them as the
main objective, the number of targets of all sorts that had to be
attacked finally reached the formidable figure of twenty-four –
eight lock gates, four bridges, six power installations and six gun
positions (thirteen guns), apart from purely fighting tasks. We
must bear these figures well in mind when we come to see what a
tiny force was to be expected to do it.

This formidable programme of havoc called for a highly
detailed and technical plan of demolition by means of explosives
and the planners were therefore fortunate to be able, at the very
outset, to seize upon the ardent young Royal Engineer officer
whose 'availability' the Chief of Staff had noted on 29 October.
Captain Pritchard, by a remarkable, and even dramatic, chain of
circumstances, which will be narrated later, had made a plan for
these very tasks long before the strategic requirement had arisen

and thus had the answers to most of the technical problems all ready to hand according to the planners' requirements.

With these and other helps the inter-Service planners formulated their preliminary proposals remarkably quickly. The means of carrying them were also soon agreed upon. A powerful force on conventional lines to fight its way through was neither available nor appropriate. The utmost economy of force was demanded. The planners therefore decided to attack the main target – the southern caisson – by what has aptly been called the 'terrifying solution' of ramming it with an 'explosive ship'. By this was meant an old destroyer (no smaller ship would make sufficient impact) with her bows packed with high explosive, which should be detonated by a delayed-action fuse after she had been evacuated. The shore targets were to be destroyed by parties of commandos landed from the destroyer and carrying prepared charges according to a plan formulated in its technical needs by Pritchard under Haydon's direction.

Whatever the targets were, and however they were to be attacked, the force had to be got there. The course to be followed at sea, the methods of avoiding enemy forces there and other related factors were not for COHQ to decide, but for C-in-C Plymouth, Sir Charles Forbes, who would automatically be 'patron' of this enterprise if the Chiefs of Staff sanctioned it. Hughes-Hallett and his co-planners, however, looking speculatively at those dangerous, wide-open jaws of the Loire estuary, saw at once that the deep-water Charpentiers Channel, running under the very teeth of the guns on the west bank, must be avoided and that therefore the craft to be employed must be able to negotiate the large expanse of the only less dangerous shoal waters, which, even at high tide, gave a maximum depth of water of only ten feet.

Quite clearly, to escape destruction from the guns that lined the jaws of the estuary and, still more, the massed dual-purposes weapons assembled in its throat at St Nazaire itself – an analysis of which is given in Chapter 11 and the locations of which may be seen in the map on pages xii and xiii and in Figs 9 and 13 – some means of surprise or deception was an imperative requirement. Granted that the force escaped observation at sea, how could it expect to sail through those last six miles of highly sensitive and protected waters, past batteries of guns and searchlights, ram the caissons and actually land its troops unseen and unheard?

In other days, even by employing all the technique of a stealthy approach, with a clouded sky, perhaps some rain and wind to impair the perceptions of lookouts and patrol boats, a good deal of luck would still have been needed to get through unnoticed. By 1942 the hazard had been added to by the invention of radar, allowing the approach of an enemy to be detected by day or dark without searchlights, telescopes or any other aid to human sight or hearing. At first sight, therefore, an unobserved approach against an alert and first-class enemy seemed unlikely, although the extreme improbability of such an apparently foolhardy exploit was in itself a partial assurance – as Mountbatten noted.

To carry out the whole operation, however, it was not enough to have an unopposed approach. What hope was there that the commandos, if landed, could penetrate several hundred yards into a dockyard full of Germans and proceed to blow up lock gates, bridges, guns and power-houses under their noses?

Thus the means of taking the enemy by surprise gave the St Nazaire planners a lot to think about. Old principles still stand and it is only the means that alter. There remained the method of surprise by diversion; and the means of diversion proposed was a bombing raid.

It had been remarked by several observers that an air-raid, or even the expectation of one, was apt to blind the force attacked to anything that was happening on the ground. This phenomenon (or is it a phenomenon?) had been observed by Mountbatten himself at the bombardment of Cherbourg by HMS *Revenge*, when, although no air-raid was in progress, the Germans' searchlights remained directed upwards. 'I know myself,' he said on this point, 'what happens when explosions go off and you don't know what's up. I am jolly sure that if there are a lot of bangs going on the Germans will look up in the air and won't think of the sea, when no reason at all exists to imagine that an attack from the sea is likely.'

Henriques also, going out into the streets during raids on London, had found the same thing. 'You could,' he said, 'go into any house, commit any crime, do anything you liked, and no one would take the slightest notice of you.'

What was proposed, therefore, was that Bomber Command should be asked to support the operation by a raid which should not only cover the approach of the ships up the estuary by bombing the docks, but which should also be continued while the commandos were actually at their demolition tasks ashore, during which the bombing should be on the town instead of the docks. By this means, it was hoped, the enemy's guns and searchlights would be so occupied with engaging the aircraft overhead that both ships and men would be able to steal swiftly in unobserved. This bombing raid was, of course, an integral and essential part of the whole operation, as essential as the fire of its artillery is to infantry in the assault. No man worked harder for its accomplishment than Willetts but, among various other obstacles and resistances, it was to be the factor that at all stages most bedevilled all those who strove for the success of the great enterprise.

These critical factors demanded also a close study of the tides, the moon's phases, dates and times. The tide must be at high water springs. The advantages of a moonlight night were preferred to those of a dark one. To these requirements of high tide with full moon were added the need to keep out of sight of land until nightfall and to be away out of sight again on the following morning; and this meant that the attack could not take place much before midnight and must be over not much after 3.30 a.m. British Summer Time (which is the time used throughout this narrative). These conditions of a full tide and full moon at St Nazaire between midnight and 2 a.m. were found to exist in the last week of March, the best date being the night of 29–30 March. After that period in view of the shortening nights, there would be no suitable opportunity until the autumn. There was not much time to lose.

*

On 31 January, after 'looking at the thing again', Mountbatten had instructed Hughes-Hallett, as chairman of the committee, to draft a plan. It was ready by 6 February and the next day Mountbatten sent a draft of it to the Vice-Chief of Naval Staff, Vice-Admiral H. R. Moore, and asked for his views. This was the plan:

A gutted and 'expendable' destroyer of light draught, carrying a commando force, was to cut through the anti-torpedo net and ram the outer caisson. A large weight of explosives would be packed at the point of impact and the ship blown up by delayed-action fuses. Through the breach thus made a specially adapted motor-torpedo-boat – the very peculiar MTB 74, commanded by a cheerful young daredevil named Micky Wynn – was to pass and attack the inner, or northern caisson of the lock. The troops in the expendable destroyer would meanwhile have landed and would proceed to destroy with explosives all lock gates leading into the Submarine Basin, with the intent of making it tidal. Bomber Command would be asked to engage the attention of the enemy's guns, searchlights and radar by a bombing operation to be begun before the expedition entered the estuary and to be maintained throughout the assault. Finally the commandos and the skeleton crew of the expended destroyer would withdraw in a second destroyer, which would have followed up and proceeded alongside.

This was the core of the plan originally devised in this revival of the St Nazaire enterprise. It was simple and audacious, counting on the achievement of surprise, on the resolute handling of ships and bold leadership of the troops to be landed. In retrospect one may say that it was certainly the best plan of all, but, paradoxically, it was the Admiralty itself which upset it. But its essential features of an explosive destroyer and bombing support were stuck to tenaciously by the COHQ planners all through. They were the features that characterized it and differentiated it from earlier proposals and, although the bombing operation was to go awry, the first and dominant feature is one that in its subsequent execution under the cool hand of Sam Beattie was to be brilliantly successful.

From there onwards things moved fast. It was that dark and heartbreaking period when the nation heard, first, of the escape of the *Scharnhorst* and her dangerous companions from Brest on 12 February, and, next, of the far more dread and humiliating fall of Singapore three days later. A section of the Press was raising a violent clamour and many a Londoner wore a sombre face as he made his way to work past the great piles of brick rubble and the staring, vacant spaces in the bombed City streets. But the nation as a whole looked forward, confident in its star. It was angry, not downcast. Accepting with equanimity all its domestic trials – the short rations, the lack of petrol, the oppressive gloom of the total blackout, the interrupted services of trains, telephones, light and heat – it demanded, in the phrase of the day, that Britain should show that she could not only 'take it' but also hand it out.

Returning from Scotland, where he had gone to watch the final dress rehearsal for the invasion of Madagascar, Mountbatten became immediately absorbed again in Chariot. To his concern, he found that the Admiralty, having themselves asked for the job to be done as a matter of high strategic importance, were now showing the strongest reluctance to providing the means – a reluctance that was to vex the whole of the planning stage and one which, in the end, was to be overcome only by something very much in the nature of an ultimatum. The naval staff, admittedly hard pressed for ships in their innumerable tasks in the oceans of the world, grudged the loss of even one for purposes to their own benefit. The only suitable craft that they could suggest as the explosive ship for ramming the caisson was the *Ouragan*, belonging to the Free French.

As for the second destroyer, for the withdrawal of the commandos and the crew of the first destroyer after the demolition, that was quite out of the question.

This was the major topic of discussion at a critical conference of the Chariot committee and Admiralty staff officers on 19 February at which Mountbatten presided. Haydon having outlined the assault plan and Hughes-Hallett having explained the naval requirements, the meeting discussed an amendment to the plan in which the second destroyer was replaced by a flotilla of twelve motor launches; some of which, if the *Ouragan* was used, would have to be French.

The employment of these little craft – the famous 'Fairmiles' of 'our light coastal forces' – which will occupy so vivid a place in our picture, was not much to the liking of the Chariot planners, particularly to the naval members. Their small fuel capacity gave them a very limited range. They were extremely vulnerable and inflammable, being built of mahogany and run on petrol, so that if hit they were liable, in the phrase of one young officer who took part, 'to go up like a box of matches'. They were also highly vulnerable to aircraft, having nothing to fight them with but a light twin Lewis machine-gun of the previous war's vintage. For surface action their only armament was an antique little Hotchkiss 3-pounder, of Boer War date, quite inadequate against the shore batteries by which they must expect to be engaged on the way out. When Hughes-Hallett observed: 'We may lose every man,' Mountbatten replied thought-fully, with a slight movement of the shoulders:

'I'm afraid you're right, but if they do the job we've got to accept that.'

There seems, however, to have been no alternative, since Combined Ops' own assault craft were out of the question. Two measures to improve the motor launches, however, were now proposed. To enable them to get to St Nazaire and back, extra petrol tanks were to be fitted on deck (thus increasing their inflammability also). For armament, in order to give maximum defence against aircraft while the force was at sea, the Hotchkiss was to be sacrificed and replaced by two Oerlikon guns. These were heavy machine-guns firing a 20 mm, half-pound explosive bullet at 470 rounds a minute, capable of engaging air to surface targets, and it was calculated that the concentrated fire of twenty-four of them from twelve MLs would see off most aircraft. The angry clamour of these fierce little guns is to echo stridently through our later pages, though it was little enough against aircraft that they were used.

The decision to employ these vulnerable motor launches meant that the plan for bomber support from the air became even more important. 'It should,' as the minutes of the meeting of 19 February record, 'take the form of a really heavy bombing raid on the dock area, later moving to the town itself for the period troops were ashore.' The detail of this bombing support had still to be worked out by Haydon and Willetts after the meeting, but we may note here that Bomber Command were asked to provide not fewer than 350 aircraft. Observe carefully also, that at this stage – and until nearly the last minute – the bombing in the second phase was to be on the *town*, for that point is soon to become of critical import by a decision of Mr Churchill himself.

Before the conference of 19 February closed Hughes-Hallett

was instructed to embody the decisions in a formal Outline Plan for submission to the Chiefs of Staff. This plan Mountbatten forwarded on 24 February, and on 25 February the Chiefs of Staff gave their approval.

'This,' said the First Sea Lord, Sir Dudley Pound, 'is a most important operation – worth an army corps.'

'You mean,' parried the quick-witted Sir Alan Brooke, 'two battleships.'

The Chiefs of Staff were not, however, in favour of the idea of using a Free French ship and Sir Dudley undertook to try to find a British one. The Prime Minister was also informed of the plan and was well pleased. The audacity of its conception and the calculated acceptance of known risks heartily appealed to him. The King also was informed and took the greatest interest in the operation.

*

So far, however, all was merely paper. The men, the ships and the equipment to transform it into actuality had still to be found – and to be trained for this very special task. Combined Ops could supply no more than the troops to carry out the shore demolitions; it could provide no expendable ship and no motor launches. Only the Navy could provide these and the men to man them. Their provision and the method of executing the plan, with the great volume of detail that was to involve, would now become the concern of Sir Charles Forbes, with continued co-operation from COHQ.

Now, Forbes was due to attend an extremely high level conference at COHQ on the morning of 26 February at which commanders-in-chief were going to consider future operations against Northern France. Mountbatten accordingly asked Sir Charles to remain for a meeting in the afternoon to advance the Chariot enterprise, and to this meeting a very special importance is to attach.

Before C-in-C Plymouth came into the picture again, however, Hughes-Hallett began negotiation with the Admiralty for the necessary craft and officers, doing so verbally or by private note. Clearly it was important that the officer who was to command this daring exploit of high importance, this 'enterprise of great pith and moment', should be appointed and briefed as soon as possible. Accordingly, almost immediately after the Chiefs of Staff had given approval, Hughes-Hallett telephoned Captain L. A. Ashmore, the Naval Assistant to the Second Sea Lord who dealt with officers' appointments and said:

'I want an able Commander for a special job. He must be a really first-class man.'

To which Ashmore replied somewhat cynically:

'Oh, I know these special jobs. They are always getting cancelled.'

'This one won't be. Much too important.'

'I'll see what can be done, but, as you can well imagine, the best men are pretty well booked up. Is it really so necessary to have a specially able chap?'

'You can count on a VC for him, if that's a guide.'

'Oh, well, if you can guarantee a VC—'

'Obviously there's no guarantee, but that's the size of the job.'

Not even Hughes-Hallett, however, could foresee that the outcome would be not one Victoria Cross, but five.

5. ROBERT RYDER

Meanwhile, a frustrated young naval officer was sitting at the headquarters of Southern Command at Wilton House, near Salisbury, the ancestral home of the Earls of Pembroke. There he was Naval Liaison Officer on the staff of General the Hon. Sir Harold Alexander, his duties being to advise the Army on naval matters affecting the shore defences against invasion.

This tame employment was hardly to his appetite and, at the height of a great war, when every man of spirit was eager for the relish of active employment against the enemy he was bound to look upon it as a step in the wrong direction, however temporary. To outward seeming the direction of that step would certainly appear to have been intentional, for Commander R. E. D. Ryder, having recently lost a ship, had 'incurred the displeasure of Their Lordships' of the Board of Admiralty.

However, this time-honoured pronouncement is not one which is normally taken by naval officers with that degree of gravity that one might suppose it should compel. Indeed, most officers of spirit might be said to take the view that it is better to incur the displeasure of Their Lordships than never to risk doing so. What bothered Ryder, therefore, was not the triviality of official displeasure but the fact that he was not at sea.

Robert Ryder, whose initials led inevitably to his being called 'Red', was then just thirty-four years old, below middle height, dark-haired, clean-featured, square-rigged, deep-chested and of determined and forthright character. He had just married Hilaré Green-Wilkinson. He had been to school at Cheltenham and as a boy had been touched by the magic spell of the sea. Especially did he come under the enchantment of sailing ships, an enchantment that has never left him. At fifteen he went sailing with an elder

brother in a converted Fleetwood fishing smack and thereafter
sailing ships became the call and rule of his life. He joined the
Navy by public school entry and grew up to be what a fellow-
officer describes as 'a man of calm and rock-like reliability, with
immense reserves of courage and endurance'. Buoyant in spirit,
he was nevertheless self-contained, inward-looking, not wearing
his heart on his sleeve. Here was no jolly sailorman of fiction, but
a dedicated professional naval officer, closely attentive to detail,
strict in his own performance and with a sharp eye for the
performance of others. 'When you served under Red Ryder,' said
a fellow-Charioteer, 'you jolly well had to keep your eye on the
ball.'

Sail, however, continued to fill the avenue of his vision and in
1933, after three years in submarines, he spent his leave, together
with four other officers, sailing from China to England the ketch
Tai Mo Shan, built specially to their order at Hong Kong. He then,
when only twenty-six, volunteered and was selected for command
of the research yacht *Penola*, an auxiliary topsail schooner fitted out
for a long expedition to the Antarctic, led by John Rymill, the
Australian explorer. For three years, from 1934 to 1937, Ryder
was on this very hard service in the stormy waters and icy winds
from Cape Horn to the southern pole, commanding a ship's
company made up mostly of adventurous young men from the
universities, with a bearded ex-Guards officer, the memorable
James Martin, as boatswain. For this service Bob Ryder wears the
rare ribbon of the Polar Medal.

At the end of this period of semi-independence, the Admiralty,
in Ryder's own words, 'thought it was high time I came back to
naval discipline' and he found himself back again in big ships. The
war found him serving in a Mediterranean flagship, 'a service to
which I was totally unsuited', and when he received a signal from
Vice-Admiral Gordon Campbell, the famous Q-ship VC of the
First War, asking if he would like to join him, he eagerly accepted,
without knowing what was afoot.

Before long he was given command of one of the new Q-ships,
a Cardiff tramp named *Willamette Valley*. In her, with guns concealed beneath dummy deck cargo, according to the daring
practice of the First World War, he went out as bait for German

submarines. But in the dark of a June night in 1940 he was suddenly attacked by two U-boats and sunk 200 miles west of Ireland. Some twenty-five of the crew got away safely in a boat, but his old guardsman-boatswain James Martin, who was serving with him again, was lost and Ryder himself was left in the sea clinging to one of the large wooden chocks that wedge ships' boats on deck. To this he clung for four days without food or water, steeped in oil and his life-jacket perished by its action. A ship ironically named *Empire Courtesy* passed him by. After this most astonishing feat of endurance, he was picked up, just alive, by a British tanker. He was taken below by a deckhand who, having put him in dry clothes, offered him some rum, which Ryder declined. Having drunk a good swig of it himself, the rascal enquired:

'What are you, mate? Fireman? Seaman?'

'No, master of a tramp-ship,' replied Ryder.

'Master! Blimey! Don't tell the Old Man about that rum, will you?'

There followed the command of the frigate *Fleetwood* for six months and promotion to commander before Ryder was appointed to command the *Prince Philippe*. This was a Belgian cross-Channel ship that had been fitted out at Penarth to carry infantry and their special landing craft for raids on the Norwegian coast. She had scarcely been commissioned and manned, however, before, in the summer of 1941, she was rammed in thick fog off the Firth of Clyde by the *Empire Wave* and sunk. Then had followed the letter of 'displeasure' and the months of tedium with the Army at Wilton House while the winter dragged its course, the tale of disaster overseas gathered volume and 'the aery devils of the sky' poured down their mischief on our ports and cities. Ryder, bred to horizons of adventure, fretted at his chains.

Then, one day in February 1942, he received a surprise signal from the Admiralty ordering him to attend a conference at the headquarters of Combined Operations at 3 o'clock on the 26th. Wondering what it could be all about, he took a train to London.

6. 'A TRUE SOLDIER APPEARETH'

An officer in another Service, though more actively employed, was also fretting at prolonged frustration.

Lieutenant-Colonel A. C. Newman, a Territorial officer of the 4th Battalion The Essex Regiment of sixteen years' standing, was by normal profession a civil engineering contractor. Thirty-eight years old, he was married and had a small family. He was of middle height and solid build and his fair hair was beginning to retreat from his forehead. His face, of which his pipe was almost a permanent feature, was illumined by a lively intelligence and a quizzical good humour. He had a warm, genial and gay-spirited disposition and brought to the business of war, not a grim intensity, but the temperament of what Bridges has called a keen-hearted sportsman, 'whose joy danceth on peril's edge'. For to Charles Newman, as to most officers and men of his force, the Territorial Army offered both the enchantments of the most spirited of all games and the most companionable of all clubs. Few commanding officers can have enjoyed so much as Newman not only the regard, but also the warm affection, of all who served under him. His own affection towards them glows movingly in his little diary, where, at the start of the war, he writes of his 'desire to soldier with one's friends, to have under one's command all these lads from Barking and East Ham and outer London whom we had trained; we knew all their families and loved them all'.

Newman was at this time commanding No 2 Commando, one of the twelve Commandos that constituted the Special Service Brigade, under Brigadier Charles Haydon, which had been raised specially from picked volunteers for the 'offensive defence' that we have discussed. These new-born units, soon to become famous throughout the world and to find their imitators everywhere, aimed at developing the highest reach of physical endurance, an eager fighting spirit, a self-reliance not based on the discipline of mass-battle tactics, a mobility not dependent on the paraphernalia of a military commissariat, together with many other special qualities – in short, all the qualities of a highly trained professional soldier combined with those of the hardiest and most austere guerrilla. And let us record with special emphasis that the commandos, who came from every corps and regiment in the Army, were no gangs of bandits. No Hemingway guerrillas, no thugs, scallywags or taproom heroes were wanted, and the gruelling tests to which all were put very soon hoed out the tares from the corn. For the training was of the most rigorous and from the beginning the highest standards were demanded of morale and of soldierly integrity and bearing. There resulted in each commando unit a tremendous pride which had its foundations in a superb physical fitness and in every man's dedication to fight, without which he had no place in a Commando.

Of this spirit, common to all the Commandos, were the men who in time gathered round Charles Newman in 2 Commando in the various stages of its evolution. The unit had had its origin in No 3 Independent Company, which Newman commanded as a major and which had been blooded in the brief campaign in Norway in the early days of 1940. In the autumn of that year the Independent Companies were absorbed into the new Special Service Battalions, within the Special Service Brigade, which Haydon was appointed to command. Newman, appointed second-in-command of 1 SS Battalion under Lieutenant-Colonel W. Glendinning, moved to Dartmouth and there had his first meeting with Lord Louis Mountbatten, who was then commanding the 5th Destroyer Flotilla. His famous *Kelly* was under repair and he was at that time in HMS *Jupiter*. Hearing that *Jupiter* had come into harbour, Newman went out in a dinghy and asked Mountbatten if he would take some of his men to sea to get experience.

Lord Louis replied: 'You're a soldier and your job is to defend Great Britain against an invasion. Don't waste time in ships; that is our job.'

Newman explained that the battalion was designed for

offensive raids; familiarity with the sea was very important, and it was for this reason that he asked for his co-operation.

'I suppose,' said Lord Louis, 'that you want your pongos to learn how to be seasick like gentlemen?'

Newman answered with a smile: 'Actually, sir, one of the objects is that they should learn *not* to be seasick.'

From that moment the two officers met several times and Mountbatten could not have been more helpful. Every destroyer in his flotilla took a few commandos when it went to sea; other men went out in submarines or in the motor launches that by night took Allied agents to and from the coast of unhappy France.

The Special Service Battalions, however, did not last long. Over one thousand strong, with fifty officers, they were too large and unwieldy. They were accordingly divided up into smaller units now officially designated Commandos, though Haydon's head-quarters, under whose command they remained, kept its title of Special Service Brigade. On 5 March 1941, 1 Battalion was split into 1 Commando and 2 Commando, Newman being promoted lieutenant-colonel and appointed to command 2 Commando.

The command of a battalion or its equivalent is a moment in an officer's life which is at once critical, anxious and inspiring. Newman, like many others at such a moment, made a searching examination of himself and the objectives that he would set for his new command. These he embodied in what he called his 'ideal' for the Commando unit, covering several sheets and set out in twenty-two points. It embraced complete efficiency in all the techniques of the soldier's trade, the special skills demanded of the commandos in cliff-climbing, the handling of boats, swimming in full battle order, moving across country by night with complete confidence, the use of explosives, and the attainment of that 'extra scruple of endurance' that often makes the impossible possible. He would be ruthless in getting rid of any man not dedicated to the fighting spirit and eager to attack the enemy closely. Officers and men must be very close to each other, enjoying 'mutual respect and friendship' and with 'complete understanding and confidence in each other, so that men would follow their officers in complete faith'. Above all, every officer and man must be filled with pride in his unit and feel that it was 'a privilege and honour' to be admitted to its ranks.

Notice the emphasis on relations between officers and men, which was one of the hallmarks of commando units. There existed a very special kind of discipline and relations between all ranks. To all his officers and men (though not to his face) Newman was 'Colonel Charles', as Copland, the second-in-command, was 'Major Bill', and Day, the adjutant, was 'Captain Stan'. Officers would let their hair down with NCOs and men at the 'troop dinners' that occasionally took place and in many other ways mix in a comradeship of human relations.

But no man ever stepped over into the province of familiarity, simply because the 'mutual respect and friendship' was instinctive and based upon example and worth. Otherwise the outward forms of soldierly discipline were strictly observed. Least of all was there any doubt at all about 'spit and polish'. Men were at all times expected to be correctly and smartly turned out, with webbing scrubbed and all brass parts polished. No guerrilla slovenliness was tolerated. In a formation commanded by a Guardsman, as Haydon was, there could be no doubt about the standards of turnout and soldierly bearing expected. Under him, what had been a number of private armies in the days of the Independent Companies was rapidly formed into a force with a common doctrine, training and a high discipline, though he encouraged each unit to develop its own individuality.

Among these men of mixed regiments, awkward and sometimes laughable problems arose. One of these was dress. A parade represented a sergeant-major's headache, for almost every cap-badge in the Army was represented and every kind of coloured 'fore-and-aft', together with a liberal sprinkling of Scotch bonnets. However, 2 Commando soon had its own badge of a dagger between the letters SS, designed by Newman, Copland and Day on the tablecloth of a café at Paignton. Later, when they went to Scotland, the Balmoral was adopted as the parade head-dress for all ranks, though when 'walking out' each man continued to wear his own regimental fore-and-aft or bonnet.

The 'Jocks', however, presented a special sartorial problem, for, although it was forbidden on operations and on exercises when concealment was important, the kilt was normally allowed to all ranks entitled to it. Needless to say, it was worn with *brio* in all its colour variations of Argyll, Black Watch, Gordon, Cameron, Seaforth and others. These Highland troops together formed 5 Troop under Captain D. W. Roy, Cameron Highlanders, a young officer of great dash and *élan*, perhaps the most colourful figure in 2 Commando, tall, heavily moustached and known throughout it as 'The Laird'.

However, even this apparently orderly arrangement had its serious problem, for in 5 Troop, not content with a common Scottism, the sparks of antique tribal rivalries were rekindled and old Highland feuds broke out into flames. Campbell and Gordon were at each other again.

Newman was very angry. He had the whole Troop out and told them that this sort of nonsense had got to stop. 'You must make up your minds,' he said, 'whether you are going to fight each other or the Germans. If each other, back you all go to your units tomorrow.'

Donald Roy, very stiff, erect and troubled, said: 'Colonel, you can rely on us.'

'I mean it, Donald. This sort of thing can't go on. I shall RTU every man jack of you if you don't stop it.'

'Returned To Unit' was the most dreaded phrase to every man, for throughout the commandos virtually the only punishment ever imposed was to return him to the unit whence he had come.

Such outbursts, however, and certain colourful pranks were incidents in an otherwise gruelling life cheerfully accepted. They marched the one hundred and twenty miles from Paignton to Weymouth in two and a half days, sleeping in ditches. Challenged by a letter in *The Times* that the longest non-stop march in British history was the sixty-two miles said to have been made by Crawford's Light Brigade to Talavera in 1809*, they beat it by marching sixty-three miles in twenty-three hours. They went for running matches in hill country at 'seven miles in the hour'. They swam in icy seas in full kit. They learnt to move at night over open country across all obstacles with confidence. And after all exer-

---

* The claim was made by Sir William Napier and is not justified. The march was spread over more than one day, with long rests, and only the last forty miles was continuous.

cises, however gruelling, they cleaned and polished their weapons and equipment before bedding down.

Much the same kind of existence was being pursued by all the Commandos of the Brigade under Haydon's training directives. Nearly all of them were to be represented in the St Nazaire Raid and we shall meet several of them as our story proceeds, but it is now time that we made the acquaintance of others of the gallant company of 2 Commando, of whom we shall see so much.

Newman was extraordinarily fortunate in having a second-in-command who was in every way his complement in personal qualities. Major W. O. Copland, a Territorial of the South Lancashire Regiment, was works manager of a large engineering firm in Warrington. A man of high ideals, strict in behaviour, tall, erect, iron-haired, his was the steel gauntlet that upheld the gay banner of Newman's leadership. A veteran of the First World War, he was forty-four years old, yet to everyone's astonishment he stood up to the rigours of commando training with complete equanimity. As hard as the nails he manufactured and of incredible vitality, 'Major Bill' was quite fearless, unexcited by a crisis, inclined to be severe and had a most convincing presence which showed all these high-spirited young colts that the bit had a curb as well as a snaffle. He was, said Newman, 'a hell of an inspiration to everyone and did more than anyone else to lick the Commando into shape.' He was also, like a great many first war soldiers, a cordial hater of the Germans.

Adjutant to Newman was Captain Stanley Day, Royal Corps of Signals, as ardent and energetic on the battlefield as upon the rugger field of Birkenhead Park; and in Regimental Sergeant-Major A. Moss, a strapping six-foot-three-inch Liverpool Scot, we behold a man of heroic mould and splendid character. These were the senior ranks on Newman's headquarters. The greater part of the Commando had derived from the 54th (East Anglia) Division, the 55th (Liverpool) Division and the London Divisions. Like other Commandos, there were six Troops besides the Head-quarters Troop – 1 Troop commanded by the splendid and fearless Captain R. Hodgson, admired and loved by all; 2 Troop by the wiry keen-hearted Captain David Birney, a winner of the King's Prize at Bisley; 3 Troop at the time of St Nazaire under the acting command of Lieutenant John Roderick, a stalwart bank clerk of six feet three inches and fifteen stone; 4 Troop by the solicitor, Captain R. H. Hooper; and 6 Troop by Captain Michael Burn, son of Sir Clive Burn and a foreign correspondent of *The Times*.

Roy's Troop, the kilted 5, had originated, like himself, from the Liverpool Scottish and had been augmented by recruitment elsewhere, though the London Scottish elected to remain with their London comrades. Here we must notice one of the most remarkable of all figures in 2 Commando – Roy's Troop Sergeant-Major, whose altogether splendid qualities as a sheer, fighting soldier enrich the story that we shall read of the combined Commandos' break-out from encirclement. Troop Sergeant-Major George Haines was no Scot himself, but came from the East Surrey Regiment. A south-country farmer, he was short and square and had enormous hands. As a sergeant, it was he who had marched in volunteers from the East Surreys when Newman went to interview them at Kingston-on-Thames. When the interviews appeared to be over, Newman asked:

'Any more, sergeant?'

'Yes, sir; me.'

'You sergeant? I'm sorry, but I couldn't possibly take you. I've no vacancies for sergeants.'

Haines laid a large right hand on the chevrons of his other sleeve and replied quietly: 'I'm quite ready to take these off, sir, if you'll take me as a private.'

Come he did, in spite of his CO's protestations at the loss of 'one of my finest NCOs'. In a very short time he had regained his sergeant's stripes and advanced further, and in battle was to win from his commanding officer the highest possible of all commendations.

These were some of the men of 2 Commando, hardy, high-spirited, filled with a bubbling vitality, scorning the organized comforts of cookhouse, canteen and 'welfare', who worked and played and laughed at Paignton and later at Weymouth. About mid-summer 1941 they went off to Scotland, where they remained, training very strenuously in the mountains and in the cold seas until, after several disappointments of raids promised and cancelled, Hooper's troop and half Birney's took part in the successful Vaagso raid in December.

A sudden call took Newman to London to meet Glendinning and get orders for another operation, but the long journey was wasted, for yet again the operation was no sooner planned than it was cancelled. He took his Commando off for stiff winter landing exercises in the Outer Hebrides in HMS *Prince Charles* and then back again to their normal location at Ayr in mid-February. He was beginning to be a little 'browned-off', but he had no sooner set foot in Ayr than he was summoned by Charles Haydon to a training conference at Irvine. The conference over, he was told to stay behind and when they were alone Haydon ordered him to take the train to London that very night and to meet him at COHQ the next morning.

More significantly, he gave orders for a hundred picked men from Newman's Commando to be specially trained in street fighting by night and for a squad to be sent to Burntisland, in the Firth of Forth, for a course in demolitions. 'You must make it perfectly clear,' he said, 'that it is a case of "No questions, no answers".'

Speculation and excitement ran high in Newman's orderly room when he went back to Ayr to give the necessary orders for these details, but he himself was slightly cynical. 'Is this,' he asked himself as he entrained for London that night, 'going to be just another false dawn?' On arrival in London, he took a room, by a quirk of chance, at the Normandie Hotel and soon afterwards made his way in the cold winter sunshine to COHQ. He found that Haydon had not yet arrived, but his pulse quickened as he listened to veiled remarks by the staff.

'Do you know what the job is?' asked one of them.

'I haven't a clue,' Newman answered breezily.

Another said: 'What a very, very lucky chap you are.'

A third handed him a fat file, and said: 'Perhaps you would like to look through this, sir, while you are waiting.'

It was the St Nazaire Intelligence file. A very interesting docket, thought Newman as he glanced through the voluminous reports, the photographs, the engineer drawings of lock gates, and the maps and plans, but he was not much illuminated. While he was still wondering what it was all about Haydon arrived and they went together into a private room, where Haydon broke the great news.

After outlining the plan he said: 'The dock demolitions are to be carried out by combined demolition squads from the Brigade that Pritchard is to train at once. Your Commando is to provide the fighting troops for the operation and you are to be the Military Force Commander.' He added: 'This is by far the biggest job yet attempted by the Commandos.'

Newman was electrified. 'I was,' he says, 'filled with elation. Here was a goal as exciting as any man could wish for.'

He was then firmly locked into a small room and there, filling it with the aromatic fumes of John Cotton, he gloated eagerly over the air photographs, the plans of the great caissons, the spottings of enemy defences, the information from secret sources and, above all, the beautiful little model of the docks made by the RAF, which he took wholly to his bosom till he had learnt it by heart so well that he could have walked about the docks blindfold and placed his slabs of explosive unerringly on the vital spots.

Then, with a smile of anticipation, he awaited the conference that had been called for 26 February, when he was to meet his co-driver of this daring and spirited 'chariot of fire'.

7. THE LEADERS MEET

No such easy briefing of the part for which he was to be cast in the unfolding drama was given to Robert Ryder.

We have seen him, chafing at Wilton House, receive a sudden signal to attend a conference at COHQ at 3 o'clock on 26 February. Normally punctilious in being on time for any engagement, he arrived at Richmond Terrace fifteen minutes late through the aberrations of war-time transport. He moved quietly into the room to which he was conducted, took an obscure seat at the back and beheld to his surprise an imposing gathering of twenty or more senior officers of all three Services, headed by an Admiral of the Fleet, in whom he recognized Sir Charles Forbes. He saw also Rear-Admiral A. J. Power, Assistant Chief of Naval Staff, Home Waters.

Mountbatten was in the chair. There was a model of some sort in front of him. He was outlining to the meeting some operation that was to take place, clearly a raid on some port in which commando troops were to be landed for demolitions and aircraft were to drop bombs. Ryder listened with interest but with limited comprehension. What had all this to do with him?

Towards the end of his exposition of the plan, Mountbatten said tersely:

'The Naval Force Commander appointed for this operation is Commander R. E. D. Ryder.' Then, looking up: 'That all right with you, Ryder?'

To which the startled officer replied: 'Certainly, sir.'

Mountbatten asked: 'Has this been mentioned to you yet?'

'No, sir,' Ryder answered, 'but I'm quite ready to take it on.'

Mountbatten having finished his outline, Sir Charles Forbes was invited to give his views. Before the meeting he had made it

very clear to Mountbatten (very much his junior) that the operation still found no favour with him. He thought it extremely rash
and likely to end in total loss. 'It is not,' he said with emphasis, 'an
operation of war. But as it's got to be done, we must make the best
of it.'

To the meeting he put two problems of particular concern.
First of these was how to plot a route to St Nazaire that would be
free from German attack, especially air attack, but one which
would not be too long. The second was the still intractable
problem of the ship that was to ram the caisson, since the Chiefs
of Staff were opposed to the use of the French *Ouragan* and since
the Admiralty, in spite of Sir Dudley Pound's assurance to the
Chiefs of Staff, still obstinately hung back from providing even the
one essential explosive ship. Why not, it was now suggested, an
old submarine? To this Hughes-Hallett immediately opposed
critical objections: a submarine could not keep pace with motor
launches, was a bad platform from which to land troops, might
not be able to penetrate the anti-torpedo net and would not have
sufficient impact on the caisson.

Nor was the explosive ship the only essential at which the
Admiralty jibbed. It was even most improbable, Admiral Pound
said, that any escorting destroyers could be found for protecting
this very vulnerable force during its sea voyage; but he would see
what could be done.

The meeting over, Haydon introduced to each other the two
men who were to be closely bound together in this exploit and
upon whom all now centred – Ryder and Newman. It was a
memorable meeting in their lives and a vital one for those whom
they were to lead, for the fate of the expedition might well have
depended on their relationship. As it was, the two men shook
hands, sized each other up and were satisfied. It was the beginning
of a warm friendship, quickly generated, each man recognizing
the other's qualities. So different on the surface – the one self-
contained and somewhat introvert, the other genial and plainly
extrovert – Ryder and Newman were yet brothers under the skin.
In Haydon's own warmhearted words, 'they were both pure gold;
each in his own way was a model of the finest type of Englishman'.

The moment they met Newman subjected Ryder to a barrage

of questions – how do you propose to do this and what do you think of that? But as soon as he could get in a word, Ryder himself asked:

'Look here, where the hell *is* this place we are supposed to attack?'

For throughout the time that Ryder had been present at the conference the objective had not been mentioned.

Newman laughed. 'Good heavens! Haven't they told you? It's St Nazaire.'

'Nobody's told me a damned thing. What are we supposed to do in St Nazaire?'

'Blow up a lot of dock gates and so on. A really saucy job – the sauciest since Drake.'

'Are you in on it already?'

'Rather. Brigadier Haydon has briefed me. Outline Plan, big Intelligence docket and a splendid model. Quite a plateful for both of us.'

Ryder thought a minute, the immensity of his task beginning to dawn on him. Then: 'God! Where do I start? I've no staff, no office, not even a clerk or typewriter.'

This was to be one of Ryder's most vexing handicaps. Unlike Newman, who had a second-in-command, an adjutant and a small office staff, Ryder was a lone hand, with no status, no apparatus for executive action, and actually no authority to give orders to anyone, for he commanded no unit or formation. At this stage he had stalwart support from Luce, but it was one of the practical difficulties for which no provision had been made, and out of Bob Ryder's experience a lesson was learned.

There followed for both of them several weeks of desperately hard work, the days and nights spent in a whirligig of journeys, conferences, specialist consultations, arguments, long hours of hard thinking and the study of charts, plans, air photos and intelligence reports. There was only a month to go. Newman summoned his adjutant, Stanley Day, to come up from Scotland to help with the multitudinous detail, and he sent to Copland, without revealing anything, special instructions on the types of training on which the picked men were to concentrate – night movement, street fighting, weapon training.

For several days the whole prospect was bedevilled by the Admiralty's stubborn objection to providing the explosive ship. Two days after the meeting Rear-Admiral H. E. Horan, who directed Combined Ops' Landing Craft and Bases, told them on Mountbatten's behalf that a submarine really would not do and that if no suitable surface craft could be definitely allocated within two days, the CCO 'intended to plan the operation with the use of coastal craft [motor launches] alone'. Newman and Ryder, in fact, actually prepared a plan that they liked very much to do the job with small craft alone, Newman being prepared to destroy the big caissons with his commandos, according to a plan which, as will be seen, had long before been prepared by Pritchard. Hughes-Hallett and his colleagues, however, remained firmly opposed to this notion. 'No destroyer, no operation,' he said, rolling his gold pencil between his hands. Motor launches were far too vulnerable. It was all very well to risk losing the men after they had done their job, but if the MLs were spotted going in the troops would never get ashore to do it. 'They will all,' he said, 'go up in flames.' In the outcome, Mountbatten personally ordered a compromise by which half the troops were to go in motor launches and the remainder in the explosive ship.

The destroyer was provided at last. Mountbatten would have fought it out through the Chiefs of Staff, but he had to leave London and in his absence a telephone signal was made on his behalf to Admiralty that, unless a destroyer were provided, the operation would be cancelled as far as Combined Operations were concerned. Time was desperately short and thus the matter was brought to a head. In fact, the Chariot committee knew privately that a destroyer had already been earmarked should the issue be forced. This was HMS *Campbeltown*, formerly the American destroyer *Buchanan* ('old Buck' to those who had sailed in her under that flag), one of those fifty ex-USA obsolete four-funnelled ships for which, in a time of dire need, we had bartered away to the Americans the use of certain of our Caribbean ports for a hundred years.

There is one final and important COHQ conference at which we must look in before we leave London to see the plan – still far from complete in its details – being translated into action. This was on 3 March. Ryder and Newman – the latter unaccountably very nervous – explained their own plans for carrying out their tasks. But by far the most important matter discussed was the air plan. Significantly a representative of the Director of Plans, Air Ministry, was present (Wing Commander J. M. Tomes), but a certain amount of unease was experienced by many, especially by Newman. It was becoming clearer that Bomber Command was not as keen as had been hoped. The aircraft that they were prepared to offer rapidly dwindled under the stresses imposed on their own programme of operations. For the time being the plan held that the bombing attack should be directed on to the docks until just before *Campbeltown* rammed and should then switch to the *town*. We shall see in due course not only how that was altered but also what severe restrictions were to be imposed on pilots.

Newman particularly asked that some low-flying aircraft should be put in at the critical period of fifteen minutes before Zero (as it was then called) until fifteen minutes afterwards. 'After all,' he said, '*we* are going in pretty low.' But he received an arid answer. It was perhaps after this meeting that he said to Robert Henriques – and was to say it again later – 'I don't believe this bombing will come off.'

*

Paper now began to be translated into action. There was a mountain of work to be done in very little time. The resourceful Intelligence machine produced nimble answers to the many problems of detail that still bothered Newman in particular. Most insistent of the tasks were the drastic modifications to *Campbeltown*, whose strange metamorphosis from a 'four-stacker' American to a bogus German we shall shortly witness. Quantities of stores had to be collected under the veil of secrecy. Naval stores officers could be given no reason or authority why extra petrol tanks should be sent to Poole and Appledore, nor why the country had to be scoured for the scarce Oerlikon ammunition. No one must be told why special explosives of curious shape and sizes were demanded. Specialists must not know the purposes for which their brains were being picked. Doubts had to be referred to many and sometimes peculiar consultants – such as the gentleman at the

Admiralty with the Canute-like title of Superintendent of Tides, the officer at the War Office known even more mysteriously as the Controller of Deception, the Inter-Services Security Board, Home Office experts on the killing range of explosive blasts (lest our own men ashore should suffer when *Campbeltown* blew up), the Director of Signals for secret information on German naval signal systems, and so on.

Ryder and Newman, accompanied by Constructor-Commander A. J. Merrington, an old friend of Ryder's, and Captain (E) A. L. F. Mark-Wardlaw, who was to keep liaison on matters material, paid their first visit to *Campbeltown*, lying at Portsmouth. There we get a first glimpse of Ryder's keen security-mindedness when, to Newman's amusement, he would not let him go on board the destroyer. 'Charles, I can't possibly let anyone in khaki go on board that ship!'

On 10 March *Campbeltown* arrived at Devonport Dockyard, where her conversion was to be carried out, and on that day Ryder and Newman attended a conference at Fort Egg Buckland, Forbes's headquarters nearby, with Sir Charles himself in the chair. Chariot was now under his command and he gave to its problems all his experience and the services of an able staff. Among these Ryder was to find a tower of strength in Commander C. R. McCrum, a tall, spare, loose-limbed officer, grey-haired, with not only a fertile brain but also the ability to get things done. In him and David Luce, who was also present, Ryder had two stalwart pillars.

But a figure even more significant to the grand design was also met at this conference. Lieutenant N. T. B. Tibbits was a brilliant product of that establishment which the Royal Navy calls HMS *Vernon*, where they study not only torpedoes but also other forms of explosive destruction. He had been hand-picked as the specialist officer to devise the means of blowing up the *Campbeltown* after she had rammed the caisson, and it was the greatest good fortune for the expedition, if not for the gallant young officer himself, that he should have been selected. Nigel Tibbits was twenty-eight years old, of middle height, fair, with a long, sensitive and intelligent face and a slow, quiet smile. The son of an admiral, Robert Roxborough prize-man cadet, winner of five firsts in the sub-lieutenant examination, Ogilvie medallist in torpedo gunnery, he had also a passionate interest in mathematics, the higher abstractions of which he would discuss with verve and gusto and often with great bursts of laughter. His intellectual grasp of things was instantaneous and sure. Through all the searching tests that Ryder, so meticulous in detail, was to put him, he was found to have an easy mastery of technical detail and a resourceful answer to any problem. He was one of several who on the eve of this exploit was to have that queer premonition of death that men sometimes do before battle, yet he was utterly cool and possessed till the last moment and it was, indeed, to be his hand upon the wheel that finally laid *Campbeltown* upon her altar. To him and to Pritchard the splendour of the Charioteers' achievement is largely due.

Ryder had now thankfully finished with London, and he presently repaired to Falmouth, where, it had been decided at the COHQ conference of 26 February, the combined force should assemble. 'The only way,' said Ryder, 'to get anything out of the Admiralty is to get as far away from them as possible and make signals.' Newman, however, had to go back there for a while. He sent Stanley Day off to Ayr to rejoin the Commando and sail with it to Falmouth in the *Princesse Joséphine Charlotte*, one of the 'carrying ships' for commando landing craft. Then he, too, quitted London by car, but before doing so had an interview with Mountbatten, which Newman was always to remember. They met on the steps of Richmond Terrace as Newman was about to walk down to his car and Mountbatten called him back. Lord Louis was always very forthright and did not 'wrap things up'. He was especially straight-to-the-point on this occasion.

'I want you to be quite clear,' he said, 'that this is not just an ordinary raid; it is an important operation of war.'

Nothing could have enchanted Newman more. He listened, absorbed and intent, as Mountbatten went on:

'It is also a very hazardous operation. I am quite confident that you will get in and do the job all right, but, frankly, I don't expect any of you to get out again.

'If we lose you all, you will be about equivalent to the loss of one merchant ship; but your success will save many merchant ships. We have got to look at the thing in those terms.'

Deeply impressed, Newman listened on.

'For that reason, I don't want you to take anyone on the operation who has any serious home ties or worries. No married men. Tell all your men that quite openly, and give every man the opportunity of standing down if he feels he should. Nobody will think any the worse of him and we must have that quite clear, too.'

Newman promised soberly to obey, but he knew without the least scruple of doubt what the answer would be. No doubt Lord Louis did also.

Noting ironically that it was Friday the 13th, Newman drove off to Falmouth, calling on his way at Marlow for the latest RAF reconnaissance photographs. He noted that a ship was now in the Normandie Dock and he noticed also new gun positions disclosed on the tops of buildings. He was not alarmed. He stopped for the night at a Tavistock hotel, very ill at ease because the door of his bedroom, which was filled with maps, photographs, the model of the St Nazaire docks, and four of the latest and extremely secret type of wireless sets, had a defective lock. He spent an uncomfortable and anxious evening guarding his life-or-death secrets, and arrived next day at Falmouth to find the *Princesse Joséphine Charlotte* already there and his men in fine fettle and longing to know what it was all about.

8. THE DESTROYERS

While Newman, Ryder and the staffs of COHQ and Plymouth were working hard at their plans and preparations, the officers and men of eight Commandos were preparing themselves with vigour and gusto for their splendid adventure. In Ayrshire the hundred picked men of 2 Commando, knowing nothing yet of what lay ahead, were training intensively under Copland, especially on the craft of street fighting by night. This was but a continuance of the sort of work they had long been practising, but over on Burntisland, in the Firth of Forth, a very special form of training was going on by a very special body of young men, the like of whom has seldom before or since been assembled together.

On orders issued from Haydon's Special Service Brigade head-quarters at Castle Douglas, seven Commandos, in addition to Newman's, had sent to Burntisland small, selected parties of officers and men for a specialized study and practice in the destruction of dockyards. These were 1, 3, 4, 5, 6, 9 and 12 Commandos. To all of them, about ninety in number, it was just a course in another type of task that commandos might be called upon to do. They were about as hardy and fearless a gathering of young fellows as one could imagine. Their tasks, which many of them were to carry out with such brilliant dash and precision, required the handling of the most modern types of high explosives, a blindfolded familiarity with the objects, as yet unseen, which they were to attack, a cool nerve and a complete disregard of whatever might be going on about them.

The guide and tutor of these men was perhaps himself the most remarkable of them all, and one to whose memory there is owing a tribute too long unpaid, for he was one of the most assiduous and inspired designers of the 'deed of glory'. Captain W. H. Pritchard was a Territorial officer of the Royal Engineers, aged twenty-eight. He was tall, strongly built, dark-haired, dark-complexioned, with brown eyes that glowed with an ardent fire for any purpose he had at heart or glinted with humour when about the pranks or rags that he enjoyed. As his father said, 'he lived and loved hard and every moment seemed of importance'. He would enjoy a turbulent party till midnight, then douse his head with cold water and work till morning on his plans and calculations. He had great charm of manner and, in the words of Bob Montgomery, who knew him intimately, had 'a wonderful smile and mischievous eyes'. This Celtic fire and charm broke through the surface on the least occasion; to quote Montgomery again, he was both a romantic and a fanatic, born a hundred and fifty years too late. To Ronald Swayne he was 'most inspiring', to Stuart Chant 'damned good', to Corran Purdon 'a magnificent chap', to little 'Tiger' Watson 'a vivid personality'.

Bill Pritchard was the son of Captain W. E. Pritchard, MBE, Dock Master of Cardiff. He had thus not only been brought up in docks but also, on apprenticeship to the engineering branch of the Great Western Railway, had spent five years in their dockyards. In September 1939 he had gone to France with the British Expeditionary Force and had won the Military Cross for the demolition of a bridge under fire during the withdrawal to Dunkirk. It was the Dunkirk evacuation that first filled him with enthusiasm for dock demolition. 'Why the hell,' he asked, 'didn't we blow up all the Channel docks before we left them to the Hun?'

On return home Pritchard was posted as an instructor to Aldershot and there met, as a fellow instructor, Captain R. K. Montgomery, a very tall and well-built young Regular officer of the Royal Engineers, who became his fast friend and disciple – indeed, his hero-worshipper. When home on leave in Cardiff Pritchard witnessed a heavy air-raid on the docks, and became more than ever a fanatic for dock destruction by engineer methods. He said to Montgomery on return to Aldershot:

'You'll never destroy docks by bombing. It's a complete waste of time. You make a lot of big holes and create a nuisance but you don't stop the dock from working. The only certain way is to send chaps in and place explosives right on the vital parts.'

Thus we very soon find him going to the Transportation branch (which is a Royal Engineer branch dealing with docks, canals, railways, etc., not motor transport) at the War Office, and, junior though he was, getting himself listened to. What he put up to them and what they were interested in, was the destruction of our own docks in the event of invasion. He was told to study the problem and began to do so in company with Montgomery. He was given the plans of a dockyard which, by one of those dramatic coincidences that seem too unlikely for an authentic narrative, were the plans of St Nazaire itself. By a further coincidence Montgomery had himself been at St Nazaire immediately before the British evacuation. On these plans the two officers worked night after night before at last they put up their demolition proposals to Transportation. It is of particular interest that they proposed the use of two destroyers, though all the demolitions were to be carried out by troops landed from them.

In 1941 the two friends were separated, Pritchard being posted to a Transportation unit in London, Montgomery to 3rd Division. Later Pritchard trained a party of twenty-six Royal Engineer NCOs for three months in dock demolitions and an association with COHQ began. Late in January 1942 he was posted to a unit in Leith, but was intercepted en route and told to report to COHQ at once. A day or two afterwards he telephoned his friend Bob Montgomery and said:

'It's on. Would you like to come?'

Thus, having 'prised himself loose' from 3rd Division, Montgomery returned to help his friend in the study of a problem with which both were already familiar. Under Haydon's direction, Pritchard had already completed a plan setting out the weight and shape of plastic explosive for each target, the precise spot on which each was to be placed, the number of men required for each, the manner in which they were to carry it out and the detailed load for each. To a large extent, he was merely putting into effect the plans already put up to Transportation after cautious consultation with technical specialists. The explosives, 'tailored' for each job, were made up by Major David Wyatt at the Stevenage SOE depot, each charge boosted with a dry guncotton primer and wrapped separately in mackintosh sheeting, with detonating cord sticking out for quick attachment to the firing system.

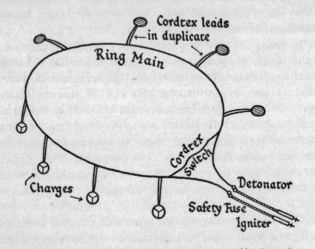

Fig 3. Diagrammatic sketch of multiple charges connected by ring main.

Many of these charges were of a like nature, such as those for blowing up the several hinged lock gates and the dockyard bridges, by the destruction of which the commandos would seal themselves off against counterattack from beyond the Submarine Basin. Others were of different and special natures, such as those for the big impeller pumps in the pump house, to attack which Stuart Chant and his sergeants would have to descend forty feet deep in the bowels of the earth. For the destruction of guns, 'sausage' charges were to be fixed round the barrel. Similar charges were to be wrapped round the pipes of machinery, blowing inwards. There were magnetic 'clams' for attacking ships and small 'limpets', also magnetic, for blowing open doors; and for motors in powerhouses there were charges that lifted the machinery off its bed.

For major tasks several charges were required to be linked together in one firing system, comprising a length of the instantaneous and waterproof detonating fuse known as 'cordtex', a detonator, a short length of the slow-burning safety fuse and a hand igniter. A length of the cordtex was attached direct to each charge and each length secured by a clove hitch to a 'ring main', also of cordtex, so that all charges went off simultaneously.

For the two big caissons, a very special charge, known as a 'wreath', had been devised. This resembled not so much a wreath as the steering-wheel of a motor car, on the spokes of which magnets were fixed, so that the wreath would cling to the internal perpendicular face of the caisson and blow a hole in it. There were twelve wreaths for the interior faces of each wall of both caissons and others were to blow holes in the internal decks or floors. Thus the wreaths required descent into the inside of the structure. For the wet, outer surfaces (both walls of both caissons would be wet if the dock were filled), twelve 18-lb charges, looking in their mackintosh wrappings like large plum puddings, were to be suspended twenty-seven feet below water.

All these charges were connected to a ring main of cordtex, so that the whole formed one firing circuit. The ring main was laid out by one man, while the others fixed the wreaths and lowered the underwater charges by lengths of ordinary cord, secured these cords and then connected all the cordtex fuse leads of the charges, which were always doubled, to the cordtex ring main. The method is shown diagrammatically in Fig 4. Quite obviously, this was a complicated and tricky job. There was well over 1000 feet of fuse and cord to handle; and to put all this correctly into position under fire without becoming hopelessly entangled needed not only a practised and a steady hand, but also a cool nerve and unshakeable determination.

Remember that the farther, or northern, caisson was positively designated as a commando task, but also that the commandos had to be prepared to attack the more important outer caisson, should *Campbeltown* not succeed or should the caisson be found to have been withdrawn into its camber. These two tasks were in due course to be assigned to teams from Harrison's 12 Commando, largely from Northern Ireland, and Sanguinetti's 5 Commando, who were mainly Regulars and reservists from the Dunkirk divisions.

The orders for their special training having been issued by

Brigade headquarters, Pritchard went to Burntisland for the course and there walked his students round the bleak Rosyth dockyard.

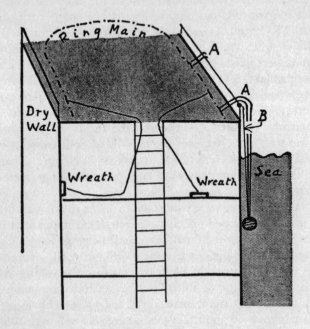

Fig 4. How it was intended to blow a caisson by commando action.

A Cordtex leads in duplicate.
B Cord for suspending charge. Diagrammatic only; precise details not now known.

Under his tutorship they became immediately enthralled, for he had, said Swayne, 'a great gift of commanding men and getting them to do just what he wanted'. Nearly all were subaltern officers or NCOs, endowed with tremendous guts, superbly fit, high-spirited, always ready for some fun. They also had considerable intelligence. Conspicuous among them were the tall, scholarly Gerard Brett, an archaeologist, Assistant Curator at the Victoria and Albert Museum, and known as 'The Byzantine Job'; Ronald Swayne, the history student, tall, strong, black-haired, just married, an Oxford rugger trial, reading Burton's *Anatomy of*

Melancholy with Brett; Harry Pennington, the dark, broad-shouldered Oxford rugger Blue who foresaw his death; Stuart Chant, the lively 'gay Gordon', of the London Stock Exchange,

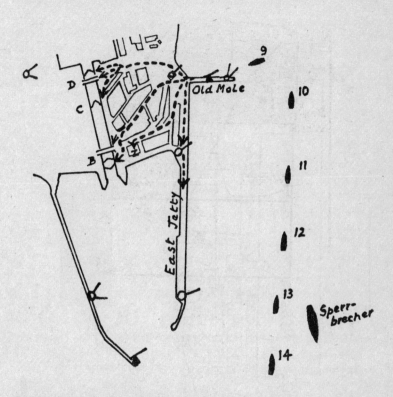

Fig 5. Group One tasks as intended to be carried out, but showing enemy defences as they actually were. (See Chapter 10)

sufficiently swarthy to be known as 'Stewie the Wop'; the golden-hearted, monocled giant Robert Burtenshaw; Corran Purdon, baby of the party, a Regular officer of the Royal Ulster Rifles, very fair, handsome, with a relish for modern poetry; Bill Etches, another fair young Regular, called 'Smoothie' from his immaculate appearance; Philip Walton, the quiet schoolmaster; Christopher Smalley, reserved, heavily moustached, walking with a rolling gait

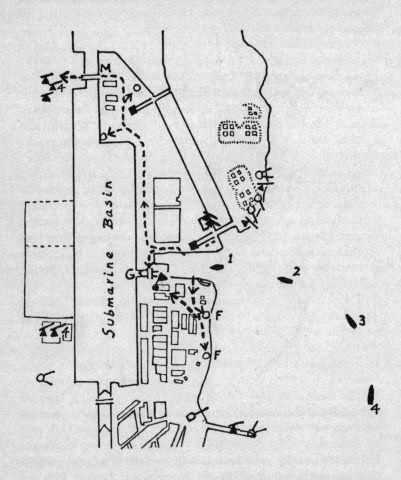

Fig 6. Group Two objectives as intended to be carried out. Flag indicates Newman's designated HQ. Enemy defences as they actually were. Small circles are gun positions found to be vacant. (See Chapter 10)

resolutely to his last assignment; and Mark Woodcock, officially on sick leave after a climbing accident, who, when peering from the big caisson's lip down to the bottom of the King George V Dock fifty-four feet below, exclaimed: 'Good God! To think that I fell five times that distance with only one bounce!'

No less remarkable were some of the NCOs who worked with these young officers – Corporal Ronald Chung, half-Chinese, broad, strong, staunch and fearless; little Corporal 'Jumbo' Reeves, ex-RAF pilot, a talented guitarist and proprietor of a fine moustache; Sergeant Frank Carr, a stalwart, erect, strong-jawed Regular sapper; Sergeant McKerr and Corporal Wright, also sappers, self-reliant and ready for anything; Sergeant Deery, the red-haired and valiant Ulsterman; Corporal 'Jones the Post', singer of songs, whose lips were so soon to be for ever stilled; Corporal Maclagan, the little Scot who was to be at Pritchard's side at his last hour; Corporal George Wheeler, the spectacled graduate in economics who was to make so remarkable an escape; Sergeant Bright, the Nottingham miner, and the four gallant East Anglian sergeants who accompanied Chant on his memorable descent into the pumping chamber – Sergeants Dockerill, Butler, King and Chamberlain.

These are but random pickings to show what manner of men were these who gathered round Pritchard in Scotland. But without doubt the most remarkable of them all was the intense person of Tom Durrant, a Regular sergeant of the Royal Engineers, who acted as sergeant-major and who was destined to win in death the only Victoria Cross ever awarded to a soldier in a naval engagement.

Like Swayne, and like Chant's East Anglian sergeants, Durrant came from Glendinning's 1 Commando and he was, Swayne tells us, 'without doubt the most loyal and efficient NCO I ever encountered'. Aged twenty-three, Tom Durrant was of average height, well set-up, well-knit, strong, as dark as a gypsy, with a thin line of moustache. His whole inner self burned with the dedicated intensity of a crusader and he would burst out violently against any man who faltered in zeal and against anyone who criticized those to whom he owed loyalty. He had a granite-like determination, was himself a very fine technician and was steeped in that high code of soldierly integrity and devotion which is the

hallmark of his Corps. But he had also a strong strain of independence and self-reliance and when his opinion was asked by an
officer answered like an equal. Again in Swayne's words, he was

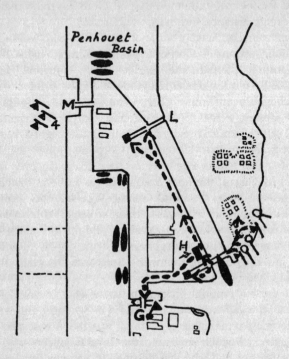

Fig 7. Group Three objectives and actual enemy positions. Guns on roof of pumping-
house not shown. (See Chapter 10)

'a formidable character and was treated carefully by all ranks, yet
his charm and good humour were evident to everyone in his
infectious smile'.

Durrant, who came from the village of Green Street Green, in
Kent, had been a butcher's boy and a builder's labourer before
enlisting in the Royal Engineers on 1 February 1937. He had a
brother, Jack, also a Regular soldier and at that time a Staff-
Sergeant in the RASC. Through him we discover another of those
long-armed coincidences that enrich with their significance and

imaginative flavour the whole story of St Nazaire. Jack Durrant had won the Military Medal only a few miles from St Nazaire itself on 17 June, 1940, when the Cunard liner *Lancastria*, in which nearly all the crew and more than 3000 soldiers had met a ghastly death from burning oil, had been sunk by bombs while evacuating our troops on the surrender of France. The *Lancastria* twice makes an appearance in our story and there is therefore a relish of prophecy in the words of Tom when he accompanied Jack to Buckingham Palace to see him decorated by the King. When his brother had told him the tragic story, Tom said nothing for a moment and then burst out:

'Jack, when we go back to St Nazaire we are going to knock seven hells out of them.' That was a year and a half before the Raid.

With such an ardent spirit animating all, the training was quickly mastered and the pace accelerated. The young destroyers learnt the difference between a caisson and the type of double lock gates that fold or swing back on hinges, they studied the machinery for opening and closing them, examined steel bridges and power stations. Using plasticene for practice purposes, they learnt how to mould the new plastic charges to the most vulnerable part of any equipment, choosing, wherever possible, a metal casting as the point of attack, since castings were irreparable (the castings of the big impeller pumps below ground at St Nazaire being irreplaceable in less than a year), and choosing, on all targets that were identical, the same point of attack, so that subsequently the enemy should be unable to interchange parts. They learnt the simple lighting by fusee of slow-burning safety fuse, which looks like a length of cord and burns at two feet per minute, and then firing by a percussion igniter by pulling out a pin to strike a spark. Gaining confidence and dexterity in the handling of all this dangerous material, they were taught how the safety fuse, when ignited by fusee or percussion igniter, burnt for its set distance till it set off the small tubular No 27 compound-explosive detonator into which it was crimped, thus initiating a detonating wave through the instantaneous cordtex and thereby blowing the main charge.

Thence they went on to learn that, for any major task, everything must be duplicated – two cordtex leads for each charge, two initiating points for firing the charge, two directions of impulse through the ring main, provided by means of a cordtex switch across the loop. Thus, whichever initiating point fired first, and whichever way the detonating wave went, the plastic charges would go up. Fig 3 illustrates this in diagrammatic form.

Cranes, ships, buildings, guns, electrical equipment – all had their own methods of destruction. Not all required explosives. Destruction by fire with 'tar babies', 'firepots' and petrol ampoules also had its part; and for delicate machinery sledgehammers and axes, duly insulated against electric shock, were adequate.

It was not long before Pritchard had all these men thinking, talking and dreaming explosives, instinctively assessing the means of destroying anything they saw. All the time there was no hint that anything was afoot, nor that these mysteries were anything more than normal education for commando soldiers. At the end of February the demolition course split into two parties, one going under Pritchard to his home ground at Cardiff and the other to the shattered docks of Southampton, where Montgomery had gone soon after joining, to meet Mr M. J. McHaffie, the Docks Engineer, and to study the King George V Dock.* Although the guise of normal training was maintained, various security precautions were taken, such as the removal of Commando shoulder flashes, and when some pompous official at Cardiff enquired what right they had to obstruct roadways with their queer and apparently senseless bits of string, they quietly folded up their gear and melted away. Dockers and other onlookers gazed indulgently at the silly soldier games as, hour after hour, officers and men played with funny brown paper parcels, handled with care and precision, all tied together with long coils of wet string.

The object was to train each man to complete nearly every demolition in the dark in under ten minutes. Each task was reduced to a drill for a set party and in all exercises men were dropped as casualties as they ran up to their objectives, so that, if necessary, one man could do at least the most vital part of the whole task. They learnt the drill first by day, then carried it out blindfolded and finally by night. Thus Brett and Burtenshaw and their men descended into

* The plans signed for by Montgomery are still there.

the eerie, hollow, steel heart of the caisson at Southampton, thus Chant and his sergeants, trying to hurry without losing balance, went dizzily down the precipitous way to the underground cavern where the pumping impellers lay. The sheer physical effort required for these performances may be judged by the fact that the average load of the explosives, carried in rucksacks by officers and men alike, was 60 lb per man, and in some cases as much as 90 lb. This heavy encumbrance meant that none of them could carry any arms except a Colt automatic pistol as a personal weapon, and strongly armed protection squads were therefore to be provided by 2 Commando to cover them as they worked.

To all this work the eager young commandos, intelligent as well as fit, took as ducks to water. They found it highly exhilarating and their night practices had an atmosphere almost as tense and dramatic as the real thing. The eeriness of the dark and empty docks, the challenges of suspicious sentries and the constant threat of attack from the air lent similitude to the scene. Thus they crept round the cliffs at Penarth and plodded across the blacked-out docks at Southampton, among the bomb-craters, the wrecked sheds and the twisted railway lines, as if they were in hostile territory in France, imagining an enemy in every shadow and prepared to deal with him.

After about a week the Cardiff and Southampton parties changed round, so that all should be familiar with every task. About this time one of the officers wrote to Robert Henriques, the brigade major of the SS Brigade, saying: 'All this is a bloody waste of time. This chap Pritchard is damned good but he just makes us do the same thing over and over again. Absolutely pointless.' Henriques smiled, for at the same time he was getting reports from Pritchard telling him by how many minutes each task had been reduced.

The time came when Pritchard was able to report by telephone to Newman that all parties were now thoroughly competent to do their tasks in less than the times allotted, in complete darkness and under the full adversity of casualties. Accordingly the two parties assembled at Cardiff on 12 March and thence journeyed to Falmouth to meet their comrades of the fighting parties from No 2 Commando newly arrived in HMS *Princesse Joséphine Charlotte*.

9. THE GATHERING OF THE FORCES

By 13 March, in a spell of warm spring sunshine, nearly all the elements of the mixed naval and military force had assembled at Falmouth, ignorant of what was afoot and ignorant even that they had anything to do with one another. In the old-fashioned, unwarlike *Princesse Joséphine Charlotte*, which we shall abbreviate, as the troops did, to *PJC*, speculation was inevitably afoot among the lively company of the soldiers, but, as they gazed over the rails, soldier-fashion, in the genial weather and saw the trim motor launches with their flared bows and workmanlike cut gliding over the quiet, sunlit waters of the harbour, they took small notice. There was no reason to suspect that the launches were any concern of theirs, for that was not the kind of chariot by which the commandos were accustomed to being carried into battle. For the first few days the *PJC* stayed berthed at the quayside, while quantities of stores poured in by every train, and then she moved out and anchored in the Sound, well isolated from the shore.

The MLs, for their part, were equally unsuspecting. The modifications which they had just undergone in the form of extra petrol tanks and Oerlikon guns fore and aft suggested nothing more than some mission that required extended cruising. They sailed quietly in, enjoying the fair weather and the mellow sun, moored or berthed and awaited the call for orders. Red Ryder, a pile of burdens on his shoulders, settled himself in the conservatory of 'Tregwynt',* which was the Falmouth Naval Headquarters, and was provided with a chart table and the bare necessities of an office, and here he collected together as best he could all the secret gear that must not yet be disclosed – the German ensigns, the

---

* Together with 'The Haven', now the Membley Hall Hotel.

special explosives, the charts, the Intelligence material and much else. He had not only to complete his own detailed orders, much of which depended on decisions still to be made by the C-in-C, but also he had, in scarcely more than a fortnight, to mould into an expeditionary force the mixed assemblage of craft and men that had been allotted to him.

The little force had swollen considerably from the early conception of one destroyer and eight motor launches. A Combined Operation Order, finally formulated on 16 March, had been worked out by Mountbatten's and Forbes's staffs jointly. One result was that the force was to be considerably strengthened and improved by the additions of two Hunt class destroyers as escorts while at sea and of a motor gunboat as a small headquarters ship for Ryder and Newman. Four more motor launches had been added to accommodate the additional soldiers who were needed for the formidable list of harbour demolitions; and now, after arrival at Falmouth, a further four were provided by Forbes at Ryder's special request. No provision had been made in the COHQ plan for offensive craft to deal with unexpected emergencies or any chance encounter with enemy patrols, guard-ships or 'examination vessels' such as are to be expected at the approach to a defended harbour. Forbes therefore fortified him with four motor launches equipped with 18-inch torpedoes, but time did not allow the mounting of Oerlikons and they therefore retained their antique Hotchkiss 3-pounders. Thus there were now sixteen motor launches in the expedition, plus others we shall very specially notice presently.

*

These motor launches were 'B' class Fairmile boats provided from three Motor Launch Flotillas of Coastal Forces – the 7th which provided the four torpedo craft, and the 20th and 28th. They came from that service whose little ships kept a coastwise watch off the shores of Britain, maids of all work on the sea's fringe, fighting fierce little battles with the enemy's small craft in the narrow waters, protecting merchant convoys, hunting submarines and rescuing from death the crews of wrecked aircraft. They were anything but ideal craft for an assault upon a defended harbour and, of course, were not intended for such a purpose, for we must at all times remember that the factor on which the whole operation was planned was surprise. Though very handy and sea-worthy, their hulls were built of two thin skins of mahogany, with a lining of calico between, so that they would not resist even a rifle bullet, though some light plating round the bridge and a few coir-filled splinter-mats were provided.

Measuring 112 feet by 19 feet 6 inches, these little boats were powered by two 650 hp Hall-Scott petrol engines, giving them a maximum speed of eighteen knots. From the well-equipped little bridge the captain, usually a lieutenant, passed his helm and engine orders by voicepipe to the small wheelhouse, a few steps down and forward of the bridge, where the coxswain stood at the wheel, and where also were to be found the engine-room tele-graphs, which rang down to the engine-room the speed ordered from the bridge, the two engine revolution counters and the control for actuating the foamite fire extinguishers below deck. The boats of 20 and 28 Flotillas were fitted with an additional wheel on the bridge.

The wheel itself actuated a Lockheed hydraulic steering gear, which we shall see being put out of action again and again as shells or splinters smashed its oil-filled pipes. When this occurred, the only manner of steering was by hand – a very exposed and dangerous performance not to be attempted by the chicken-hearted. For this purpose an iron tiller had to be fitted on to the rudder-head on the open deck, and the helmsman, standing completely unprotected, then actuated the tiller by hand on orders shouted back from the bridge.

Besides their new Oerlikons, the 'B' class Fairmiles were armed also, as we have briefly mentioned earlier, with a twin Lewis light machine-gun of the previous war's vintage, intended primarily against low-flying aircraft and sited amidships. In the wings of the bridge there were stripped Lewis guns, fired from the hand as in infantry work. They were equipped also with depth charges for use against submarines and with a projector for tossing hand grenades at aircraft. They had wireless, of course, as well as signalling lamps and flags, but no radar.

Normally manned by two officers and ten ratings, their com-plement was increased for the St Nazaire operation and, in addition, each of the troop-carrying boats took about fifteen commandos, so that the total of all hands on board amounted to about thirty. They were then very crowded and the upper deck was much encumbered by the extra 500-gallon petrol tanks and the Oerlikons. The deck tanks also sharply increased the boats' already high inflammability, in spite of being covered in self-sealing material of crêpe rubber laminations, and Ryder accordingly ordered that these tanks were to be used up first and then filled with sea water through the fire hoses. He also ordered that, in order to make room for the after Oerlikon, every motor launch was to land its dinghy.

All motor launches, and similar Coast Forces craft, were designated by a Navy List number, but, as these numbers are liable to confuse the reader, we shall identify them instead by the names of their commanding officers or by the simple tactical numbers by which they were designated in their cruising order; thus Stephens's boat was ML 192, but for our purposes it will be No 1. A record of their Navy List numbers is given in the diagram on page 121.

Such were the little ships that assembled under Ryder's command at Falmouth in that sunlit March. He very soon discovered, however, that an unexpected difficulty faced him. For none of these craft had ever before manoeuvred together in large formations. This shortcoming was most apparent in the 20th Flotilla, which had only recently been formed. These had been employed in rescue work and had seldom been to sea in more than pairs; few had operated with more than three or four other craft. 'I realized at once,' said Ryder, 'that it would be a great mistake to underestimate the difficulties of handling this untrained and heterogenous force. Their weakness in signalling and their inexperience in maintaining contact at night had somehow to be remedied, and remedied in a fortnight. So I determined to work them as hard as I could in that woefully short time.'

But of one thing Ryder, unlike Wellington, could not complain – the quality of the human material allotted to him. Himself a lover of small ships, he took an instant liking to these young men of Coastal Forces and found, he said, 'their attitude most refreshing'. There was nothing stuffy or conventional about them.

Unlike the commandos, the officers and ratings of the motor launches and of all the naval force were not volunteers or picked men. They were simply the augmented crews of the craft on everyday Coastal Forces duties. Yet, if there had been a selection board, it would have been difficult to have found a gathering of young men more excellently suited. Nearly all were 'hostilities only' officers and ratings of the Royal Naval Volunteer Reserve – a force composed largely of what one calls 'sporting types', renowned for its fine natural qualities and ideally suited to the companionable service of small ships. A sprinkling of them came from New Zealand, Canada and Australia.

The senior of them was Lieutenant-Commander W. L. Stephens, one of the two flotilla commanders, a delightful and spirited Irishman from the Northern Counties. The other flotilla commander was Lieutenant-Commander F. N. Wood, but illness robbed him of his part in the Raid at the last moment and his place was taken by Lieutenant T. D. L. Platt, an RNR officer and a professional Merchant Service seaman. We shall see a great deal of Lieutenant Tom Boyd, the robust, rugged, strong-nosed Hull trawler owner, a born fighter and commonly called Nero; Lieutenant Ted Burt, the Metropolitan Police detective, steady and reliable as one expects a policeman to be; Lieutenant Leslie Fenton, the film actor; Lieutenant Tom Collier, the Scottish yachtsman; Lieutenant Mark Rodier, the lover of music; Lieutenant N. H. B. Wallis, the Australian; Lieutenant Ian Henderson, the Lloyds underwriter; and many gallant ratings such as Chief Motor Mechanic Lovegrove, Able Seaman Savage, Leading Seaman Fred McKee, Able Seaman Lambert, Ordinary Seaman Albert Tew, Petty Officer Lamb and many others.

*

Such were the motor launches destined for St Nazaire and such the men in them. To these were added two other small motor craft of peculiar interest.

The first, arriving at Falmouth on 14 March, was that very peculiar and temperamental little craft which was included in the very first plan of all made by the Chariot committee. This was MTB 74, commanded by Sub-Lieutenant R. C. M. V. Wynn – Micky Wynn to most people and even Pop-eye Wynn to his intimates.

'Mad as a hatter,' Casa Maury had said when he brought him to the notice of Hughes-Hallett, 'but he has a very useful toy.'

Wynn, a young Welshman of Merionethshire, was a complete individualist. He had been a Regular officer in a cavalry regiment, but found that the Army was not his avocation and he had quitted early in the war and signed on as a deckhand in a civilian motor boat for the Dunkirk evacuation before joining the Navy. He was not at first much liked by the commandos, a few of whom had met him before at Dartmouth, because of his derogatory remarks about 'pongos', but that all changed later. He was equally disparaging about admirals.

Wynn was fair-haired and stockily built with a face in which you could easily trace the delineaments of a quiet stubbornness. Withal he had a quick eye for a pretty face – even a German one, which he was to find much to his cost when, having successfully escaped from prison in Germany, the hailing signal customary on such encounters was intercepted by the fräulein's boy friend.

Wynn's first lieutenant, and his 'dear and personal friend', was the gallant Arthur O'Connor, a tall, dark and slim New Zealander. Their 'toy', MTB 74, was a small Vosper-built motor boat, which, as the outcome of a wild suggestion by Wynn after an hilarious guest night, had been specially modified for a clandestine attack upon the *Scharnhorst* in Brest harbour. For this purpose the torpedo tubes had been dismounted from their customary positions in the boat's hull amidships and mounted on top of the fo'c'sle, the intent being that the torpedoes, gutted of their engines, stuffed with 2200 lb of explosive and fired at extremely close range, would jump over the anti-torpedo net with which the battle-cruiser was surrounded, sink to the bottom and go off on a time fuse. Clearly a 'suicide job'.

When *Scharnhorst* had escaped from Brest early in February, the disconsolate Wynn appeared to be out of a job. However, the Chariot committee at COHQ saw in him a very useful desperado for some task of destruction. After several suggestions, these tasks were finally determined in Forbes's Operation Order of 23 March; if the outer caisson were found to be open, the MTB was to enter the lock and attack the inner caisson, or, if she were able to pass through the Old Entrance, she was to fire her delay torpedoes at the U-boat kennels.

These, however, were not the only peculiarities of 'Wynn's

Weapons', as the MTB became known among the Charioteers. Smaller even than an ML, she was of doubtful seaworthiness in rough weather. She had no fewer than five engines, but they were so temperamental that a defect in any one of them communicated itself to all the other four, like measles among children. For some very mysterious reason, she was incapable of any speed in between a sluggish six knots and a furious thirty-three, so that, when sailing in company with other craft, she had to keep leapfrogging and waiting. She consumed vast quantities of petrol, so that she had a very short range, and, if taken on Chariot, would have to be towed most of the way.

Small wonder, therefore, that when Ryder was offered this odd craft he gave it a cold welcome. 'What earthly use can you be to me?' he asked Wynn. Liking the young man's spirit, he gave way to his pleading, but when he learnt of a serious engine defect a few days before sailing, he gave a decisive 'No.' Undefeated, Wynn, entirely off his own bat, and against official resistance, obtained a new engine just in the nick of time; under the guidance of the brave and devoted Chief Motor Mechanic Lovegrove, with only improvised lifting gear, the little crew worked all the last night to install it and, a few hours before the expedition was due to sail, Wynn reported to Ryder:

'Ready for sea, sir.'

*

Much more orthodox in character, but in fact much more important to our story, was the second of the two special craft added to the force. McCrum, of Sir Charles Forbes's staff, had seen that some sort of headquarters ship would be essential for Ryder and Newman and the C-in-C therefore provided them, at the last minute, with MGB 314. From this memorable little ship we shall see a great deal of the battle.

MGB 314, which belonged to the 14th MBG Flotilla, was a 'C' class Fairmile motor launch, differing a good deal from the 'B' class. Two feet smaller both in length and beam, she was powered by three 850 hp supercharged Hall-Scott engines, giving her a maximum speed of twenty-six knots. She had a long and rather deep keel, three screws and twin rudders, with a poor turning circle. Her hull was built of two skins of thin mahogany, like those of the 'B' class, but was of hard chine design, so that she rolled with an irregular rhythm and the sea slapped noisily against her angular but graceful hull. Her engines and petrol tanks took up so much space that accommodation was very cramped and uncomfortable and permeated by the condensation from human bodies. The ship's company got so used to their food being flavoured with paraffin, which was the sole means of cooking, that they complained when the flavour was lacking. Bridge and wheelhouse were arranged in much the same manner as in the 'B' class, but in the 14th Flotilla it was customary to steer from the bridge and not from the wheelhouse. The three engine-room telegraphs were also on the bridge, usually operated by the captain himself, who stood to port.

As one might expect from her designation, the gunboat was quite strongly armed for a small craft. Forward she carried a 2-pounder hand-operated Vickers pom-pom, very exposed and prominent, capable of firing about 120 rounds a minute. Aft there was another 2-pounder, this time a Rolls semi-automatic, and amidships two twin power-operated heavy machine-guns of half-inch calibre, but these and the Rolls were to be out of action for the whole battle.

What made the gunboat particularly suitable as a headquarters ship was that she was also equipped with a radar set and an echo-sounder. She was thus well-fitted to lead a force of small ships over the shallows of the estuary, the echo-sounder telling her the depth of water underfoot among the dangerous shoals and the radar giving warning in the dark of the proximity of enemy vessels or other objects, though the radar proved of little value, for it was a primitive type fixed fore-and-aft.

With all these advantages of speed, armament and navigational aids, however, the gunboat, like Wynn's MTB, suffered from a very short radius of action. By some adroit quick thinking, extra petrol tanks were secured on the very eve of departure, but she would nevertheless have to be towed if taken on the expedition. Ryder and Newman, however, were in complete accord that she was the best craft available for the job, especially as they both were convinced that this was an occasion when the two leaders should themselves be in the van – or, as one of them put it, should 'lead from the front'.

For the great raid the crew of the gunboat was augmented to a total of twenty-four all hands. Her spirited and dashing young captain was Lieutenant D. M. C. Curtis, an old Etonian who wore a red-gold beard of true Captain Kettle cut. He had also the same small, trim figure and his gay and easy disposition seemed to belie his trade as an international lawyer but was very well suited to the cloak-and-dagger traffic in which he had been hitherto engaged of running Allied agents to or from remote parts of the French coast by night. He had actually just returned from a mission in which he had taken off the patriot Pierre de Vomecourt and the traitress Mathilde Carré, who, it was alleged later, on suppositions for which this narrative will show that there are no grounds, had alerted the Germans by disclosing to them a British request for information on the St Nazaire defences. Dunstan Curtis had also, though he did not know it at the time, ferried over several times members of the *réseau*, or group, that had been responsible for providing much of the Intelligence used in preparing the Chariot raid.

If we now move from the bridge of the gunboat and go forward to the Vickers pom-pom, we shall meet the entirely different man who was destined on that dark March morning to win in death the Victoria Cross. Able Seaman William Savage, to quote the words of an old shipmate, Donald Mackenzie, 'always looked a proper sailor with his stocky build, his beard and his pipe'. He was twenty-nine years old and was the youngest of a large family who lived in Smethwick, where his parents kept a general store. He was employed by the brewing firm of Mitchell & Butler and was essentially a quiet, steady fellow whom everyone liked, good-natured and good-hearted, married, a member of his firm's water polo team and secretary of the local darts club. After he grew his square-cut reddish beard, which so well matched his broad shoulders and his fresh complexion, Savage became known to his shipmates usually as 'Henry VIII', or more simply 'Beardy'. He had a brother, Jack, who was also in the Navy.

Just before she sailed, a very special hand, to whom a dramatic rôle had been assigned, joined the gunboat. This was Leading

Signalman F. C. Pike. He was what the Navy called a headache rating – a specialist and not a seaman – but he was also a very staunch character. He had been employed in that secret department of the Admiralty which has certain dealings with enemy wireless signals and he had been sent to Ryder's force in answer to a request for someone who could signal in German.

Another specialist whom Ryder was particularly glad to get was Lieutenant A. R. Green, an officer of the Regular service and a specialist in navigation. It would be his special and vital business not only to pilot the little fleet at sea but also to guide it over the dangerous shoal waters of the Loire estuary and at the last moment to direct *Campbeltown* on to her target. With his unruffled temperament and nice sense of humour, Green was just the man for the job. Ryder seized upon him also to act as his sorely needed staff officer – his adjutant, as it were – and he took from his shoulders much of the detailed administrative work, for he was the only naval officer in the expedition, other than Ryder and Tibbits, who so far knew what it was all in aid of.

*

For the inevitable gossip in a small port about 'what it was all in aid of' constantly haunted the two leaders. Falmouth did not have a good name for secrecy, and it was said that there was a known spy there. Moreover, it was not a purely naval port and was open to mercantile shipping, including foreign ships, and indeed a convoy arrived while the Chariot force was assembled. In the naval boatyard and among members of the new force itself, speculation was inevitable. Thus Tom Boyd, meeting Swayne, whom he had known at Dartmouth, exclaimed: 'Why, Ronnie! You here too? The plot thickens!'

The first precaution to be taken, therefore, was to keep the khaki and the blue well away from each other as far as possible. Ryder, who had a keen sense of security, devised a special cover plan to account for the new craft and, with the C-in-C's approval, a bogus command was established under the title of the Tenth Anti-Submarine Striking Force.

It was put about, in order to explain the additional petrol tanks and the extra anti-aircraft defence, that the flotilla's mission was to carry out long-range anti-submarine sweeps in the Bay of Biscay. For such a mission Falmouth was a perfectly natural base. Thus Ryder was able to make and receive signals freely and to obtain stores, and the naval headquarters staff, including the Wrens who handled the signals traffic, were presented with a plausible answer to their speculations. A few bogus signals also helped and tropical kit was issued openly in the technique of the double-bluff.

Under cover of this plan the motor launches were put through a stiff programme of training. They carried out anti-aircraft practice with their new Oerlikons. They were taken out to sea to practise station-keeping in formation, at which they were very bad, they were exercised in manoeuvring after dark and, under Ryder's exacting eye, were drilled again and again in running their craft alongside jetties at night, not knowing that it was operational practice and thinking that it was only a Regular officer's tiresome insistence of the smart handling of their craft. On 16 March, after having put about a suitable training pretext, they went for a two-days' cruise in vile weather to the Scilly Isles and back, taking the commandos with them and 'vomiting till it hurt'.

It was the first time that the commandos and the men of the motor launches had come together and they took to each other immediately. A few, such as those who had served at Dartmouth, already knew one another. The RNVR men of the small ships had, indeed, much in common with their spirited new comrades in arms and the fellowship spontaneously generated between Newman and Ryder spread quickly to every private soldier and ordinary seaman, welding a bond which is today as strong as ever in what Mountbatten has called 'the most exclusive Society in the world'. Jack Tar and Thomas Atkins were firm friends.

They came together again on 21 March for the final and much more significant Exercise Vivid, in which, under a suitable cover plan, they carried out a night raid upon the Devonport defences as a rehearsal for the real thing. Haydon and Henriques were present and valuable lessons were learnt.

But the blinding dazzle of the massed searchlights, in which the boats could not satisfactorily navigate, keep station or land their troops, was a vexation to which they knew no answer and a foretaste of sharp realities to come.

10. 'THE SAUCIEST JOB SINCE DRAKE'

It was now Sunday, 22 March. A warm spring sun continued to bathe the southern coast with its genial rays. On shore the crocuses flowered in the gardens, the early shrubs were bursting into bud and here and there an almond tree spread its pink mantle for the awakening year. 'The whole earth,' wrote one of the soldiers, 'seemed to be wishing us well.' From the *Princesse Joséphine Charlotte* some of the commandos bathed hardily in the cold March sea. Once or twice the shore anti-aircraft batteries blazed off into the night sky at German raiders passing over, but no bombs fell.

On board their ship the soldiers had at first no need to be as hard driven as the sailors. Until the secret was disclosed they had little to do but some routine training, learning to use the Oerlikon gun and to keep fit. They were all as hard as nails and in the idyllic condition of physical well-being. They went for route marches in the country, walked in the woods in the hot sunshine, exercised their several dogs and kicked footballs about. Swayne and Sergeant Durrant, both fine shots, practised with their Colts on Cornish turnips which they bowled down a hillside. Roy took his Jocks on a long march which ended, by chance, at a convenient tavern. In the evenings the officers played liar dice in the wardroom. After an uproarious St Patrick's night Pritchard threw a jug of cold water over Montgomery's head and said: 'Now then, Bob, to work!' They enjoyed their tough PT ashore. 'We came back,' wrote Corporal Wright in his diary, 'with bones and muscles aching, but it did us good . . . Most of the fellows are writing or playing cards on the mess table where I write. I have just finished a pipe on deck and shall now sling my hammock.'

But, though the sailors may still have been unsuspecting, the soldiers had little doubt but that something was afoot. They had not, they knew from the pulse of recent happenings, been put on board their landing ship and brought, from eight Commandos, to the warm south for any trivial purpose. They waited on tiptoe, and they did not have to wait long, for the very detailed nature of their parts required that they would have to study and rehearse them again and again until they could carry them out almost blindfold.

On the evening of the 18th – the day after the return from the Scilly Isles cruise – while the men were off duty in the mess decks below, the thirty-nine officers – an enormous proportion for so small a force – were summoned to a CO's conference in the wardroom after dinner. They trooped in and sat down round the big table. In a corner they saw a blackboard on which had been drawn the map of a river mouth. Beside the blackboard stood their Colonel Charles in very good form, smoking his pipe, laughing and talking to Copland and Day. When they were all in, he ordered the door to be locked, put his pipe aside and began to speak.

'Gentlemen,' he said, 'I know jolly well you have all been wondering what we are up to down here, and now I'm going to tell you. You will all be delighted to know that we have been selected for a really lovely job – a saucy job – easily the biggest thing that has been done yet by the commandos. You could say it is the sauciest job since Drake.'

You could have heard a pin drop. There was not a man whose heart did not quicken its beat. In dead silence and with rapt attention they listened as Newman went on:

'Look at the blackboard. That is the map of a French port. I am not going to tell you what it is – not until just before we sail. But you have all got to learn the geography of the port by heart, with the help of that very fine model over there, so that you will be able to move about in it in the dark as though it were your own back garden. The code name of the operation is "Chariot", and you are not to discuss it with a single soul except among yourselves – not even with the Navy, who don't yet know anything about it.'

He went on to explain the background and conception of the operation and, using map and model, described in general terms the purpose of the raid, pointing out the targets and emphasizing that the primary one, to which all others were subsidiary, was the outer caisson of the big dry dock. He explained also how what at first appeared to be a preposterous undertaking was immediately made feasible by a surprise approach and a diversionary bombing attack. Coming to the method, Newman went on:

'As there are about twenty-four objectives, the detailed plan is a fearfully long one. I shan't attempt to go into the detail tonight. You'll be getting an Operation Order of 40-odd pages of foolscap, and I shall take you all through your separate parts later on. All I shall do now is to give you the general outline of the military plan.

'This is essentially a mission of demolitions. Our job is to blow things up and, as we have got to do so right in among the Jerries, the chaps doing the demolitions must be able to do so undisturbed. So the military force is to consist of two types – demolition troops and fighting troops. The demolition chaps will not be expected to fight, as they will be too heavily laden to carry any arms except a Colt.

'The fighting troops, who will be provided by 2 Commando, have got to do two jobs. The first is to assault enemy gun positions and hold a perimeter of bridges until they are blown, against counterattack from the town side of the docks.' He pointed out on the blackboard the bridges at the northern and southern ends of the Submarine Basin and the main caisson, which was itself a road bridge. 'These assault parties will be the first ashore and have got to be pretty slippy. You, Johnny Roderick, have got to be off like lightning, because you've got to tackle a gun position right slap alongside *Campbeltown* after she has rammed the near caisson.

'The second job of the fighting troops is to provide protection squads for the demolition teams. They will stick close alongside the demolition chaps and guard them against interference while they lay their charges.

'That is the general idea of the military plan. The parties will be awfully small – only about a dozen in each assault party, one officer and four men for most of the demolition jobs and the same number for the protection squads. What Brigadier Haydon calls "boy scout parties". If we make up our minds to be quick in and quick out under cover of the bombing diversion, we shall have done the job before the Jerries realize that we have paid them a visit at all.'

At about this point, we are told – and we may scarcely wonder – it came home to Newman's audience, despite his buoyant and confident manner, that the raid was not merely 'the sauciest job since Drake', but also an extremely difficult and dangerous one. To more than one of these highly intelligent young officers it had all the appearance of so many suicide jobs. Thus the battledress audience sitting round the big wardroom table, with here and there a kilt to contrast with the khaki, continued to listen with all the more rapt and concentrated attention, filled with elation and pride that they had been chosen for a task that would challenge any man's courage. Cigarettes and pipes went out and lay unheeded as they heard their Colonel Charles go on:

'So much for the general idea. Now a few words on how we are going to tackle the job. To make the thing manageable, all these targets have been divided into groups, which will correspond to the most suitable landing places for them. Those on the left, or south, situated on the Southern Entrance, will be Group One, under you, Bertie Hodgson.' He looked towards his friend, the stalwart, fearless and much-loved leader of No 1 Troop. 'Those in the centre, a rather mixed bag, stretching right up to the Penhouet Basin, will be Group Two, under Micky Burn. Those on the right, which are associated specially with the big Dock, will be Group Three, under Major Bill Copland. All these groups include assault parties, demolition chaps and their protection squads.'

He went on to enumerate the other tasks in outline. Young 'Tiger' Watson, one of the two 'babes' of the party, sat with his heart in his mouth till he heard his own name, fearing that he was going to be left out.

'Now about getting there,' Newman continued. 'Groups One and Two are to make the passage in MLs – in fact, in the MLs in which we made yesterday's seasick trip to the Scillies, although they don't know it yet. So don't go talking to them. We shall enter the Loire in two columns of MLs – Group One in the port column and Group Two in the starboard.

'Group Three, however, is to take the passage in a destroyer, HMS *Campbeltown*, whose job is to ram the near caisson and to blow herself up by delay fuse, after we have all gone. Not, I hope, before. The further caisson, as well as the pumping-house and the winding-huts, which house the machinery for operating the caisson, are our birds. The near caisson – the really important job – will be our bird too if anything should go wrong with *Campbeltown*.

'Each of these groups will have a separate landing place. Group One is to be landed at the Old Mole, here, where there is a landing slip, Group Two in the Old Entrance, here, and Group Three will land from the bows of the destroyer on to the caisson itself.

'I myself, with Stan Day, shall be with Commander Ryder, the Naval Force Commander. For the outward passage we shall be in HMS *Atherstone*, one of the escorting destroyers, and on the second night we shall transfer to an MGB as headquarters ship. My headquarters after landing will be this building beside the Old Entrance and close to the bridge marked G. Bill Pritchard will have general control of the demolition tasks, except for Group Three, which will be looked after by Bob Montgomery.'

Newman paused a while, as though to emphasize the close of a phase, then he continued:

'As you can imagine, in a party like this communications will be very important but limited. Once ashore, Sergeant Steele will open up from my headquarters with three other stations – Commander Ryder in the gunboat, Major Bill and the Beachmaster on the Old Mole. For this purpose we have been issued with some new and extremely hush-hush portable radio sets with a microphone operating on the larynx. They must on no account fall into enemy hands.

'Well, gentlemen, having done all our jobs, we have to get home again, and smartly, too. As each demolition team completes its job it is to come in to my HQ to report. When they are all in I shall give a withdrawal signal by means of 35-star rockets to the assault parties still out on the perimeter – green for those on my right, red on my left. We shall then all assemble at the butt end of the Old Mole and re-embark in the MLs under the orders of the Beachmaster, Lieutenant R. E. A. Verity.

'One last thing, and this is awfully important. Remember that we shall all be milling about in the dark, with Jerries all round us. In fact, in this show the danger of shooting up one's own chaps will be at the maximum. So recognition will be terribly important – faces clean, not blacked, all webbing equipment scrubbed and blancoed white. Secondly, every man is to carry a blue pinpoint torch. Thirdly, the answer to any challenge will be the name of the officer in charge of the particular sub-group. Fourthly, I've concocted a password that I defy any German to pronounce who is not an expert English linguist, even if he ever finds it out.' He smiled. 'The password will be "War Weapons Week" and the countersign "Weymouth". A good mouthful of W's!

'But, apart from these devices, there will be the characteristic silhouette of our tin hats. And remember that, as we shall be wearing the new-issue rubber boots, the sound of any hard-soled boot will be as good as a loudspeaker shouting: "Here comes a Jerry!"

'I think that is enough for tonight. Tomorrow I shall talk to the men and then you will all have some jolly hard work to do practising your parts until you can do them blindfold.'

The next morning Newman broke the news to the men, mustered on the messdeck by RSM Moss. He told them to sit easy and then began, Sergeant Butler tells us, with the words:

'Well, chaps, this is it!'

As he unfolded the story in simple terms they listened in the same electrified silence as the officers had done. The crowded messdeck, close and shuttered, stark and astringent, lit with up-turned faces, became in imagination a vaster field. They were filled, Sergeant Butler records, with 'a spirit such as I had never before experienced – a sort of swelling that our bodies were too small to contain. Before he had finished it came home to us how difficult it was going to be ever to return, but this did not detract from the general determination one bit. I felt proud to be there.'

In fulfilment of Mountbatten's instruction, Newman ended his exposition by saying:

'There's one last thing I've been ordered by the Chief of Combined Operations to say to you. This is going to be a dangerous job. In fact, the CCO told me that he did not expect any of us to come back. He therefore doesn't want anyone who is married and has family responsibilities to go on it; nor any man who thinks he ought to stand down for any reason at all. Nobody has *got* to go on this party if he doesn't want to and neither the CCO nor I nor anyone else will think any the worse of him if he elects to stand down.'

For a moment there was a stunned silence. This was not the way that they were used to being talked to. Then, simultaneously, spontaneously, there was an astonishing response, a response never to be thought credible of a disciplined unit and one that would never have been given by a unit not on such unique terms with its officers—

'GURTCH!'

Newman beamed and as he left the messdeck they all stood to attention.

That evening Corporal Wright, as he wrote up his diary in the messdeck, said of the plan: 'A most audacious one; it almost takes one's breath away (like the rum that I am now drinking) . . . Everyone is happy, this is real commando stuff. Tonight most of us are speculating about the scheme and looking forward to the leave that will follow. . . . This is a strange life – as I sit writing a lieutenant is playing draughts at my elbow and our other "two-pipper" is drinking tea at the bottom of the table. And so to my hammock.'

Thus, as one might expect, officers and men reacted alike. 'Undoubtedly,' Tiger Watson records, 'many of the older hands realized that it was a pretty desperate undertaking, but most of us' – like Mountbatten – 'felt that it was so daring that we should get away with it.'

From then onwards, except for Vivid, the commandos plunged into an intense concentration on their various tasks, a detailed summary of which is set out in Appendix C. Newman had each of the 'boy scout' parties into his cabin, the model on his bed and the map and air photo above it, and went through its task in detail, with Pritchard in attendance for demolition matters. The squads went away and rehearsed their own tasks again and again, squatting on deck in little groups all over the ship, putting test questions to each other. 'You would have thought,' wrote Swayne, 'that a dozen conspiracies were going on at the same time.' The model, the air photographs and the maps were burnt into every man's mind, so that each knew exactly where he ought to land, where else he might have to land, the route from that point to his objective, the buildings that he would meet in the dark and the ways round them, the places where the enemy was to be expected

and the route back to the point of re-embarkation at the Old
Mole.

Sergeant Steele, Newman's signal sergeant, began training on
his new No 38 portable laryngoscope radio sets with Lance-
Corporal Fyfe, who was to be Copland's operator, and, later on,
with the naval operators who would be with Ryder in the gunboat
and with Verity on the Old Mole.

The two doctors, Captain G. M. Barling and Captain D.
Paton, prepared their gear, together with the three medical
orderlies, Corporal Simister (remarkable among commandos
for declining on religious grounds to bear arms, though he was
to win the Military Medal later), Lance-Corporal Everett and
Lance-Corporal Mills.

For the demolition parties the orders to be studied were minutely
detailed. From Pritchard's hand there were exact descriptions of the
docks equipment and how they were operated, precise instructions
where to place each charge, the weight and nature of each charge,
where precisely and how to fix them, the manner of their firing,
together with lists of what each individual officer and man in the
demolition parties had to carry of explosive, adhesive tape, cordtex,
detonators, sledgehammers, firemen's axes, ML flares for burning
out electric windings, boxes of fusee matches, 'tar babies' for setting
oil on fire, rubber gloves for those who would have to handle electric
apparatus, and so on in infinite detail.

Quantities of stores were coming on board – bamboo scaling
ladders, grapnels, explosives, weapons and ammunition, special
clothing, the new type of rubber-soled boot with rubber crampons,
emergency rations and a multitude of other items that kept
Regimental Quartermaster-Sergeant Seaton working day and
night. The ordinary web equipment had to be altered to take the
formidable amount of ammunition, grenades and trench-mortar-
bombs that men in the fighting parties were ordered to carry,
special pockets being added for the extra Bren and Tommy-gun
clips and the whole equipment 'built to the man'. Blue sweaters
were issued to every soldier, a box of morphine syrettes to every
officer and a haversack of shell dressings to a trained first-aid man
in every party. Excitement mounted as the days passed, and all
were on tiptoe to learn when and where they were to go.

The day after Vivid – 23 March – it was the turn of the naval force to be admitted to the secret.

In contrast to Newman's orders, which had to be minutely detailed, Ryder's were short and simple. He briefed only the commanding officers and first lieutenants of each vessel, taking six at a time. They in turn were to brief their own ships' companies, but not until after sailing. The main requirement was that they should be able to recognize their proper landing places in the glare of the searchlights, of which they had had such a trying experience the night before. These searchlights Ryder simulated with electric torches placed in the model, while the officers looked at the harbour approaches at eye level.

The probable date of departure, Ryder told them, was Friday, the 27th – only four days hence – and Zero Hour – the hour at which *Campbeltown* was to hit her target – was fixed for 1.30 a.m. two nights later.

On that day Forbes's operation order was issued. The routes laid down for the outward and return passages (shown in Fig 11) had been skilfully calculated and timed in order that the force should escape enemy observation aircraft, on the movements of which he was particularly well informed, or, if observed by chance aircraft or ships, that its direction and demeanour should give no clue to its purpose. By day the flotilla was to adopt the broad arrow-head cruising order of an anti-submarine sweep. The force was to part company with the escorting destroyers at Point E at 8 pm and thence proceed on its own. In order that Green should have a precise fix of his position on the chart, vital for the final run-in over the shoals, HM Submarine *Sturgeon*, commanded by Lieutenant-Commander M. R. G. Wingfield, was to serve as a navigational beacon, surfacing at Point Z, forty miles from St Nazaire, to meet the force at about 10 p.m.

On that same day also – 23 March – the two escort ships sailed into Falmouth. These were the Hunt class destroyers *Atherstone* (Lieutenant-Commander R. F. Jenks) and *Tynedale* (Lieutenant-Commander H. E. F. Tweedie). Ryder, together with Green, moved his headquarters to *Atherstone*, where he felt much more at home. The motor launches were now anchored in Cross Roads and, as a result of Vivid, had all been repainted that shade of mauve known as Plymouth Pink or Mountbatten Pink to make them less conspicuous under searchlights. Throughout the whole force there was now a throb and bustle as the last-minute preparations were made.

Other late arrivals came in about the same time. Two of these were French-speaking liaison officers for whom Newman had specially asked for reassuring civil inhabitants and seeing that they kept indoors. These French faces were Captain Vicomte Peter de Jonghe (in fact a Belgian and a well-known steeplechase rider) and 2nd Lieutenant W. G. Lee. Soon after them there came two Press representatives sent from the Ministry of Information in the persons of Mr J. M. G. Holman and Mr E. J. Gilling; Newman interviewed them on board and allotted Holman to the head-quarters gunboat and Gilling to the motor launch of Wallis, the Australian. Almost last of all came Captain Anthony Terry, a liaison officer from the War Office.

And now at last, on 25 March, HMS *Campbeltown* arrived with her gallant ship's company. She sailed quietly into the golden bay with the sun behind her, astonishing the older naval hands who saw her in the distance. For from a little way off she looked very like a German destroyer of the *Möwe* class, with two rakish, cut-back funnels of unequal size, instead of her normal four. Even stranger changes had taken place on her upper deck. All her guns were gone, their places usurped by a little 12-pounder forward and eight Oerlikons mounted high on bandstands. Her bridge and wheelhouse superstructure were sheeted with armour plating as a shield against small-arms bullets. Less obvious, riveted to the deck amidships, were long, low armour-plate fences behind which the commandos were to lie down as they faced the hail of close-range fire before they clambered ashore.

Equally strange sights were to be seen below deck – her bows packed with high explosive ready at short notice to be made alive, her torpedo-tubes and all other heavy gear not essential to her task removed, her magazines emptied, her fuel oil and boiler water reduced to the calculated minimum for reaching her objective. Riding very light in the water, she was stripped and ready for the last race of her life. She drew only eleven feet of water, or twelve feet at the stern when moving fast, but even that was risky for her ride over the dangerous shoal waters, for the tidal calculations had shown that she would have only ten feet of water.

These sweeping changes in her cut and trim had been made in phenomenal time by the hands of Devonport Dockyard, giving her new captain, whom we are about to meet, a few days in which to take her to sea and handle her. He found that, like all these old American destroyers of her class, she was anything but easy. Compared with our V and W class destroyers of the same date, she was, in his own words, 'a bitch'. At a cruising speed of twelve knots she had a turning circle as wide, it seemed, as a battleship's. Only when reaching about seventeen knots did she handle with the suppleness of an ordinary destroyer. Moreover, ruthlessly lightened as she was, she skidded badly, needing frequent corrections to her helm.

To his own distress, *Campbeltown*'s former captain, a thoroughly able officer with whom Ryder would have been perfectly happy to sail, had been displaced, as, in the Commander-in-Chief's opinion, his years were against him. In his place Forbes had appointed Lieutenant-Commander S. H. Beattie. Nothing could have delighted Ryder more, for he and Sam Beattie were old friends and shipmates, cadets of the same term in the training ship *Thunderer* when they had joined the Navy together as boys from school.

In him Ryder had complete faith, for Beattie perfectly suited the part in character and temperament. In his early thirties, he was tall, slender, black-bearded, blue-eyed. With his handsome presence he matched a charming personality, a serene and even temperament, a sound and sensible judgment and a retiring manner. Nothing rattled or ruffled him and he could be relied upon to carry out the great test of nerve and fortitude to which he was committed with a steady hand and a calm precision.

Beattie was the son of a Herefordshire parson, and had taken no small risk to his career in marrying very young. Indeed, he had had at first to hide his wife, as it were, from senior officers. He and Philippa Beattie were devoted to each other, and already had a jolly family of three small children. At home he was a completely domesticated animal and was as ready to deal with nursery tasks as he was to con a ship.

This was the officer chosen to lay his ship upon her sacrificial altar. For the final act of destruction Tibbits had meanwhile been working with great ingenuity at an explosive scheme that seems to have been almost entirely his own, consulting with Pritchard from time to time. COHQ's first tentative plan of placing the explosive after the ship had rammed was too chancy and there was very little experience to go upon. No one knew, for example, how far back the ship's bows would buckle. Since *Campbeltown*'s immolation was the kernel of the whole business, Ryder demanded an absolutely foolproof scheme, designed to meet every foreseeable contingency. He examined every proposal under the microscope of his criticism, shooting searching questions at Tibbits from day to day.

'How can you be sure,' he demanded to know, 'that the charge will be in intimate contact with the face of the caisson but yet not be smashed by the impact? What happens if we run into heavy fire and the fusing system gets shot up? Or the chap responsible – that's you – gets shot up? If the delay action has to be long enough to save our commandos from being blasted when ashore, how can we prevent the Germans from disarming the fuses when they board the ship after we have gone, as they certainly will? How do I know that this cordtex stuff is really waterproof? Demonstrate it to me.'

To all these and other posers Tibbits supplied answers, conferring with Pritchard on methods of fusing. In the outcome the explosive charge was placed immediately abaft, or behind, the steel column that supported the ship's most forward gun, on the argument that this was the first obstacle of strong resistance to the momentum of the ramming impulse. The charge was made up of twenty-four Mark VII depth-charges, as used for attacking submarines, weighing 400 lb each, so that the total charge weighed four and a quarter tons. It was enclosed in a special steel tank on top of the fuel compartments and cemented in, as shown in Fig 8. The fuses used were the Army's new long-delay 'pencil' fuses set to act after eight hours, at least three being inserted in the charge, and the whole connected together with cordtex. To safeguard against casualties to vital personnel, the fuses would be actuated at about 11 p.m., before the ship entered the estuary, and to safeguard against disarming by the enemy the ship was to be scuttled after ramming.

Some mystery still remains today on exact points, and particularly as to whether the alternative 2½-hour fuses were ever used. A paper inquest was held after the raid on this point, but the only men who knew the answers, and to whom the brilliant success of the exploit is so largely due, were dead.

The time was drawing very near. There was no more shore leave. Personal affairs had been settled. Wynn and Boyd had 'dated' some Wrens for a party on a night after their return. Stuart Chant had put his Lakeland terrier Spiff into the care of his friend Mr George Green, the Falmouth Docks Manager, and the crew of 'Wynn's Weapons' had entrusted their Scruffy to the Wrens of the duty boat (though he got away from them and actually took part in the raid in another boat and was shipwrecked and rescued).

On board the *PJC* the soldiers listened to a very poor lecture by an officer from London on the technique of escaping should they fail to get home in the motor launches, but were given none of the customary escape aids. Newman, to his relief, received at the last moment, a clear direction from COHQ, through Henriques, defining the priorities of the tasks and emphasizing that if only the big lock gate were destroyed the mission would have been fulfilled. If necessary, everything should be sacrificed to that aim. By the same letter Henriques told him the final bombing plan, of which we shall read in a moment, and passed on to him the considerations that Haydon had laid down for abandonment if that should appear necessary.

*

Away in London, meanwhile, no little anxiety was being experienced at COHQ over the proposals for providing support by bomber aircraft. Up to the last minute these proposals were clouded with doubts. The really heavy support that had been asked for early in February, and the seventy aircraft that had later been considered adequate, dwindled week by week as Bomber Command, hard pressed for machines for their own campaign and obliged to transfer some to Coastal Command, found itself

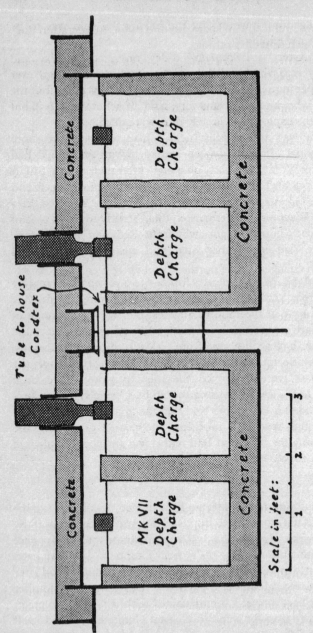

Fig 8. Sectional view of one section of *Campbeltown's* charge; there were six such sections. Thick lines show steel plating; light shading shows concrete filling and heavier shading wood blocks.

more and more reluctant to spare any forces for an operation not within their own scheme of things.

Moveover, a new dilemma had arisen about the target that was to be selected for bombing while the commandos were about their business in the dockyard. As late as 16 March, when, as we have seen, the Combined Plan was issued, the bombing in this second phase was to be on the *town* of St Nazaire. About that time, however, Mr Churchill himself gave a direction that, in order to avoid casualties to Frenchmen, the town was not to be bombed.

Thus on 22 March – four days before the Charioteers were to set out – we find Air Vice-Marshal Robert Saundby, Senior Air Staff Officer, Bomber Command, having received the Combined Plan, forwarding to COHQ the suggested new basis of bomber participation. In this the number of aircraft to take part had shrunk to thirty-five and the target for the second phase – Target B – had been changed to the northern end of the Penhouet Basin and the adjoining building slips – more than a mile away to the north of the selected landing places.

This proposition was received at COHQ with concern. In conjunction with the reduced number of aircraft, it altered the whole complexion of the affair. On 24 March Haydon urged strongly that thirty-five aircraft were quite insufficient and that the change of Target B was also very unsatisfactory; the purpose of bombing in this phase, he observed, was to draw the enemy's attention away from the docks and not to them.

'I recommend very strongly,' he wrote, 'that we should hold to our original request – even though it may run counter to political opinion.'

Haydon was further disturbed by Forbes's proposal that, if bad weather prevented the bomber force from starting, the naval and military force should still go in, if it had not been spotted on passage. The essence of the military plan, however, was that the enemy would be unable to take counter-action against the commandos quickly; if no bombing took place enemy reaction would be swift and would be far too strong for the very small and scattered commando parties. 'I do not consider, therefore,' Haydon wrote, 'that the assault without air support is a fair proposition. I therefore recommend the recall of the force should air support be impossible.'

Henriques speaks of the 'ferocity of our arguments' at this stage on the bombing needs. This was not just another Lofoten or Vaagso pinprick; it was a sabre-cut of serious strategic importance. 'If we only drop soda-water bottles on the town,' Haydon said, 'or harmless objects that will scream through the air, that would serve the purpose. Anything to distract or mystify the German defences in the vital two hours.'

Such unorthodoxy, however, received no welcome.

The attempt to change Target B therefore failed. As Willetts pointed out, nothing short of a Cabinet decision could permit Bomber Command to accept the bombing of the town.

Other representations, however, succeeded. That same day – the 24th – Mountbatten attended a meeting of the Chiefs of Staff and he emphasized that 'the success of Chariot depends very largely on the success of the diversion created by air bombing'. He asked for a ruling as to what should be done if weather prevented bombing aircraft from participating and the Committee agreed 'that Operation Chariot should not be undertaken unless the diversionary air bombing could be carried out'. Mountbatten appears, however, to have been reluctant to abandon the operation altogether and in the event the orders received by Ryder and Newman, from Forbes, gave them discretion to press the operation if they had not been spotted at sea.

The urgent request for more bombers was also successful. Bomber Command responded to it by raising the number to sixty-two. When their Operation Order was issued on 25 March, however, very severe restrictions were imposed on pilots. They were to bomb no other targets than those specified, they were not to come below 6000 feet and they were to drop their bombs singly on separate bombing runs.* Moreover, in the subsequent briefing, it was impressed upon pilots that they must not attack at all unless they could clearly identify their targets and they were told nothing at all about the main operation, or the critical importance of it, beyond the fact that 'a night operation by naval and military forces has been planned'.

---

* The timings of the bombing programme are briefly outlined in Appendix C.

Thus, although provision had been made for cancellation of the expedition if the bombers should be unable to take off, and although Bomber Command laid on a modified programme should some of the airfields be fogbound, no provision was made for advising the two force commanders what was to be done if the pilots were able to take off but were unable to see their targets on arrival.

'I bet you anything you like,' Newman said when bidding goodbye to Henriques after Exercise Vivid, 'that the bombing won't work.'

*

Down at Falmouth everything was now ready, ahead of time. The statistics of tide and moon had shown that the first night of the most favourable spell at St Nazaire was that of 28–29 March, which would have required sailing from Falmouth on the 27th. The suspicion of a break in the weather, however, the arrival of *Campbeltown* and the impulse to be gone moved Ryder to suggest to the Commander-in-Chief that they should leave a day earlier. Forbes agreed.

That day, 25 March, therefore, with all safely 'locked up', Newman caused his commandos to be mustered in the *PJC* and he told them their destination. To them St Nazaire was but a name; most of them had expected that it would be Brest. But 'a mighty cheer went up which nearly lifted the messdeck and we all felt very glad that there would be no more waiting about'.

Many witnesses bear evidence of the extraordinary and moving sense of exaltation that animated the commandos in these last days. That exaltation which is known as euphoria, occasioned by the perfection of physical well-being, was already known to them all. The exhilaration of the golden spring, in the midst of which new life was to be seen and felt bursting in every bud, gave stimulus to that high condition. And now at the summons of a high purpose and the challenge of the last enemy it reached its highest sublimation. Only too clearly did that map on the blackboard resemble the jaws of death.

One who declared himself in a moment of self-revelation, but whom we need not name, observed: 'I felt quite ready to die, in fact that I should be happy to do so.' He did not die, but Harry Pennington, the Oxford Blue, who did, was of a like mind, dour and tough though he was. Coming back from a spell ashore, where he had lain in the sunshine in contemplation of the awakening woods on almost the last day of all, he remarked to Gordon Holman, the journalist, in a manner perfectly matter-of-fact: 'Well, that is England.'

'Why, whatever do you mean?' asked the journalist.

'Oh, I've just said goodbye to her; that is all.'

'But surely you don't think you are not coming back?'

'My dear Gordon, you haven't seen what I have got to do. But it's quite all right. I don't mind a bit. Only I hope I do the job first.'

Holman was troubled, not knowing what to say, and Gilling, the other journalist, noted with distress that Pennington 'wore the mask of death'. Pennington added thoughtfully: 'You see, lying out there on the edge of the woods, I decided that England was worth it.'

Pennington and Tibbits were not the only ones. Bertie Hodgson, splendid, fearless and much loved, and Tom Peyton, model of a keen and selfless young Regular officer, came to Newman at the last minute, saluted smartly and said 'goodbye' in a manner that left him deeply troubled.

*

In this spirit and atmosphere was this last day spent by the commandos, amid the whirl of the final preparations. Reminded to make their wills, most of them did so – the soldier's paybook will, which needs no witness. Barling, the doctor, who had a fractured ankle, ignored the hurt. Every man bathed and put on clean underclothes, to lessen the chance of infection from wounds. All badges were removed, except those of rank. Kits were minutely examined to make sure that each man carried all that he should and nothing that he should not. Grenades were primed with all due care. Webbing equipment was blancoed white. When all was ready and done, RQMS Seaton and Corporal Crippin, the orderly-room clerk, earnestly appealing and inventing quite unnecessary jobs for themselves, persuaded Newman to allow them to join the great enterprise for which they had worked for so many sleepless nights and days.

Just after nine that night Newman received the signal from Ryder: *Can you come over to* Atherstone *with your magnifying glass?* He went at once and found Ryder in the Captain's cabin studying a set of new air reconnaissance photographs taken that morning. Robin Jenks, *Atherstone*'s commanding officer, was there, too. Pointing to one of the photos, Ryder said:

'Look at that, Charles.'

There in the Submarine Basin, right alongside the spot chosen by Newman for his battle headquarters, were berthed four German destroyers of the *Wolfe/Möwe* class. These, as we learnt later, were part of the 5th Torpedo Boat Destroyer Flotilla, commanded by Korvettenkapitän Moritz Schmidt and consisting of *Seeadler, Falke, Kondor, Jaguar* and *Iltis*. They were to play no small part in the Chariot story.*

Newman looked at him quizzically. It was characteristic that to him they were not a new menace but a new opportunity; fresh victims for his bag. He said cheerfully:

'We'll slip on board and sink them with limpets.' Then reflectively:

'How many men should I need to capture them, Bob?'

'Well now, how many have you got in reserve?'

'Twelve.'

'Then I suggest, Charles,' said Ryder with a smile, 'that you will probably need all of them.'

Ryder just had time next morning (26 March) to go ashore to telephone this troublesome news to Pat McCrum at Plymouth. There was nothing that the Navy could do about the ships while in the docks, but McCrum promised to ask the Commander-in-Chief to procure two more destroyers to reinforce the escort on the return voyage. Ryder returned to *Atherstone*, little imagining under what curious and moving circumstances the enemy destroyers were to be met. The signal *Preparative Chariot*, which required the

* Referred to sometimes as torpedo-boats and sometimes as destroyers they will be called destroyers in this book, to mark their comparative relation to the Hunts and the sharp dissimilarity from our motor torpedo-boats.

expedition to be at half an hour's notice for sea, was received from Plymouth at 9.30 a.m. At 11.03 Ryder in *Atherstone* made to Newman in *Princesse Joséphine Charlotte*:

Request troops may be sent now.

At 12.30 p.m. came the executive order from Forbes:

Carry out Chariot.

A few minutes after one o'clock, Copland, last to leave the *PJC*, climbed aboard *Campbeltown* and made to Newman, now in *Atherstone*:

All troops embarked.

At two o'clock, under a genial sun, with a light breeze from the east-north-east, and with Spitfires circling a few feet above the water, the Charioteers sailed quietly out into the English Channel, followed by the three destroyers an hour later. They numbered, apart from the escorts, 611 souls – 345 naval officers and ratings, 166 all ranks in the fighting parties from 2 Commando, 91 all ranks in the demolition teams of the combined Commandos, together with the medical party, three liaison officers and two Press representatives.

Had the spirit of Hotspur been with them, he would surely have said as he did of old:

'Our plot is a good plot as ever was laid; our friends true and constant – a good plot, good friends, and full of expectation.'

11. THE ENEMY

Very soon now we shall meet the enemy. Hitherto his defences have been spoken of only in general terms, but it is essential for our narrative that, without further delay, we should look more closely at the men, the weapons and the ships that defended the stronghold which Ryder and Newman were about to assault.

Not all the information now presented, which is taken from German documents, maps and personal reports, was in the hands of our planners at that time. Our information on the enemy's fixed coast-defence gun positions was good, but it was far from complete on the locations of all the small, rapid-firing guns of Bofors and Oerlikon types, which were not only difficult to spot among buildings in air photos, but which were also liable to be moved from day to day. Nor were the planners or leaders able to assess the opposition that might be met from ships in harbour at the time of the attack, which proved to be very troublesome and responsible for the repulse of Burt's and Beart's commandos and which added considerably to the opposition encountered by the motor launches. The positions of these ships in harbour are given in Fig 10 and those of the enemy guns and searchlights in Fig 9, both taken from the German maps and lists used by the German naval staff in their subsequent tactical study of the operation. In all diagrams in this book, the enemy guns are shown as they actually were.

The defences of St Nazaire and the seaward approaches to it were entirely in the hands of the German navy, being manned by what the Germans describe as 'naval troops', organized on an army basis and dressed in the field-grey of the army, but wearing gilt-coloured naval buttons and badges. The Germans had no marines as we know them. These defences were under the command of the

See Kommandant Loire, Kapitän zur See Zuckschwerdt, whose headquarters were at La Baule. Under him were a battalion of coast-defence artillery, a brigade of flak, or anti-aircraft artillery, and the minor forces of the Harbour Commander.

The coast-defence guns were manned by 280 Naval Artillery Battalion under the command of Korvettenkapitän Edo Dieckmann, with headquarters at Chémoulin Point. He disposed of twenty-eight guns, of calibres of 75 mm, 150 mm (5.9 inches), 170 mm (6.6 inches) and a powerful battery of 240 mm (9.5 inches) on railway mountings at La Boule. All these guns were to be engaged in the action, though the big railway guns fired only a few rounds on account of their slow traverse.

The anti-aircraft, or dual-purpose, guns were manned by 22 Naval Flak Brigade under the command of the shrewd and able Kapitän zur See C. C. Mecke, with headquarters at St Marc. He had three battalions in position in and close around St Nazaire – 703 Battalion commanded by Korvettenkapitän Thiessen, 809 by Korvettenkapitän Lothar Burhenne and 705 Battalion by Korvettenkapitän Koch. The German maps show forty-three guns of 40 mm and 20 mm, with a few 37 mm. The 40-mm and 20-mm were very similar to our Bofors and Oerlikon guns and for the convenience of the narrative we shall use these terms, although they were not always so called by the Germans. In addition, the enemy had some heavy AA batteries, but these could not engage surface targets. Many of these guns were mounted on the tops of concrete bunkers, on rooftops or on flak towers. These were not only formidable objects to attack, but also added the extraordinary difficulty of securing an actual hit on the guns themselves from water level.

The ears of all this artillery were provided by two main radar stations – one at Le Croisic and another, for seaward observation, under Dieckmann's command at St Marc. Mecke's flak brigade had also three other radar stations, for air shooting only. At Chémoulin Point was a naval signal station.

Harbour defence appears to have been the responsibility, at least to some extent, of the Harbour Commander (Hafenkommandant), Korvettenkapitän Kellermann. He commanded no troops other than guard companies and the like, but disposed of some small

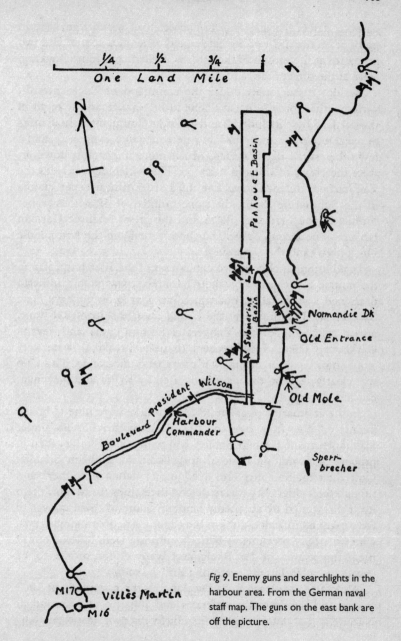

Fig 9. Enemy guns and searchlights in the
harbour area. From the German naval
staff map. The guns on the east bank are
off the picture.

harbour defence boats (*Hafenschutzboote*), of which four were in
harbour on the night of the battle (and came into action) and two
on patrol at the mouth of the estuary. Kellermann himself was on
leave at the time of the raid.

Besides these forces under the command of Zuckschwerdt,
various other forces were available in St Nazaire on the night of
the battle. These included 2 and 4 Works Companies, small units
of naval technicians who had an emergency rôle as infantry, and a
few other small detachments. Much more important, however,
were the crews of ships in harbour. These included, besides the
four harbour defence boats, five ships of 16 Minesweeper Flotilla
in the Submarine Basin, the same number of 42 Minesweeper
Flotilla in the Penhouet Basin and the crews of three German
tankers – the *Passat*, *Schledstadt* (both actually in the Normandie
Dock itself) and the *Uckermark*.

In addition, anchored two cables east of the East Jetty, slap in
the course to be taken by the Charioteers, was a ship hitherto
described as a flakship, but which we now know to have been
Sperrbrecher 137, formerly the *Botilla Russ*, a ship of 996 tons,
armed with one of the dangerous 88-mm guns and several
Oerlikons. These Sperrbrechers (barrage breakers) were very
stout ships used for dealing with magnetic minefields. This ship
was clearly seen on the air photos used by Ryder and Newman,
but not identified.

In the submarine pens on 28 March there were nine U-boats,
mainly of the fully operational 7 Submarine Flotilla under
Kapitänleutnant Herbert Sohler, and partly of 6 Flotilla, then in
process of formation under Kapitänleutnant Wilhelm Schultz.
Only their maintenance and headquarter hands were there and
though their chief duty was to defend their ships (or to blow them
up if threatened by an enemy landing) some of them appear to
have manned machine-guns in the action. The operational crews,
who were very precious to Hitler's purpose, were billeted out of
the danger area in La Baule and were under orders to be
evacuated inland in the event of a British landing.

Altogether, we learn from Dieckmann, there were about 5000
troops and hands in the defences and ships in and around St
Nazaire and about another 1000, chiefly his own, disposed along

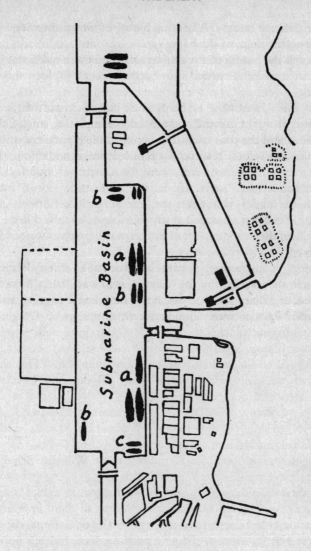

Fig 10. Ships in the Submarine Basin on the night of the attack.

a   Five minesweepers of 16 MS Flotilla

b   Four harbour-defence boats

c   The tugs *Champion* and *Pornic*. Three other tugs also in basin. In Penhouet Basin to the north are three ships of 42 MS Flotilla. From German naval staff map.

the shores of the estuary. A balloon barrage unit was provided by the Luftwaffe.

Such was the citadel that was to be assaulted by an old destroyer and by 257 soldiers, carried into battle by light wooden motor launches.

Eight miles westward of St Nazaire lay a cluster of headquarters that might critically affect the battle. Here, among the sand dunes and the pine trees that fringed the Atlantic coast was the fashionable seaside resort of La Baule. Here, in addition to the headquarters of Zuckschwerdt, were the Corps headquarters of General Ritter von Prager. Under his command, 333 Infantry Division was stationed to cover the area St Nazaire–Lorient, one of its brigades being stationed at towns a few miles inland from St Nazaire, and the headquarters of the brigade being just west of La Baule itself.

Entirely unsuspecting, secure in their hold upon France, revelling in the successes of the German armies in Russia, Hitler's forces on the Loire went about on their normal rounds while Ryder and Newman were slipping quietly out to sea.

12. TO SEA

Ryder shaped course south-westerly at thirteen knots to follow the long route ordered by the Commander-in-Chief, giving the Lizard a wide berth to keep out of sight of land. He was quite happy about the weather prospects. The easterly winds prevalent at that time and the bright sun, making the land warmer than the water, promised him a protective haze, with low cloud and patches of fog off the western coast of France. This was precisely the weather that he wanted. He was in HMS *Atherstone* as guide of the fleet, standing on the bridge with Robin Jenks, her captain, Green, his specialist navigator and staff officer, and Sub-Lieutenant J. E. O'Rourke, his Canadian signals officer. With them were Newman, glad to have a few brief hours of ease after the exhausting days and nights of preparation, Stanley Day, Terry, the War Office representative, and Gordon Holman, the journalist.

Immediately astern, in tow by *Atherstone*, they could see Dunstan Curtis's MGB 314, the headquarters ship to which the two Force Commanders would transfer for the approach and the assault, and in which were the remainder of Newman's headquarters party. Astern of *Atherstone* was *Tynedale*, followed by *Campbeltown* towing 'Wynn's Weapons'. On either hand of the destroyers were the two flotillas of motor launches in line ahead, that on the port hand carrying the soldiers for the Group One objectives, that on the starboard those for Group Two. A strange force, one might well say, for 'the counterpoise of so great an opposition', composed of more than 60 guns and 6000 troops. A single Hurricane continuously circled the little fleet at nought feet, knowing nothing of its purpose.

England was out of sight and all the ocean was before them. Gone were the bustlings and the hurrying to and fro, gone the exercises, the lectures and the drills, gone the streets, the pubs and the verdant hills, gone for over three years for more than half the men who sailed, gone for ever for more than one man in four. A sense of freedom possessed them all, except for those intent upon their tasks on bridge or in engine-room or who kept unceasing watch for enemy craft on the water or in the air. For the soldiers it was a time of momentary relaxation, of enjoyment of the warm friendship and hospitality of the seamen. They bore themselves like a team travelling to play in some great cup-tie, not indeed in the presence of cheering crowds, yet a match that was to bring the eyes of the world upon them. This they had trained for. This they were eager to begin. 'They were,' said Pritchard's father, who had met many of them, 'men who feared nothing and inspired one to believe that they would move mountains.'

For the sailors it was no time for relaxation, but in the moving waters they were in their element, already engaged in their part of the game, moving upon the field with ordered unison, preparing for the great moment of the move into the mouth of the goal. In the *Campbeltown* the ship's company had been reduced to seventy-five, all ratings not required having been transferred to the *PJC* at the last moment – to their bitter disappointment, for it was clear that some special service was afoot. Sam Beattie mustered the reduced ship's company on the quarter-deck and broke the news to them. They it was who were to put the ball into goal. They broke into broad grins and returned to their stations with pert little jokes and a quickened pulse. Revolvers were issued and practice conducted.

The sun shone. As the afternoon wore on the breeze freshened to Force 4 – a moderate breeze of 11 to 15 mph. The motor launches rolled a little and from time to time their bows lifted out of the moving sea. As a precaution against observation by enemy aircraft, the commandos were not allowed on the upper deck unless wearing oilskins or duffle coat, of which they had been provided with a small supply, and steel helmet. One or two borrowed from the sailors the white sweaters that the Navy calls submarine frocks.

Ryder presently hoisted the signal (F Pendant One) to adopt the broad arrowhead formation of cruising order No 1, in order to simulate a normal anti-submarine sweep. Speed was reduced to ten knots. In order to avert the danger of wireless signals being picked up by the enemy, no ship-to-ship signals were allowed except visual signals – by flag or Aldis lamp by day or a screened and subdued light by night. Newman, on *Atherstone*'s bridge, watched absorbed as the signal was repeated back along the line by ship after ship, and then, when all had received it, he watched with delight the 'fine sight of each vessel changing speed and direction to take up her new position' on the screen two cables* apart, with the three destroyers astern. The spectacle, he wrote afterwards in his report, 'is imprinted on my memory. The thrill of the voyage was upon one – the study of the navigational course with the Navy, the continuous lookout for enemy aircraft, the preparation of one's own personal kit to land in and the deciphering and reading of W/T messages from the C-in-C brought nightfall upon us in no time.'

Tired though he was from the laborious time in Falmouth, Newman was too absorbed to seek sleep, though from time to time he retired to the charthouse to smoke a quiet pipe. Day, however, was worn out from nights without sleep and turned in. To Ryder the whole proceedings seemed 'faintly unreal'. On this fine, sunny spring day, with a fresh breeze that would have been ideal for a ship in sail, he found it hard to believe that it was not merely some pleasant cruising exercise and that, before many hours had passed, they would be engaged in a desperate undertaking 'at the cannon's mouth'.

Dunstan Curtis in his gunboat astern of *Atherstone*, which had often been his parent ship in operations off the French coast, had the same sense of unreality. 'We sat about gossiping,' he said, 'as though it were a pleasure party, helping ourselves to the raisins that I always had in saucers on the bridge.'

Everyone, Ryder records, was feeling pretty confident. Neither he nor Newman now concerned himself greatly with the discretion given them to abandon the operation if the bomber support raid did not materialize. The notion of abandonment scarcely registered. The Chariot was under starter's order and

* A cable = approximately 200 yards.

they were determined to reach the winning post. What gave greater concern to Newman was the realization that he was now cut off from the troops he commanded and that he could no longer influence or co-ordinate the dismembered fragments of his complicated jigsaw. Nor was there any possibility of changing the design as might be required by the unforeseen. Such pitiably small parties! All these subalterns and NCOs thrown into action on their own in little packets! He had complete confidence in them all but hated the idea that he might not be at their side if they were in trouble.

Others also had their small misgivings or anxieties. The burly Tom Boyd in ML 8 admitted that he set off with apprehension, because 'I felt that the Force, as regards the Navy, was insufficiently trained, and this was borne out by the frightful station-keeping'. Ian Henderson, in ML 14, remarked to Swayne that he thought motor launches were 'hardly the best vessels for this sort of job'. Swayne himself experienced the sensation of being watched all the time by some malevolent eye, expecting a German aircraft to drop out of the clouds at any minute. But these were exceptions and the 'pre-examination feeling' upon which the gallant and stalwart Sergeant Butler remarked was but the common sensation on the eve of any stirring event.

Thus the golden afternoon wore on. At 3.30 Horlock, the 'spare commanding officer', took over ML 13, since Platt had to lead the port column in the absence of the sick Wood. Ryder rebuked the motor launches for excessive lamp signalling. Newman similarly made the signal: *Too many obvious soldiers on deck in all boats*. On board the little MTB 74, in tow by *Campbeltown*, Lovegrove and his engine-room hands, after a night without sleep, were tuning and adjusting their new engine ready for the first and last race of her life; and the remaining hands laboured to remove the warhead of one of their special torpedoes and to fit a new fuse, obtained at the last minute by Micky Wynn's pertinacious independence 'and the influence of a certain admiral, in an effort to prolong our lives'.

Soon after seven o'clock on the evening of 26 March, as night approached, having reached Point A in his orders, Ryder altered course almost due south. A haze had developed over the sea and the breeze abated, to the greater comfort of the motor launches. Just before dusk the lone Hurricane, for ever circling, straightened out and, roaring low above the little fleet, flew away northwards into the gathering gloom. To Ryder it was 'the last visible link with the homeland we had left six hours before'; and he added, with characteristic understatement: 'Much lay ahead and even the least imaginative of the company present, alone with his thoughts, must have speculated as to his future.'

As darkness fell Ryder made the signal to change to the night cruising order, and, as all ships took it up, they manoeuvred gradually into three columns, the destroyers in the centre column, one and a half cables astern of each other, and the motor launches out on either hand, a cable between each. Speed was increased to fourteen knots, in order that it might be reduced the next day; for heavy wash from the vessels by day would instantly attract the eyes of scouting aircraft. The haze persisted, but the wind eased further to a mere sigh and the misty moon palely lit the scene as through a blue-black filter. No sound could be heard but that of the engines and the swish and slap of the water against the ships' hulls. Lovegrove, covered in oil, slept fitfully on the gearbox of his treasured engine. To Ryder and Newman in *Atherstone* the destroyers astern stood out as solid, black shapes against the night sky. To port and starboard the dim shapes of the motor launches could be discerned keeping station, a faint phosphorescence gleaming from their ruffled stern waves. All who had no duties to do turned in for the night, the soldiers reluctantly, for the spell of the moment was on them, accentuated by the inevitable wakefulness of the night before a great event.

*

To Ryder's disappointment the morning of Friday, 27 March, opened to a brilliant dawn with a cloudless sky and limitless visibility. This was particularly the day when he would have welcomed heavy clouds or a light fog. He and Newman, who, 'much against my will', had taken a few hours' sleep, were on the bridge before daylight and again Newman watched with zestful enjoyment the little fleet obey the signal to swing out into the anti-submarine formation. He chuckled, and every soldier in the force

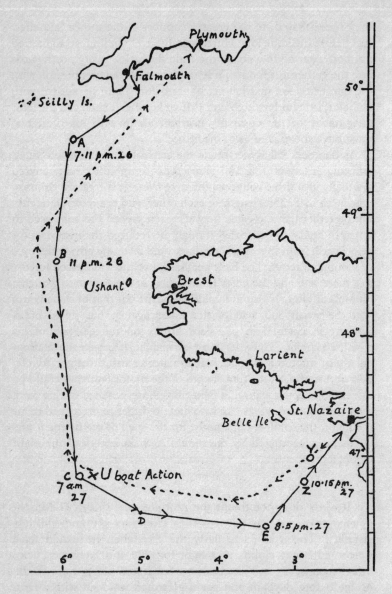

Fig 11. There and back. Outward passage shown by continuous line, homeward by dotted line.

chuckled with him, when the three destroyers, though not the motor launches, were seen to hoist the German ensign. It was now the last day.

By seven o'clock in the morning the fleet had reached Point C, some 160 miles to the westward of St Nazaire. Low down on their port hand, the sun was gilding the quiet waters, deserted of all but themselves. In accordance with his orders, Ryder altered course to 112°. Five minutes later *Tynedale*'s Gunner, Mr S. W. J. Ford, who was second officer of the watch, sighted an object, possibly a submarine, on the port beam, seven and half miles distant at a bearing of 37°.

Ryder ordered *Tynedale* to close and investigate and he himself, after the gunboat had been cast off, followed her at speed in *Atherstone*, with Nock's and Falconar's MLs in company. As *Tynedale*, still wearing German colours, closed the distant object, Tweedie, her captain, identified it as a submarine, surfaced and apparently stationary. When she had closed to about five miles, the submarine saw her coming bows-on and fired a rocket of five white stars as a recognition signal. *Tynedale* replied with five long flashes of her signal lamp – a pure guess.

The U-boat seemed to be satisfied and she remained innocently on the surface until 7.45. *Tynedale* had now closed to about five thousand yards and Tweedie, hauling down the German colours and breaking the White Ensign, opened fire with the forward mounting, much too soon. Columns of water spouted up around the submarine, which immediately crash-dived.

Tynedale, continuing at speed till she had reached the submarine's estimated position, dropped a pattern of depth-charges thirteen minutes later. The shock forced the U-boat to break surface again and *Tynedale* opened fire on her a second time at short range and with all the guns that could bear. The U-boat, said the watching Newman, was enveloped in 'a mass of large columns of water', but she was on the surface for only a few seconds before diving again, apparently hit.

The expedition was not out after submarines, but what concerned Ryder was the chance that, before diving, she might have seen them and might later make a sighting report by wireless to the German Naval Commander-in-Chief West (General-

Admiral Alfred Saalwächter). He therefore ordered *Tynedale* and *Atherstone* to carry out a 'square search', but *Tynedale*'s asdic went out of action and contact was lost. After two hours Ryder called off the hunt. As both the submarine herself and the launches lay low in the water, with limited horizons, he hoped that she would have seen only the destroyers. Tweedie thought it looked probable that she had been sunk or mortally injured. Ryder, however, was far from convinced and, with a shrewd instinct, he ordered the two destroyers to steam off on a south-westerly course, so as to deceive the U-boat, should she have them under observation from her periscope.

This quick-witted decision had a vital effect. Had it not been made, the whole expedition would surely have been imperilled, for the submarine, which postwar evidence showed to have been U 593, homeward-bound, had in fact sighted some of the motor launches before she had been attacked but had not reported them, not supposing that they could conceivably be British. Nor had she been sunk. After the attack she remained submerged for five and a half hours and at 1.47 p.m. reported by wireless:

0620 (7.20 a.m. BST) *three destroyers 10 MTBs, 46° 52′N., 5° 48′W. Course West.*

The effect of this report, which was received at German Group Command West, at 2.20 p.m., and the error in judging the course of the Charioteers, was to cause the enemy to suppose that the British force was withdrawing after a minelaying operation, or else that it was on passage to Gibraltar. 'An imminent attack from the sea on a port on the French west coast,' we are told in the report of the German naval staff, 'was never anticipated.' This was exactly what Ryder wanted, but it had been a very near thing. We shall see very soon what course was taken by the German command.

After abandoning the hunt, *Atherstone* and *Tynedale* rejoined the force by a circuitous route. *Atherstone* once more took the gunboat in tow. Ryder felt sure that, as a result of the encounter with the submarine, he must very soon expect enemy reconnaissance aircraft to appear, but he had now to turn his glasses to a new cause of apprehension. On the port bow there appeared a fleet of French fishing trawlers.

He had given careful thought to this likelihood, for he was

anxious to do no avoidable harm to French interests or to any other innocent parties. It was, however, known or believed that the Germans sometimes put observers equipped with wireless sets on board French fishing boats and Ryder therefore decided that any that were met would have to be sunk. On this occasion, however, shortly before noon, he was confronted not with one or two fishing vessels but a whole fleet. Their appearance so soon after the encounter with the submarine was suspicious; they may have had a rendezvous together.

Two, however, were widely separated from the rest and he dispatched *Tynedale* to sink one of them, which was the trawler *Nungesser et Coli*, and *Atherstone*, with the gunboat in company, sank *Le Slack*. The skippers and crews, throwing their hats in the air with delight at this totally unexpected appearance of the White Ensign, which the destroyers hoisted, accepted the decision with perfect goodwill and cheerfulness. They were taken on board the destroyers and made much of, involuntary participants in the great enterprise. At its conclusion, they were taken back to England to their great delight, where most of them joined the Free French Forces. From the skipper of *Le Slack* Ryder learnt that the fishing fleet, which was from La Pallice, carried no wireless or German observers and he decided to sink no more.

*

To the relief of all, the sky had now become completely overcast with low cloud, but Ryder remained apprehensive of the danger of observation by enemy craft, particularly from the air. The encounters with the submarine and the fishing craft were disturbing, a clear sign that the nearer they approached the French coast the greater was the danger of unforeseen encounters. This apprehension was increased by news received from Plymouth soon after midday of the moves of the five German *Wolfe/Möwe* class destroyers, commanded by Moritz Schmidt, which he and Newman had spotted from the last air photographs of St Nazaire docks. Just after the trawler incident Ryder had been relieved to hear from Plymouth that these destroyers had moved up to Nantes the day before, but at 5.18 p.m. a second signal from Plymouth reported that they were now back at St Nazaire and 'might be met'.

This was disturbing news, as they were a very much superior force to Ryder's. In point of fact, however, the German Group Command West, after receipt of the submarine's report, telephoned the information to the Luftwaffe and to the admiral commanding the Protective Forces and then, on the supposition that the force had been engaged in minelaying, ordered the destroyers to carry out a 'mine reconnaissance' along the U-boat routes off St Nazaire *that night*. The submarine's report therefore worked unexpectedly to the advantage of the Charioteers, for, at the time when Ryder was beginning to steal over the shoal waters of the Loire, Schmidt's flotilla, following the orthodox Charpentiers Channel, was already at sea.*

Of these movements Ryder, of course, knew nothing. He was expecting extensive air reconnaissance at any time, and he knew that once spotted, he would be kept continuously under observation even if not attacked. The wisdom of the course selected was therefore now apparent, for, as they were now heading, they might be supposed to be making for La Pallice, a good way south of St Nazaire. Even so, the presence of the enemy ships anywhere near St Nazaire was a menacing factor, if only for the subsequent return voyage home, and therefore Ryder took comfort when another signal came from Forbes, telling him that two more Hunt class destroyers, the *Cleveland* and the *Brocklesbury*, had been sailed from Plymouth to support the withdrawal.

Many years later he was to learn that, that very day, as he was moving surely towards his objective, Admiral Doenitz, C-in-C of the German submarine forces, having left his headquarters at Kernval, near Lorient, was himself visiting the threatened docks of St Nazaire. He had come to inspect the submarine base and during the course of his inspection he asked Kapitänleutnant Herbert Sohler, commanding the 7th Submarine Flotilla:

'What are you going to do if the British attack this place?'

Sohler replied that plans had been made for that unlikely event and embodied in an Emergency Order. 'However,' he added, 'that is considered here to be highly improbable.'

---

* Six weeks later Schmidt, in *Seeadler*, was sunk by an MTB near Dover, and, he tells us, 'had to swim for my life in the cold water of the English Channel'.

'I should not be too sure,' Doenitz commented.

For, only four days earlier, Hitler had issued his personal order on 'Command Organisation on the Coasts'. In this order (Directive No 40) he warned all higher commanders that British landings with limited objectives were to be expected. Our strategic reasons for such operations were perfectly well understood by him. He therefore ordered that 'special attention must be paid to British preparations for landings . . . Large-scale parachute and glider operations are likewise to be expected.'

One need not wonder that, coming hot on top of this special warning, the events of the next few hours were to generate an outburst of fury in that satanic mind.

*

Ryder continued to take every precaution, the antennae of his senses stretched in every direction. Earlier that afternoon he had again rebuked the motor launches for too much lamp work and had ordered Tillie in ML 4: *Go round MLs telling them all by hailer to reduce Aldis signalling.* Later, as evening approached, he made to the whole force: *Glass on wheelhouses most conspicuous at night. Must be covered with paint, paper or grease on outside.*

The commandos, however, were little concerned with these anxieties. For the last time, they cleaned their weapons, checked their gear and ammunition and rehearsed their tasks. Sergeant Steele, in the gunboat, satisfactorily netted his new 38 radio sets with the operators of the other three stations that were to be set up. Throughout the fleet the commandos shared anti-aircraft duties with the naval ratings, and in the motor launches they practised the use of the Oerlikons and twin Lewis guns, fitting themselves to take part as integral members of the ships' companies in their fire plans; but otherwise they had little to do. They played brag in the fo'c'sle or sat about on deck in oilskins or duffle coats. Their only inconvenience was a prohibition of washing and shaving, since the fresh-water supplies were severely strained by so many extra hands and a strict water discipline was necessary. The officers gossiped with the troops or kept company with the naval officers on the bridge.

In the *Campbeltown*, with more room to move about, the

soldiers were even more comfortable, though here also the number of soldiers allowed on deck was limited. The scaling ladders and ropes for use in the disembarkation were brought out and put into position. The two 3-inch mortars with which the commandos were to supplement the fire of *Campbeltown*'s weapons, under Proctor, were mounted on the fo'c'sle. Action stations were practised under Gough, the tall, lithe, gay and handsome first lieutenant. Final rehearsals were held. But apart from these few duties, one might have supposed that the doomed destroyer, which in a few hours' time was to ride into the jaws of death and whose company was to leap from her deck in the face of a furious cannonade, was no more than a pleasure steamer filled with exuberant holiday-makers. Sailors and soldiers alike were in high spirits. The bridge itself became, as it were, a coffee house, where the commando officers jested with Beattie, Gough and Tibbits and drank quantities of 'pusser's cocoa'. Donald Roy, Proctor and their men of the kilted Troop of 2 Commando, added an exotic and festive touch to the stark steel walls.

But no one, perhaps, more aptly represented the air and spirit of them all than Burtenshaw, the strong-limbed, monocled subaltern of the Cheshire Regiment and 5 Commando. He stood about six feet four inches and, although powerfully built and a fine rugby footballer, stooped a little, as very tall men often do, his battledress sagging loosely on his frame, so that he was known to all ranks inelegantly as 'Bertie Bagwash'. Not, however, in derision, but rather in affection, for he had a heart of gold and the spirit of a lion. On board the *Campbeltown* he, as much as anyone, set the light-hearted tone of all these gay crusaders. Borrowing an old cap of Beattie's, and draped in a duffle coat, he walked the deck and mounted the bridge as to the manner born, for he had a quick wit and a spritely humour, and was acknowledged as 'the skipper' by all. 'Well, skipper,' Beattie himself would ask, 'what would you advise us to do now?'

Nothing stimulated the bubbling hilarity of the troops so much as the ensign of the Third Reich. Draped in all manner of 'fancy dress', picked out from ship's stores that would never now be wanted, they grouped themselves aft, mocking the ensign with the Hitler salutation, and were photographed by cameras illicitly brought by one or two. Gunner Milne, Roy's soldier-servant, looked on the emblem with a deeper design, biding his time. Above all, however, the most ardent occupation of soldiers and ratings alike was to eat. For security reasons, the ship had been provisioned on more or less the normal scale at Devonport and there were large quantities of food on board, and of sorts that the commandos, on home rations, had never seen in such abundance. Eggs, hams, 'real butter', sausages and other fare liberally supplemented the ample meals served from the galley. And after eating their fill they sat about in groups and sang songs.

The NAAFI was likewise well stocked. For some time the ratings and other ranks solemnly went on paying for their wares in the normal way until someone said: 'Hey, the ship's going to be blown up tonight – accounts and all. What are we paying for?' Thereafter, everything was 'on the house'. Nor did the fun stop there. From these doomed canteen supplies bright spirits made sandwiches filled with toothpaste, shaving-soap, and haircream to be offered to unsuspecting friends. All this harmless hilarity Beattie and Copland and their officers looked upon with indulgence, understanding the springs that fed it and knowing what was to come. Copland had allowed the soldiers a rum ration the day before, but on this last day he would not sanction it. The thirty-six hours' holiday was soon to end. They knew that they ought to get some sleep before their tasks of the small hours, but most of them were much too excited to do so.

*

Operationally only one small mishap disturbed the ordered routine. At 6.30, when the sun was very low, the port engine of Douglas Briault's ML 10 went out of action, and although one of the flotilla engineer officers, Sub-Lieutenant Tom Yendoll, came to his assistance, nothing could be done in time. In accordance with the prescribed plan Falconar's ML 15, one of the spare vessels so fortunately added late in the day, took over her troops, who consisted of Hodgson's assault party and Barling's medical party. Putting on full speed, Falconar caught up the remainder of the force two hours later, taking station last in the port column of troop-carrying boats. The unfortunate Briault followed on one engine as best he could the blue hand light put out for him by Nock, but the port engine was not repaired until 10.20 p.m., when all chance of catching up had long gone. Sadly Briault turned about and returned to England alone.

No further encounters took place and no German aircraft flew. Under the clouded sky, the Charioteers sailed on at a quiet eight knots. The team was moving steadily up the field in good order. The second night drew on. The last phase, when the dash into goal was to be made, was nearly upon them. At eight o'clock, just after darkness had fallen, they reached Point E and turned north-eastward, shaping now straight for the open jaws of the Loire. Here the whole force stopped and finally manoeuvred in the dark into the special cruising order in which they were to make their attack. Wynn's MTB was cast off from *Campbeltown* and her engines pulsed sweetly into action under Lovegrove's care. For Ryder and Newman the time had come to say goodbye to *Atherstone*. Curtis's gunboat was cast off and came alongside. Ryder, accompanied by Green and O'Rourke, and Newman, accompanied by Day, Terry and Holman, after cordial 'good luck' wishes from Jenks and his officers, jumped on board.

It was indeed a dramatic moment. As the little gunboat began to move away, *Atherstone*'s company lined the rails and gave a warm cheer that seemed suddenly to people the dark and empty sea with friends. Jenks, remembering *Atherstone*'s old status as parent ship to the little gunboat, gave a touching message to the offspring that was now to adventure into the storm of life. Standing in the wing of his bridge, he called out not, as might have been expected, 'Remember whose son you are,' but, with a touch of inspiration that filled with pride all hands upon the gunboat:

'Don't forget whose father I am.'

Very much stirred, Curtis took his gunboat to the head of the line. Astern of him the small dark shapes of the motor launches moved silently as night moths into their columns and the solid bulks of the escort destroyers slid away on either hand. Then, with *Campbeltown* two and a half cables astern, with the two columns of motor launches close in on either hand, the torpedo-carrying boats of Boyd and Irwin leading them to starboard and port respectively, and with Wynn's MTB in the tail of all, he moved on

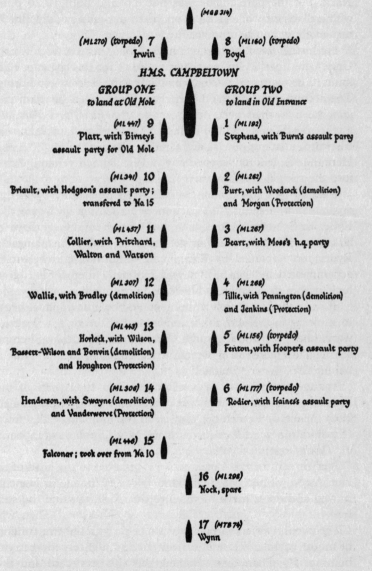

(MGB 314)

(ML270) (torpedo) 7
Irwin

8 *(ML160) (torpedo)*
Boyd

.H.M.S. CAMPBELTOWN

GROUP ONE
to land at Old Mole

GROUP TWO
to land in Old Entrance

(ML447) 9
Platt, with Birney's
assault party for Old Mole

1 *(ML192)*
Stephens, with Burn's assault party

(ML341) 10
Briault, with Hodgson's assault party;
transfered to No. 15

2 *(ML262)*
Burt, with Woodcock (demolition)
and Morgan (Protection)

(ML457) 11
Collier, with Pritchard,
Walton and Watson

3 *(ML267)*
Beart, with Moss's h.q. party

(ML307) 12
Wallis, with Bradley (demolition)

4 *(ML268)*
Tillie, with Pennington (demolition)
and Jenkins (Protection)

(ML443) 13
Horlock, with Wilson,
Bassett-Wilson and Bonvin (demolition)
and Houghton (Protection)

5 *(ML156) (torpedo)*
Fenton, with Hooper's assault party

(ML306) 14
Henderson, with Swayne (demolition)
and Vanderwerve (Protection)

6 *(ML177) (torpedo)*
Rodier, with Haines's assault party

(ML446) 15
Falconar; took over from No. 10

16 *(ML298)*
Nock, spare

17 *(MTB74)*
Wynn

Fig 12. Order of battle for the attack.

at twelve knots into the clouded night. Only seventy-five miles now.

There was only one more check point to pass now; at Point Z they were to make contact with Mervyn Wingfield in the submarine *Sturgeon*, acting as a navigational beacon from which Green could get a pinpoint chart position for the last run. She would be displaying a masked white light showing to seaward only and intermittently flashing the letter M. To broaden the chance of safely keeping their ocean rendezvous, *Atherstone* and *Tynedale* stayed near them for a little while, taking station about a mile on either beam. But so precise was Green's pilotage that, at 10 p.m., the double dashes of *Sturgeon*'s light were sighted, winking from the dark waste two miles exactly ahead.

It was a moment that impressed itself powerfully upon the expectant commandos. That, at a mere pinpoint in the ocean, the beckoning light should appear from the depths and meet them in the dark with such unerring precision seemed to them nearly miraculous. Newman, no less than the junior ranks, experienced a stirring of wonderment. They all felt tremendously set up, as though, Swayne recorded, Neptune himself had risen to guide them on to victory. Surely nothing could now go wrong. As they came closer in the phosphorescent gloom they saw the *Sturgeon* half submerged, nothing more visible than her conning-tower, looking like a mere tub afloat in the ocean, and inside it the small, dim figure of her commander.

As they passed close to her Ryder thanked her through the loud-hailer. Wingfield, in a breezy stentorian voice that seemed oddly incongruous with the tension of the moment, called back 'Goodbye and good luck', and, as the boats further astern came up: 'Good luck boys!'

The import of the occasion was on every man. Even the buoyant Newman recorded: 'One felt very much nearer the fighting and one's nerves instinctively became just that little bit tighter.'

The two destroyers turned away, to begin an all-night patrol off the mouth of the Loire, and to await such as might return the next morning. The Charioteers watched their dim shapes fade into the night, watched the submarine slip below the sea. They were alone.

13. INTO THE JAWS

Forty miles to the goal.

The little bridge of the gunboat is crowded. Dimly silhouetted against the night sky, there is a cluster of dark shapes, steel-helmeted, life-jacketed. Curtis, her bearded young captain, stands at the port side with the three engine-room telegraphs before him. Behind him is the slight figure of Anthony Terry and to his right, in the manner customary in these gunboats, Leading Seaman McKee, the coxswain, stands at the bridgewheel, instead of in the wheelhouse. Behind the coxswain is Stanley Day. The small, square figure of Robert Ryder, alert, concentrated, sensitive to all sound and movement, his active mind projected ahead, is close by and behind him the burlier Newman, biding his own time, eagerly takes in all there is to see and hear. The leaner, cheerful figure of Green is to starboard, taking observations from time to time and darting down into the little charthouse to make his calculations. Between these activities he sits casually on the rail of the bridge, hatless, his chart on his knees, relaxed and full of fun, cracking jokes with the equally buoyant Curtis. O'Rourke, the Canadian signals officer, is in the background. Pike, the specialist in German signals, is near at hand, his night lamp and his German signals ready. Within the force itself, however, there must now be no more signalling.

On the fo'c'sle Able Seaman Savage, burly and bearded and his No 2, Able Seaman F. A. Smith, took post at their pom-pom, ready for their last fight. Other hands manned the two twin .5 heavy machine-guns amidships. On deck or below, the remainder of Newman's headquarters party were gathered – Sergeant Steele with his secret portable radio ready to strap on, Lance-Corporal Harrington, the gallant runner, Privates Kelly and Murdoch, the two Tommy-gunners, and Private Peter Walker, the ex-German, sent expressly on Mountbatten's orders because 'he knew how to deal with Germans'. Newman, going below, found Kelly slipping down his trousers and about to put on the kilt. The Scot looked up a trifle guiltily, saying: 'Can I, sir?'

Smiling good-naturedly, Newman answered: 'All right, if you think you'll fight better that way.' He was glad afterwards that he had been able to grant the lad his last wish.

Glancing back from time to time to see if all ships were keeping proper station, Ryder saw the shapes of the two leading torpedo-carrying motor launches two hundred yards away on either quarter, and astern of them the troop-carrying MLs stretched back for a mile in two orderly columns, gradually diminishing in size so that the farthest were scarcely discernible as faint black marks upon the sombre grey seascape. Falconar, with Briault's troops, had just caught up. In the very tail of all, 'Wynn's Weapons' continued to hang back and leap forward by her queer jerks. The haze persisted and thickened. The clouds grew denser and it began to rain a little. The tall bulk of *Campbeltown* astern, five hundred yards away, became blurred with a thin veil of moisture. This, thought Ryder, was just the weather he wanted to avoid being seen; it did not, perhaps, occur to him in his preoccupation with the immediate present, that it was just not the weather for the bombing support that was of such critical importance.

All hands had already had their last meal and in *Campbeltown* the officers thought regretfully of the doom of their excellent La Ina sherry in the wardroom and they all had a glass or two before supper. At 11 o'clock Nigel Tibbits, assisted by Able Seaman Demmelweet, activated the eight-hour pencil delay fuses that were to set off the great explosive charge, starting the flow of the acid that would gradually eat through the copper. Their known margin of error made it possible that one of them might turn out to be a six-hour fuse, so that the charge would go up at 5 o'clock next morning, and it should not, in any case, go off later than 9 o'clock.

Just before half past eleven, while they were still several miles out to sea, the throb of our bombers was plainly heard coming over to attack. Mecke, the German anti-aircraft commander, had in fact given the alert at 11.20 and a few minutes later the horizon ahead of the Charioteers leapt into life. The sky became illuminated with the probing fingers of searchlights, followed very soon by the sharp flashes of many guns, seeming at that distance like the flickering of innumerable torches or the flashes of some army of crazy photographers. The streams of coloured tracer were seen climbing into the sky with little pinpoints of bursting shells at their extremities. Almost immediately afterwards they heard the muffled crump of bursting bombs, not in showers, but only one at a time. All hands who were on deck watched, fascinated. The battle of St Nazaire had begun.

Midnight passed and it was Saturday, 28 March.

Half an hour later, exactly on time, the gallant little force, buoyant and eager, entered the estuary of the Loire. In less than an hour they would reach their goal. The bombing raid was already faltering to its premature end, but it never for a moment occurred to Newman or Ryder to do otherwise than go straight forward.

Yet, just a moment before, a harsh reminder of the venom of the air arm lay close to their course. Montgomery, standing with Beattie on *Campbeltown*'s bridge, observed not far away the stark outlines of a wrecked liner, its masts and funnels standing acutely out of the water and outlined against the grey night sky. It was the ghost of the *Lancastria*, relic of one of the war's most cruel tragedies, now beckoning to them, as might seem, to avenge the horrors of that mass sacrifice to Moloch. Newman, who had been evacuated in her from Norway, saw her too. And in Henderson's motor launch, they say, Sergeant Durrant also observed her and perhaps his mind went back to that day, eighteen months before, when he had prophesied revenge to his brother Jack.

That time, with all its shining prowess and its gallant loss, grew closer yet. The commandos, tense and expectant, began in silence to prepare themselves. At a quarter to one, in the vicinity of Le Chatelier Shoal, they had their first glimpse of land, the low line of the northern shore being dimly discernible, smudging the leaden horizon. Green thought that the set of the sea must have carried them a trifle farther to the north than he had expected and he altered course a little. They were now in dangerous shoal

waters and speed was reduced to ten knots, in order to minimize
Campbeltown's draft as much as possible, for she settled by the
stern when at speed. Navigationally, this was the most difficult
part of the passage, for the destroyer, head and front of the whole
enterprise, had nothing whatever to spare beneath her keel.

Accordingly, ordering *Campbeltown* to steer a course of 50°,
which made allowance for a strong northerly set, and to act as
guide of the fleet, Ryder himself moved off on either bow to locate
shoals by the echo-sounder and to take ranges to the shore by the
radar equipment. He found, however, that the radar, primitive as
it was, able to read only directly fore-and-aft and subject to false
echoes from the adjacent ships, was of little value.

On slender threads do great enterprises often hang. The
destroyer did in fact ground twice. Each time, Donald Roy tells
us, 'we felt her churning and shuddering through the mud and we
had some bad moments'. Beattie, looking over the side to see if
the destroyer was still moving, noted that her speed was checked
to about five knots, but by great good fortune she drove through
without harm. Thus was one of the main hazards of the expedition
averted and in after days the professional Loire pilots declared
that Green's feat of navigation that night was without parallel in
the history of the port.

About this time yet another danger was averted. Away on the
port quarter Ryder saw the dim shape of a small ship patrolling the
entrance to the Charpentiers Channel. It was, as we now know,
one of the two harbour patrol boats numbered 414 and 415. 'We
held our course as well as our breaths,' Ryder said, 'praying that
we should go unnoticed.' Their luck still held. We know today
that the patrol boat did in fact observe them after they had passed,
but, having no wireless, she was helpless to take any action, her
attempts to attract attention by flashing her searchlights into the
sky passing unnoticed.

The air-raid had now completely stopped. Aircraft, indeed,
were still flying, but they were high above the clouds and no one
heard them now. The German searchlights had been dowsed. All
was very quiet. To the men who were stealing across the shoals
nothing broke the stillness of the night except the murmur of the
ships' engines moving through the calm, unruffled sea. All hands

were at action stations. In the motor launches the deck petrol tanks had been emptied and filled with sea water. The surgical dressings and the morphia had been laid out in each wheelhouse. The soldiers had prepared themselves, harnessed in their webbing equipment with their heavy loads of ammunition and grenades and with their fighting knives strapped to their legs. The Bergen rucksacks carrying the explosives of the demolition men were laid out on deck ready to be picked up. Bren-gunners with stocks of 100-round magazines lay on the deck. Officers waited on the bridge to take instructions from the Captain.

In the *Campbeltown* Copland, tall, erect, very cool and self-contained, had summoned all the fourteen commando officers to a short final conference in the wardroom a little before midnight. It was a calm, confident, cheerful gathering. Whatever may have been going on in the hearts of each of them, no tension was apparent. They spoke in a matter-of-fact way about final details of their tasks. It was just midnight when they finished and Copland ordered: 'Action stations, please, gentlemen.'

They jumped up and went quietly to their places with their men. Copland's place was on the fo'c'sle, where he was to direct the disembarkation of the parties in their correct order. On the fo'c'sle with him was John Proctor, in the kilt, in command of the two 3-inch mortars, manned by Corporals Beacham and Cheetham and Privates Holland and Hannon. Amidships the assault and demolitions parties took up their positions under cover of the steel fences erected for them, the assault parties outboard, the demolition teams and their protection squads inboard. Leading on the starboard side, ready to land, like lightning, was the assault party of the stalwart John Roderick, with Donald Roy's kilted party in the corresponding position to port. Gunner Milne, The Laird's batman, close to the signal deck, kept his eye musingly on that German ensign showing darkly overhead. Etches, the serious, fair-haired, handsome young Regular officer who was in charge of the two demolition teams at the northern end of the dry dock, was also close to the signal deck. Inboard also were the parties of Chant, Hopwood and Smalley. Down in the wardroom were the demolition teams of the two Royal Ulster Riflemen, Gerard Brett and Corran Purdon, looking wistfully at all the bottles that were so soon to be blown to destruction.

Burtenshaw, monocle in eye, still wearing Beattie's cap and towering above everyone, was in exalted good humour, humming:
'There'll always be an England'.

The naval officers and ratings were also already at their action
stations. On the bridge were Beattie and Tibbits, with Montgomery
as commando liaison officer. On the fo'c'sle, with Proctor's
mortars, was the ship's lone 12-pounder, manned by cooks and
stewards, but with trained gun-captain and layer. Gough, as first
lieutenant, gay and debonair, stood ready to control the fire of the
eight Oerlikons high on their 'bandstand' towers, the moment that
Beattie should give the order to open fire by the ringing of a bell.
Petty Officer Newman, gunner's mate, was at his hand. Down
below Warrant Engineer Locke looked round the engine- and
boiler-rooms, ready for the final moment. In the sick bay the
Canadian doctor, Surgeon-Lieutenant W. J. Winthorpe, waited to
perform the last duties of his life. All else – messdecks, cabins,
galleys, stores, offices – were empty, silent and abandoned. In the
heart of the great charge beneath the 12-pounder the acid was
slowly and inexorably eating through the tensed copper wire. All
was very quiet, no sound audible except the steady hum of the
ship's engines and the men's low-murmured conversation.

Was it conceivable that they would have the luck to get through
unseen and unheard? Boyd, leading the starboard column in ML
8, admits that, at this period, he was feeling very apprehensive.
'But I shall never forget,' he recorded, 'the sweet smell of the
countryside as we steamed up-river; we could see both banks now
and on the port hand could even make out trees and hedges.'
Curtis, too, could smell the land. They were within a few hundred
yards of the enemy. It was unbelievable. 'This,' said Boyd to Petty
Officer Lamb, his coxswain, 'is a queer do.' 'It will soon,' replied
the coxswain, 'be a bloody sight queerer, sir.'

It very soon was. The moon, that moon which the bombers had
needed so much, was now partially unveiled as the clouds began
to dissipate. Under the clearer light, not yet bright, but soon to be
all too bright, the two columns of little boats and their big
companion moved confidently forward up the hushed river, the
black cross of the German ensign flying loosely in the still air from
Campbeltown's stern and masthead. At 1.20 a.m. the gunboat,

now again in the van for the final dash, passed the old disused tower of Les Morées in midstream, almost exactly on time. Men spoke now only in whispers. What was going on on that dark, hostile shore? Surely the enemy must be able to see them now, or at least must hear the throb of those engines, which beat into their own ears with so loud and clear a note?

*

On that dark shore Captain Mecke, commander of the anti-aircraft brigade, had been following such events as he could hear and see from his headquarters at St Marc with perplexity and some anxiety.

After the British bombing attack had developed at 11.30 he became considerably astonished at the unusual behaviour of the aircraft. Bombs fell only one at a time, with long intervals between. Not more than thirty altogether. Some aircraft dropped no bombs at all. 'The employment of so many aircraft' – which he estimated later at eighty – 'and the determination with which the British pressed forward their attack bore no relation to the number of bombs.' 'Some aircraft,' he noted, 'flew on to Nantes.'

As one after another they flew in, flying high and apparently aimlessly, the radar trace of their movements resembling a spawn of eels, he became more and more suspicious. He formed the impression that the bombing raid was a blind for some other purpose and he said to one of his staff officers: 'Some devilry is afoot.' At midnight he made the signal to all command posts of the Wehrmacht:

The conduct of the enemy aircraft is inexplicable and indicates suspicion of parachute landings.

He noted that the night was not very dark, with no cloud below 3200 feet, except for an occasional short rain squall, and that surface visibility was fairly good up to three or four miles. By one o'clock the greater portion of the British aircraft had withdrawn and there remained only a few in the neighbourhood, flying beyond the effective range of his guns. He had already given the order to cease fire and, in order not to assist further aircraft in finding their way to St Nazaire, he had also caused the search-lights to be switched off, and not to be employed again unless aircraft were visible by the naked eye or by glasses. But he also gave the order to his troops for a continued and increased alert and – a quite exceptional order for them – to direct special attention seaward.

Perhaps as a consequence of this order, or perhaps, in his own words, 'because he was bored with looking at the sky', Korvetten-kapitän Burhenne, commanding 809 Naval Flak Battalion, from his headquarters on the east bank, turned his night glasses to the river and beheld to his astonishment a force of small ships moving up at moderate speed. As this was the concern of the Harbour Commander, he reported the fact direct to Kellermann's head-quarters, but was given the answer:

'Don't be stupid. It's not your business. You would be better employed looking at the sky instead of the river.'

He thereupon reported to his own superior, Mecke.

At 1.15 a look-out at St Marc, or the naval station nearby, or both, reported the approach of a force of 'about seventeen vessels' at extreme visual range. Three minutes later one of Mecke's staff telephoned to the Harbour Commander and asked: 'Are you expecting any German ships to come into harbour?' The answer was in the negative.

At 1.20 – the moment when Ryder passed Les Morées tower – Mecke made the signal to all concerned:

Achtung Landegefahr ('Beware landing').

On receipt of this code word, the machinery for repelling an invasion in accordance with the Emergency Orders was put in force throughout the command. More particularly, all anti-aircraft guns switched to the defence of the shores and all available troops and crews of the minesweepers, harbour defence boats and tankers in St Nazaire, many of whom were in their air-raid shelters, from which they were promptly routed out, became actuated in an infantry rôle as *Stosstruppen* (thrust troops). The most important of these were the spare hands of Mecke's own battalions – the watch off duty, the clerks, instructors, storemen and so on.

At the same time the commander of the coast-defence guns, Korvettenkapitän Dieckmann, who had become restless at the sound of engines and who had come out immediately at his headquarters at Chémoulin on receipt of the siting report at 1.15, gave the order to his batteries: 'Stand by to attack naval targets.'

Why the searchlights had not already been switched on is not explained. According to the signals log, five minutes elapsed before Mecke's order to illuminate was put into effect. Those five minutes were of priceless value to the dim shapes moving steadily onward under the misty moon.

*

On the bridge of the gunboat Ryder and his companions were tingling with suppressed elation. Damned nearly home now; less than two miles to go. The luck was incredible.

At 1.22 the big five-foot searchlight BLAU 1, hard by 703 Battalion's headquarters, flashed out. The whole force was brilliantly floodlit, showing, as upon some great arena before multitudes of an unseen public, the splendid spectacle, suddenly revealed in diamond brilliance, of the long columns of ships smoothly moving in formation over the silent water. In the cold, white beams the bow and stern waves glittered and foamed. Towering over the little ships, like some great sea bird escorting her adventurous brood, there was revealed the bulk of the German-seeming *Campbeltown*, beginning to increase speed for her final burst.

Two German signal stations, their lamps winking through the blaze of light, at once challenged – one from right ahead in the dockyard area (in fact from the *Sperrbrecher* moored off the East Jetty), the other from a position on the port beam. At the same time a few bursts were fired at the van of the force from the Bofors guns at positions M16 and M17 at Villès-Martin.

Now was the moment for Leading Seaman Pike to play his part. For this critical eventuality Ryder had made careful preparation and had given Pike instructions beforehand how to act. He was to transmit in German a long, delaying message and to give the 'Morsename' or call sign of one of the German torpedo boats on that coast, of which we knew several from documents found on the Vaagso raid. Further, as a trump card, Ryder had been provided with the cartridges for the current German Very-light recognition signal, which we also knew.

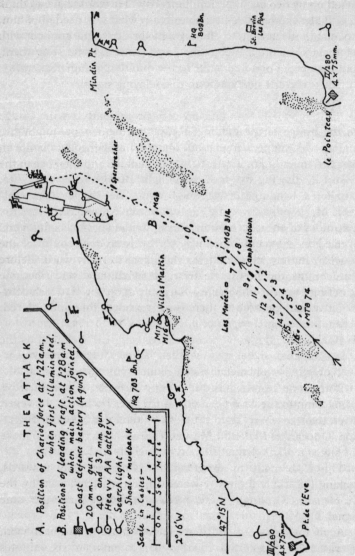

THE ATTACK

A. Position of Chariot force at 1·22 a.m.
   when first illuminated.
B. Positions of leading craft at 1·28 a.m.
   when main action joined.

▨ Coast defence battery (4 guns)
⌇ 20 mm. gun
⌇ 40 and 37 mm. gun
⌇ Heavy AA battery
⌇ Searchlight
⠿ Shoal or mudbank

Scale in Cables—
1 2 3 4 5 6 7 8 9 10
One Sea Mile

Fig 13. The attack.

What Ryder had not been prepared for, however, was being called up by two stations simultaneously. He would have to think fast. Pike, who had been quick to grasp what was needed of him, was standing ready at his elbow on the bridge of the gunboat with his night signalling lamp, as the harsh white light burst on them, and Ryder told him to answer first the station abeam of them.

'Make the call sign and then the delaying signal.'

'Aye, aye, sir.'

Pike complied. Standing up very prominently on the bridge and wearing a petty officer's cap which at that distance might give him an outline similar to a German's, he aligned his lamp on the challenging station, made the Morsename and then began the bogus signal: *Proceeding up harbour in accordance with orders* . . .

It worked like magic. At the same moment, quite unaccountably, Mecke was advised by the Harbour Commander that the convoy was, after all, German. Firing stopped at once and several of the searchlights switched off. All hands on deck could see the German station acknowledging the signal word by word. Before Pike could complete the pre-arranged signal, however, it became imperative to deal with the *Sperrbrecher* station ahead, which continued to challenge. Ryder therefore interrupted Pike and ordered:

'Make the signal to "wait".'

Pike, cool and steady, complied, making 'EB' followed by the Morsename.

'Now the station ahead. Call sign and same signal.'

With some searchlights still glaring at them, Pike turned his signal lamp to the *Sperrbrecher*. He had scarcely begun, however, when the ships were again fired on, but still with obvious hesitation. Once more Ryder interrupted Pike and ordered him to make the signal for 'ship being fired on by friendly forces'.

This Pike made by directing the lamp vertically upwards, making two short flashes repeated three times, followed by the Morsename. On board the *Campbeltown* Beattie made the same signal.

Again the firing ceased. Four precious minutes had been won. It was 1.27. Scarcely a mile to go. In another six minutes *Campbeltown* would be home.

14. CAMPBELTOWN'S ATTACK

The Germans, we know today, had been completely foxed. They did not conceive it credible that a British force could suddenly appear under their noses with such effrontery so far from home. Naturally enough, they supposed at first that this unheralded force was more probably a German one, perhaps seeking shelter after stress of battle, without having followed the proper procedure for obtaining permission to enter the port.

But the brilliant bluff was at an end. Had they been genuine, the approaching ships would have stopped when fired on. Every German gun that could bear had them in its sights and at about 1.28 the storm burst.

Ryder made one last attempt to gain time, playing what he hoped was his trump card. He had reserved to his own hand the playing of it. Raising the Very pistol in the air, he fired the recognition signal. It rose a few feet into the air and then fell sizzling into the water – for it was an aircraft cartridge, designed to be fired downwards. What the Germans noticed, however, was not its curious flight, but the fact that the red light was not the shade of red to which they were accustomed. The battle was on.

The British ships, too, were ready. Ordered to hold their fire till the last moment, they decided that the last moment had now come. On board the *Campbeltown*, the tall, bearded figure of Beattie, very calm and serene, had already ordered:

'Two hundred revolutions' (eighteen and a half knots) and to his Yeoman of Signals:

'Hoist battle ensigns.'

The German colours were run down, and as the masthead flag came to the signal deck, Gunner Milne, who had for so long been waiting for this moment, seized it, cut off a strip and gave it to the delighted Roy.

A moment later a German searchlight threw upon the mast a noose of light, which, travelling slowly upwards, came to rest on the White Ensign, old, weather stained and half drooping in the windless air. The symbolic act filled with pride the hearts of the commandos, unaccustomed to the olden time spell of the Colours, and they watched entranced as all down the double column of motor launches, which had hitherto worn no colours, the White Ensign was seen to break out astern.

Beattie sounded his bell to open fire. At once the eight Oerlikons, under the direction of Petty Officer Newman, burst into a shattering clamour. On the fo'c'sle Copland had softly ordered the 12-pounder and the 3-inch mortars, a little ahead of him, to keep the searchlight on the port beam covered but not to fire. He now, at the top of his lungs, orthodoxy forgotten, shouted: 'Let her go!' Instantly gun and mortars opened fire. Almost instantly, also, the Klaxon horns sounded all down the columns of the motor launches and in a moment the little boats were sparkling with gun-flashes from twenty-four Oerlikons, from the four Hotchkiss guns of the torpedo craft and from Savage's little pom-pom in the gunboat. To this was added the brittle chatter of the Bren-guns as the commandos joined in the common fire plan.

In a moment upwards of a hundred guns and innumerable small arms were firing, within this small area, nearly all of them rapid-firing pieces, their orange flashes stabbing the cold, white glare of the searchlights. Across this great pool of light, into which every lamp that the Germans possessed was now concentrating its shaft, there shot in all directions vivid streams of red, green and yellow tracer. They criss-crossed like lighted shuttles on some infernal loom, duplicated by their darting images on the still water. As orchestra to this dazzling and menacing spectacle there could be heard, above the drumroll of machine-gun and rifle, the prolonged bursts of Oerlikons, the repetitive thuds of Bofors, and the sharper cracks of Dieckmann's heavier coast-defence guns – 75 mm, 150 mm, 170 mm. Gun-blast and shell-burst came almost instantaneously together, so short was the range. The rugged Boyd declared: 'The weight of fire caught one's breath,' and even one so given to understatement as Ryder officially recorded: 'It is difficult to describe the fury of the attack that was let loose on either side.'

One might doubt whether in this raucous orchestra the heavier German coastal guns could bring their fire to bear upon the raiders at this stage, yet Dieckmann says that they did – even his 6-inch howitzers away at Chémoulin Point. Certainly the four 75 mm guns at Le Pointean could bear at all stages and during that night this battery fired no fewer than thirteen hundred rounds. But on any count the odds were unequal. It was a battle in which the German guns, firing from fixed and protected positions, and from behind their own lights, fought against a quantity of heavy machine-guns, half a dozen 2- and 3-pounders and a solitary 12-pounder from exposed positions on moving platforms, firing into a blinding white glare.

Yet in spite of this inequality the British gunners quickly established a temporary superiority. Their only targets were the mere flashes of guns or the direct glare of searchlights, against both of which it is particularly difficult to lay or aim any weapon. Even by day, the most expert gunner would have been severely taxed to secure direct hits on the actual guns themselves from the water level. Yet, after a three or four minutes' duel of exceptional intensity, a definite slackening of the enemy's fire was forced at the most critical moment. Some guns ceased fire. Some search-lights went out. The Germans had been taken aback by the violence of our instant reply and although they recovered quickly, the relaxation came at a moment when time was the most precious of all elements. Not a single ship was mortally hit. Through the whirlpool of light and the coloured rain of shells and bullets the raiders went undeviatingly ahead, nearer and nearer to their objective, moving faster now, the seventeen ships preserving unbroken formation. It was indeed a gallant sight and one never to be forgotten by those who took part.

At this moment, almost in the mouth of the goal, the gunboat, still in the van and under considerable fire, but with Green still keeping a cool and cheerful check on navigation, came at last nearly abreast of the long clasping, outer arms of the South Entrance. The moment had nearly come for her to swing away to

The St Nazaire docks. For identification of main features, see Fig 1.

Vertical air view of the docks just before the raid.

Port side view of *Campbeltown* rammed on the caisson and sunk at the stern.

Sergeant T. F. Durrant, VC

Lieut-Comdr S. H. Beattie, VC

Lieut-Col A. C. Newman, VC

Comdr R. E. D. Ryder, VC

Able Seaman W. A. Savage, VC

Nine months after the raid. The Germans have dammed both ends of the
Normandie Dock, at the south end by dredging up a bank of sand and mud.
Stern half of *Campbeltown* lies near the centre.

starboard to make way for *Campbeltown*'s final dash. At that moment she came suddenly upon the enemy *Sperrbrecher* anchored in the river, previously obscured but now revealed by the lights of her own side. Her solid structure sprang out conspicuously very close to the starboard bow. She opened fire at once on the gunboat, but Able Seaman Savage, at the forward Vickers pom-pom, plastered her from end to end with such accuracy that she was at once temporarily silenced. Her dangerous 88 mm gun was put out of action and its ready-use ammunition set on fire. They passed so close to her that a man might almost have jumped on board.

Meanwhile, the main weight of the German fire was being directed at the *Campbeltown*, clearly the main agent of whatever mischief the British were up to. 'Her sides,' said Newman, looking back from the gunboat, 'seemed to be alive with bursting shells.' Beattie had begun to increase speed just before the action started, having discovered, as we have seen, the inflexibility of the ship below about sixteen knots. She must now, he knew, be able to answer the wheel instantaneously. With the flood tide to help him, he intended to hit the caisson at about twenty knots.

High on the open bridge, Beattie, Tibbits, Montgomery, now in his full equipment ready for landing, the Yeoman of Signals and other ratings had been clearly revealed in the cold light as soon as the Germans had illuminated the scene. They were, said Beattie, 'too jolly conspicuous'. He sent Tibbits down into the wheelhouse, immediately below the bridge, to take charge in case of trouble, and when the German fire began to get hot, and tracer-lit projectiles of all sorts were whistling about the bridge, he said:

'I think we'd all better go below; no point at all in getting killed.'

Accordingly they all slipped down to the wheelhouse, where they had protection against small-arms fire overhead and on all sides, except for an open horizontal strip about a foot wide, which allowed them to see perfectly well ahead and on either beam. Here, therefore, they stood, with Chief Petty Officer Wellstead, the coxswain, at the wheel, the two telegraph-men on either hand and the quartermaster to one side. Beattie was concentrating his mind on the changes in course which he would have to make at any minute and which he had already worked out in advance.

The moment that the full violence of the action broke loose *Campbeltown* began to take casualties. In the wheelhouse Wellstead was shot dead. The quartermaster jumped forward to take his place at the wheel but, almost immediately, he also fell. He attempted to continue steering while lying on the deck, but he collapsed. Montgomery, nearest at hand, stepped instinctively over his body and grasped the wheel, but to his relief he felt Tibbits, who had come forward from behind, put his hand on his arm and move him aside, saying in his quiet way:

'I'll take it, old boy.'

Beattie, unmoved, remained standing at the front of the wheel-house, intent upon his task, pitting his eyes against the glare. The noise and the light were merely a nuisance. Montgomery, now standing at the back of the wheelhouse, with a few small splinter wounds in the leg, saw his solid, black, bearded profile stencilled against the brilliant light and exclaimed inwardly: 'By God! the absolute Elizabethan!'

Ahead of them, the distance between them now shortening, Beattie was watching the gunboat firing vigorously to port with her little pom-pom. He was looking for the moment when she would sheer away to starboard for his final spurt. On either bow Boyd and Irwin were firing hard with their Hotchkiss guns. On his own decks Beattie could see the cooks and stewards serving the 12-pounders just ahead of him – 'and damned well, too'. Amid-ships and astern, high up on their stages, he could hear the shattering orchestra of his eight Oerlikons.

A continuous stream of projectiles of all sorts was now striking the *Campbeltown*, but so violent was the sound of our own weapons that the ring of bullets on her hull and the crack of small shells was scarcely noticed; but when larger shells shook her from stem to stern none could be unaware, and what every survivor was to remember for ever afterwards was the unchecked flow of the darts of red and green tracer flashing and hissing across her deck and the quadruple whistle of the Bofors shells. Bullets penetrated her engine- and boiler-rooms, ricochetting from surface to surface like hornets, and Locke, the Warrant Engineer, ordered hands to take cover between the main engines of the condensers, except for the throttle watchkeepers, Engine-Room Artificers Reay and Nelson, who stood unmoved at their valves throughout. High on the exposed bandstands two of the Oerlikons were knocked out and Sergeant Butler, lying behind the steel screens amidships, watched the ratings running up to replace their shipmates as they fell, 'admired their bravery and discipline and thought what fine fellows they were'.

Through this frightful racket the group in the wheelhouse remained tensed and alert. The bodies of the coxswain and quartermaster lay at their feet. Montgomery, as a mere spectator, kept out of the way at the back, watching and admiring the cool handling of the wheel by Tibbits, the steady and motionless telegraph hands and the icy detachment of Beattie. Beattie, his pupils mere pinpoints, peered out through the slit into the glare as the minutes went by. He quietly cursed the searchlights. 'Can't see a bloody thing,' he muttered to Tibbits. A moment later his vision was further obscured as the 12-pounder sustained a direct hit from a large shell, her own crew and those of Proctor's mortars spreadeagled in death or wounds.

As the smoke cleared away Beattie saw revealed before him two stone arms with a strip of sea between. This must be the lock gate at last. He was shaping direct for the gap and he held his course to ram. Just in time, he saw that it was not the lock, but the long curving arms of the South Entrance. He ordered sharply:

'Hard a-starboard!'

Tibbits acknowledged: 'Wheel's hard a-starboard, sir.'

'Steer 055 degrees.'

Scarcely had the destroyer swung to starboard than, by one of those tricks of fortune that so influence events, a German searchlight, swinging its beam, picked out for a fleeting moment the lighthouse at the tip of the Old Mole. This was the aiming point for which Beattie had been looking. From this point he had already worked out his course according to the distance he should find himself to be from the mole. As he came abreast of it, he judged himself to be about a cable-length away, and ordered:

'Port 25.'

'Twenty-five of port wheel on, sir.'

'Steer 345 degrees.'

Before Tibbits had time to set the ship on this course, however, Beattie made a correction. He must, he decided as he looked again on the port beam, be only about half a cable from the mole. He ordered quietly:

'Steer 350 degrees.'

Tibbits swung the ship back five degrees to starboard. Only seven hundred yards now.

'Stand by to ram.'

Ahead of him Beattie saw the gunboat sheer away to starboard. The moment had come.

Campbeltown was going fast now, making good twenty knots, her bow wave splaying wide. Every German gun that could bear was now converged upon her; not now those lower down the river but those at point-blank range in the dockyard area itself – from the Old Mole, from either side of the Normandie Dock, from the top of the submarine pens, from the roofs of buildings – and from the east bank of the river. Repeatedly hit, she was now suffering very heavy casualties, among her sailors and soldiers alike, her decks spattered with fallen bodies. To Copland it seemed as though they were the converging point of one of those fountains in which illuminated jets pour continuously upon the centre; how anyone in those fiery minutes was left alive was always to pass his understanding. But miraculously *Campbeltown* escaped damage to any vital part as she raced forward. The gunboat and the motor launches of Boyd and Irwin were backing her up gallantly at close quarters. Boyd's gunner, Able Seaman MacIver, observed a Bofor immediately to starboard of the caisson dangerously engaging the destroyer. With a steady hand, he caught it in the sights of his Hotchkiss and silenced it with a direct hit.

Not till he was within two hundred yards did Beattie see the great steel gate of the lock, discernible as an indistinct black line beyond the 'spill' of the searchlights, dead ahead. At the last moment an incendiary bomb, of the nature of thermite, projected by no known agency, but conceivably dropped from one of our own aircraft, landed on the fo'c'sle and burst into flames. *Campbeltown* held steadily on her course. In the wheelhouse there was complete silence. Beattie and Montgomery propped themselves against the front of the wheelhouse, ready for the shock of impact. Throughout the ship every man braced himself; in the wardroom Brett's and Purdon's parties sat down on the deck and an unexploded shell, its red tracer burning in the base, shot through above their heads. Denser and denser grew the black line ahead. A momentary check told them that they had ripped through the anti-torpedo net. All hands could feel the wire dragging along the ship's bottom. The caisson was scarcely fifty yards away and only now could Beattie clearly see it. With extraordinary presence of mind, in order to hit the caisson in the centre and in order to swing the ship's stern to starboard, so that the Old Entrance should not be blocked, he crisply ordered at this last moment:

'Port 20!'

Instantly Tibbits obeyed and at 1.34, with all her Oerlikons blazing at the enemy guns only a few yards away, with her fo'c'sle in flames, she crashed into the caisson.

She struck with such accuracy and force that her bows, up to the level of the caisson, crumpled back for a distance of thirty-six feet, leaving her fo'c'sle deck, which was higher than the caisson, actually projecting a foot beyond the inner face.

Beattie turned to Montgomery with a smile, and said: 'Well, there we are.'

Looking at his watch, he added:

'Four minutes late.'

15. THE DOCK BUSTERS

Beattie's achievement, executed with such cool precision, marks with clear and resonant emphasis the attainment of the chief purpose of the expedition. Act One is run down with a curtain of fire. There now began a medley of events difficult to describe in ordered sequence. The battle spread like a flame, too like a flame, to the whole scene by land and water. The motor launches, coming up astern of *Campbeltown*, pressed towards their designated landing places in the great whirlpool of light with the greatest daring, adding to the lurid scene the glow of their own conflagrations and the smoke and stench of burning petrol as one by one half their number burst into flames or blew up. Events crowd upon each other as the battle splintered into innumerable little actions, each a vivid narrative in itself and more than one a minor epic. From the moment of committal command and control of the action was lost, partly through the very nature of the operation and partly through the failure of the gunboat's wireless, so that each boat and each group of soldiers pursued, or attempted to pursue, its predetermined part alone.

We shall follow with astonishment, and often with some anguish, the impressive exploits and the gallant defeats of all these small bands one by one, in such order as will allow the spectator to appraise this episodic battle as a whole, but must bear in mind always the general background of the scene and the place in the main design of all the achievements and failures of these brave young men. Not all fearless, not all undismayed, yet overcoming all. Each act falls into place in the composition; telling sometimes of tactical success, but always of the greater triumph of a high and selfless spirit that was not intimidated by the trial of death by flames, or terrible wounds or hopes forlorn or sufferings after capture. Newman laughing aloud when all seemed lost, Burtenshaw singing as he died, Hewett seeing God beside him, Copland serenely organizing order out of confusion, Lovegrove carrying his wounded officer from the flames, the perforated body of Durrant answering the call to surrender with one last defiant burst – these and many other heroic and knightly activities we shall see; others lie still hidden behind the veiled countenance of men who prefer to remain silent or died with those who performed them.

This spectacle of splendid episodes begins to burst upon us the moment that *Campbeltown* crashes into the caisson. At that moment we may imagine Curtis's gunboat and the motor launches of Boyd and Irwin standing off to support her and the two columns of troop-carrying craft coming up close astern, with Platt leading the port column and Stephens the starboard. These beheld the bows of the destroyer erupting in flying timbers, smoke and flames. They saw also the commandos leap to their feet on deck and, under a covering fire gallantly sustained from the destroyer's Oerlikons overhead, begin to move forward to disembark for their tasks. The din was tumultuous as the guns of both sides began to concentrate their fire on this small area.

Campbeltown herself began to prepare for her last moments. Beattie, excited enough beneath his icy exterior, forgot to give the order to ring off the engines, and for a few minutes there was a little confusion in the engine- and boiler-rooms, accentuated by the darkness which now enveloped the whole ship below deck. The engines might have been required to hold the ship on the caisson, but Chief Engine-Room Artificer Howard went up on deck, found Gough in the storm of fire that crackled and flashed up there and got sanction to shut off steam. The ship was still being repeatedly hit and down below, where the engine-room staff were bearing themselves with exemplary courage, shells and explosive bullets were still penetrating. Stoker Petty Officer Pyke was going about quietly, maintaining machinery by torchlight, an inspiration to junior hands. Engine-Room Artificer Nelson was killed while evacuating hands from the forward boiler-room.

The first, the most imperative duty, however, was to disembark the commandos as rapidly as possible. Not till this had been done did Beattie give the order to abandon ship. Winthorpe's medical party, their hands more than full to the last minute, were routed out. Howard and Engine-Room Artificer Reay proceeded to scuttle ship by torchlight, opening the valves that would let in the sea and removing the condenser doors. To make assurance doubly sure, scuttling charges were fired under the direction of Hargreaves, the Torpedo Gunner. Finally Beattie and Gough then went round the ship to make sure that no one was left behind. Then they themselves went on to the upper deck while the ship, held fast by the bows on the caisson, was beginning to settle at the stern. About half the ship's company, according to plan, made their way forward to the fo'c'sle, which they found enveloped in the acrid smoke that was pouring from the hole made by the mysterious incendiary. Led by Howard, they scrambled down the scaling ladders left by the commandos, and, suffering sharp casualties from the heavy machine-gun fire that was riddling the quayside, made their way to Curtis's gunboat in the Old Entrance.

The remainder, numbering about thirty and including Beattie himself, went aft. By this time the gallant Rodier, commanding ML 6, had with great coolness successfully landed Troop Sergeant-Major Haines and his party in the Old Entrance. On being hailed as he came out by Beattie, who was concerned at the difficulty of getting his wounded away safely, Rodier came alongside on the port quarter and took off Beattie's party.

Full of wounds, silent, empty and deserted by all except her faithful dead, *Campbeltown* lay patiently on her altar, waiting for the determined hour of sacrifice.

*

Meanwhile, her commandos had been taking sharp casualties before ever they landed. On the exposed fo'c'sle Proctor had been badly wounded when the 12-pounder was knocked out and lay with his leg shattered and his kilt smouldering. Amidships, where lay the assault parties and some of the demolition teams, Chant, Etches, Sergeants Chamberlain, Jones, Davies, Corporals Johnson, Donaldson, O'Donnell and several more had been hit just before ramming.

The ship was a cauldron into which light and fire were being poured from all directions as though from hoses. To starboard the

German guns were shooting from a few yards' range. The whole gun areas of Mecke's 703 and 809 Battalions were alight with illuminated jets of crackling venom, streaming through the white searchlights' staring beams. The fo'c'sle was smothered in smoke from the incendiary which had burnt a large hole in the deck, penetrated the Chief Petty Officers' mess and was threatening the great three-ton explosive charge immediately below, until a gallant damage-control party of Leading Stoker Baxter and Stokers Steven and Newbold arrested the danger.

Through this pall of smoke, confusing the searchlight glare, Gough, Tibbits and Copland at once hurried forward to direct the landings from the bows. Having seen that the way was clear to land on the caisson, the naval party began to fix iron-runged ladders over the side. Copland, as cool and self-contained as upon an exercise, then ran back amidships, through the narrow gangways and into the welldeck, to call forward the assault parties. His path was choked with wounded sailors and unceremoniously he thrust them aside. Very coolly, he ordered: 'Roderick off, Roy off.' They went forward through the smoke and the coloured darts, 'with the awe-inspiring drumming of our own Oerlikons firing overhead', narrowly escaping falling into the gaping hole in the deck, from which clouds of smoke continued to pour. As they came forward, they carried up their own bamboo ladders to supplement the ship's ladders, but several of them were smashed, either through enemy fire or by the heavy weights imposed on them. Roderick, adjured by Newman to be off 'like lightning' to attack a gun position only a few yards away, was quickly over the side to starboard. Almost simultaneously, Roy's Scots were off on the port side, he and Tibbits cursing each other freely when the steel ladder jammed. Down they all went, carrying or supporting their wounded, collected themselves, then moved off at the double against the targets that they had been dreaming of for so long.

Very calm and unconcerned, though his slung rifle was shattered to pieces on his shoulder, Copland took post on the swirling fo'c'sle, ordering off each of the parties in turn, with a word of encouragement for each, greeting many of them by name, and adding: 'Just think of this as only another exercise.' He might well, said John Roderick, 'have been seeing us off on the local bus for all the concern that he was showing.' When all were off he went in search of Beattie to report all troops disembarked. He found the bridge 'a mass of twisted wreckage' and Beattie not there. He went about the ship, calling him by name. Not finding him, he searched the ship for wounded and got them over the side with Howard's party, to make their way to the gunboat. He put a tourniquet on Proctor's nearly severed leg and, finding it impossible to carry him down the damaged ladders, threw him over the side on to the caisson.

Then, accompanied by Corporal Cheetham, Lance-Corporal Fyfe (his wireless operator) and Private Hannon, he climbed down himself and made his way into what had by now become a devil's shooting gallery.

First Ashore

From this moment we must imagine the seven parties of the commandos, steel-helmeted, with whitened webbing, scattering to their several targets, moving at the double under heavy weights of arms or explosives in the stark dockyard scene, past tall cranes, buildings, railway trucks and piles of timber, now brilliantly illuminated by the searchlights, now in a moonlike gloom, sometimes unopposed, sometimes having to fight bitterly for their objectives. Everywhere the crackle of machine-guns, the fiercer bursts of Oerlikons and the occasional crashes of high explosive poured out their mischief, accompanied very soon by the roar of the commandos' explosions and lit anew and with different tone by the orange flames of their successive destructions. In the midst we see the handfuls of the commandos, swift and soft-footed shadows, moving to their stations – Roderick scattering his enemies right and left, Roy holding his bridge, the teams of destroyers fixing their charges with swift and cool precision. Those things that impress themselves upon us are not merely their courage, which we take for granted, but their speed, their cool and steadfast balance, their indifference to wounds, their resourcefulness and, perhaps above all, their ability to achieve what they did with such absurdly small numbers.

First we shall see the dashing little party that had to be off to starboard 'like lightning'.

John Roderick was a strapping young Welshman of twenty-three, born at Neath, trained as a bank clerk and commissioned into Newman's regiment, the Essex. He looked and was a fine rugger player. At his side was young John Stutchbury, Gordon Highlanders, one of the babies of 2 Commando, senior in years only to Tiger Watson. Twelve NCOs and men made up their little assault force of Group 3c, whose tasks were to destroy the group of light guns immediately to the south-east of the caisson, of which, as German maps now show, there were four, to establish a defensive position against counterattack, and to make an attempt to fire the underground oil fuel tanks.

Roderick's party was quickly away, clambering over the fallen bodies and leaving Corporal Donaldson, the soft-spoken Scotsman with a slow, charming smile, mortally wounded on the deck. Impeded by the broken ladders, several swarmed down to the caisson by rope, Corporals Woodiwiss and Finch, Tommy-gunners, being the first of all the force to set foot on French soil, while the weapons of their comrades, to cover them, opened fire against the bursts from the enemy positions to their right.

Clearly visible in the artificial light not many yards away there stood their first objective – a light gun in a sandbagged pit. Roderick and his men went straight at it, throwing hand-grenades and then rushing in with Tommy-guns and Brens blazing. A German grenade was kicked back by Woodiwiss to burst among the enemy, and it was Woodiwiss who clapped the sausage charge on the guns to sever the barrel. All six Germans of the detachment were left for dead.*

From this first, flashing success Roderick's men swept on to the next objective, which was a 37 mm gun mounted on top of a formidable concrete bunker. This was position M 70. As the only approach up to the gun platform was by a single stairway, they were unable to assault it, but they silenced the gun with grenades skilfully thrown, killed the gun captain as he tried to come downstairs and, entering the bunker, killed three Luftwaffe men who had come to collect ammunition.

---

* In fact, three were killed, two wounded and one shammed death.

On again went the little band to the third gun (M 10). This was a Bofors gun and they found it silent, for it was the gun that had been knocked out by Able Seaman MacIver, but Roderick's men, entering the bunker, destroyed the crew. Many Nissen-type huts were here and into these they hurled grenades.

There remained yet a fourth gun (No 67), with a searchlight beyond and here the historian finds some difficulty, for while the Germans admit officially that this gun and searchlight were destroyed, 'by parties landed by raft from the motor launches', no definite claim is made by Newman's men. Roderick's party moving by small squads and giving covering fire to each other, was now extended and it is far more credible that it was one of these squads that accounted for the last targets. Whatever the truth, the simple fact remains that four guns and a searchlight were destroyed or silenced and a number of Germans exceeding Roderick's in strength were killed within a space of about twenty minutes.

By now Stutchbury, Sergeant Davies, Corporal Howarth and Lance-Corporal Simpson had been wounded and the effective strength of the party reduced to ten or fewer. Yet the oil tanks were reached and incendiaries were thrown down their ventilators, though without effect.

By now the Germans had begun to collect themselves. The troops of 4 Works Company, whose headquarters was quite close, had almost certainly come into action. Beyond the gloom Roderick found resistance stiffening and it was only by great determination that his tiny band held on so long to fulfil their purpose of perimeter protection. Some time a little after 2.30 a.m. the appointed lookout reported having seen the green rain rocket which was the withdrawal signal from Newman's headquarters ashore. He was mistaken, for the mass of coloured tracer in the rear confused him, but it was at about the expected time and, as events were to prove, it was apt to the occasion. Roderick gave the order to withdraw.

The little band began to move back, one party extricating itself at a time under covering fire from the remainder. Their way back lay across the caisson, but, since *Campbeltown*'s bows projected right across it, they had to clamber up once again on to the destroyer's fo'c'sle and down the other side. Roderick, last or nearly last, as he stepped again on that deck which he had left about an hour before, was aware of a strange sensation. The whole ship, littered with débris, her sides and works pitted and torn, smoke still issuing from the hole made by the incendiary, was enveloped in 'an uncanny silence'. Not a sign of life was to be seen or heard; signs only of death. In the midst of the hurly-burly shattering the night air on all sides, *Campbeltown* was as quiet as the grave. The deserted ship was preparing herself for her last moments as down below the acid was slowly eating its way through the copper wire.

Passing on and crossing the fireswept dockyard, Roderick was bowled over like a rabbit with a bullet in the thigh.

Roy's Bridge

No less swift and successful was the performance of Roy's kilted team, detailed to the assault tasks on the western side of the dock. Disembarking on the port side of the destroyer's fo'c'sle, and assisting between them Sergeant Jones, who had been wounded on board, they made off swiftly by the way they had learnt so well from the model, silent in their rubber boots and carrying bamboo scaling-ladders with them. Proctor having been so severely wounded, The Laird was now the only officer. They had not far to go for their first task, which was to silence the gun positions (64 and 65) on the roof of the big pumping station.

Before he could make his attack Roy saw the German teams in full flight across the shadowed dockyard, having escaped by an outside staircase. He called upon Sergeant Challington with his Tommy-gun, but the gun jammed after a few rounds. Roy then lobbed two grenades on to the roof, and, following up quickly with Randall, found the guns deserted and he blew them without difficulty.

The Laird then turned and led off his assault party at the double to Bridge G over the Old Entrance, where he was to hold a vital bridgehead, through which the demolition teams, on completion of their tasks, would have to withdraw towards the designated re-embarkation area at the Old Mole. He reached the bridge safely, finding no Germans there. His little party took post and waited in the ghostly white light, all eyes and ears – a little band of thirteen men islanded in the heart of enemy territory.

To this position, extremely exposed and with only the flimsiest cover, they hung on with great determination for a period that must have been nearly an hour and a half, suffering casualties to half their number from a galling fire that was soon directed on to them from the unreachable guns on elevated positions on the far side of the Submarine Basin, particularly the two quadruple Oerlikons, and from the ships in the Submarine Basin. The whole of the German naval forces and establishments ashore were now dashing from their shelters and running to emergency action stations as the 'Enemy Landing Alert' was circulated. Of these, the most troublesome were to be the five ships of the 16th Minesweeper Flotilla, and the four small harbour defence ships, one of which scuttled herself to avoid capture. Further off the *Stosstruppen* of Mecke's brigade were already on their way to the scene.

Of all this, save for its results, Roy at Bridge G was unaware as he held on to his position and waited for the parties to eastward to come through. Sergeant Jones, Gunner Milne and Private McCormack had already been hit and now, throughout the long stand, Sergeant Challington, Lance-Corporal Sumner and Private Ashcroft were wounded also and Private Gwynn killed in circumstances to be painfully told before long.

Forty Feet Down

Thus the two little assault parties carried out their allotted tasks with a dash and precision of the highest order. The demolition teams for whom they were designed to provide cover were hard on their heels, waiting for no man and carrying out an even more impressive mission with astonishing exactitude and daring. Let us remind ourselves what were the targets they had been ordered to destroy.

These numbered five. At the southern end of the dry-dock area was a group of three tasks entrusted to teams under officers of 5 Commando. Stuart Chant had the formidable task of destroying the big pump house; Christopher Smalley of the rolling gait and walrus moustache was to go for the winding-house where was situated the machinery for moving the big southern caisson in and out of position; Robert Burtenshaw, the tall, gangling, monocled jester, was to destroy the caisson itself with magnetic 'wreaths' and 18-lb charges if *Campbeltown* should fail to ram satisfactorily. The protection party for all these teams was provided by Hopwood, of the Essex Regiment, spectacled, heavily moustached, powerful and, in the words of Donald Roy, 'as staunch a friend as any man could wish to have in action or out of it'.

At the northern end of the big dock Etches, the young Regular officer of 3 Commando, having with him two Royal Ulster Riflemen from 12 Commando, Gerard Brett and young Corran Purdon, was charged with destroying the caisson at the end, and the winding-hut associated with it. For these demolition teams, who were to have a pretty stiff time, the protection was provided by the hefty 'Bung' Denison, of Roderick's Troop. All these five demolition tasks in the dry-dock area were under the control of Pritchard's friend, Bob Montgomery, and as an aide he had with him the stout-hearted Rhodesian, Sergeant Jameson, of 9 Commando.

*

Stuart Chant, leader of the little team ordained for the destruction of the pump house, was a young Gordon Highlander on the London Stock Exchange. Dark, good-looking and with a lively disposition, he was a rugby footballer of class and a young man of energy and drive. His team consisted of four quite outstanding sergeants, not of his own Commando, but of No 1. Sergeant A. H. Dockerill, Royal Artillery, was a plumber from Ely and a former choirboy of Ely Cathedral; we shall, indeed, hear him singing as he went about his work. His three comrades were all Norfolk men. Sergeant R. H. Butler, dark-haired and well set-up, was a village baker, whose pursuits of yachting on the Broads and swimming were apt to a commando life. Sergeants A. W. King and W. Chamberlain were two strapping fellows, as stout of heart as they were of frame.

During *Campbeltown*'s approach Chant's party were lying

behind their steel screens, face up and feet forward against the shock of impact. A moment before the destroyer rammed, a small shell burst beside Chant and Chamberlain, wounding them both. A sticky feeling running down his leg told Chant that he had been hit in the knee; splinters wounded his arm and fingers also. The bittersweet fumes of high explosive blew over him. He lay momentarily dazed, but an inner compulsion told him to rise and slip into his rucksack with its load of explosives. Three of the sergeants rose with him, but Chamberlain said: 'Very sorry, sir, but I can't move.'

Between them, however, they lifted up his thirteen stone and half carried him as they moved forward to disembark, together with Smalley's and Hopwood's teams. On the fo'c'sle Chant fell painfully into the smoking hole, as many others did, but was caught and held up by his rucksack and moved on, saying a word as he passed the blanched Proctor. Then, heavily laden with their explosives, sledge hammers, axes and incendiaries, they scrambled, slid or fell down the scaling ladders on the port side. Somehow Chamberlain was got down and the team made for the pump house by the route printed on their minds through a scene vividly lit, but chequered by the dense angular shadows of the buildings, swaying from time to time as the searchlights swung their beams.

Chant was limping but could move fairly freely. They were right on Roy's heels, seeing the kilts flying just ahead. Without waiting for him to attack the German gunners on the roof of the pump house, they went straight for the entrance, but met an unexpected obstacle when they found it barred by a heavy steel door. Chant was momentarily at a loss, but at that moment Montgomery appeared and from the spare explosives that he carried he took out a small magnetic charge, clamped it on the door and stood back. Chant made to light the short length of safety fuse, but found it difficult to strike the fusee with his bleeding fingers. He was disconcerted to find his hands trembling and he said to Montgomery: 'Bob, for God's sake help me light this bloody thing; the chaps will think I'm scared.'

With a laugh, Montgomery complied, the door was blown in and Chant and his sergeants then entered the pump house.

The very difficult task that Chant's team now had to perform they had rehearsed over and over again, including provision for casualties. The task required two demolitions – the first, that of the great impeller pumps forty feet below ground, and the second, the electrical gear on the ground floor where they now stood, particularly the electric motors that drove the impeller pumps below, and the transformers. They flashed their torches around and, with the help of the glow coming in from the searchlights and the fires outside, they noted that everything was exactly as they had seen it in the King George V Dock at Southampton – the straight line of the motors, the transformers, the switch gear, the indicators, all laid out in orderly precision.

Chamberlain was by now weak and moving slowly. Chant was reluctant to take so heavy a man down the steep, zigzag staircase that led to the pumping chamber far below, but to ease the sergeant's chagrin, he said:

'Stay up here and do guard for us. Don't let anyone in.'

The big sergeant lay down at the top of the stairs and Chant, with the other three sergeants, started on the long descent below ground, Butler and Dockerill helping him down, with King following, and carrying between them Chamberlain's 60 lb of explosive besides their own.

Utter darkness lay beneath them, a darkness that the torches at their belts penetrated only as a cold, unfocused beam. Below ground level a cold dampness at once struck their faces. Their blindfolded exercises at Southampton came back vividly to them as they counted the steps, but these were not quite the same. The impulse to make haste was upon them, held in check by the risk of losing balance and by thought of the results of taking a false step or of straying off the stairs on to the galleries that ran round the walls of the pit. Chant, limping down by jerks, fought the threat of giddiness.

At the foot of the long stairs, in the pumping chamber at last, their torches showed them that the impeller pumps were exactly as they knew they would be – four main pumps of the turbine impeller type and two subsidiary drainage pumps. They looked rather like giant lifebelts, or huge inverted mushrooms. Inside these big steel ring castings were the fast-revolving vanes which impelled the water in or out of the dock. Standing up in the middle of each ring was the long, shining, steel shaft connecting

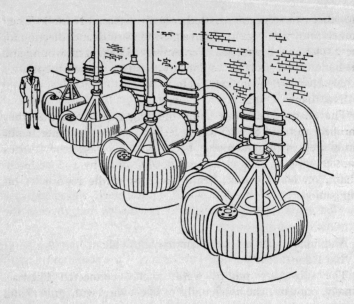

Fig 14. The four main pumps in the pumping chambers forty feet below ground. The figure of the man is included to indicate size. (By courtesy of Lt.-Col. Chant)

with the motor that drove it far above at ground level. Under the drill so often practised, each of the four sergeants was to blow up one of the main pumps and Chant himself the two subsidiaries, but Chant now took over Chamberlain's target, leaving the subsidiary pumps to be attacked collectively.

Not much need for torches now. They knew every step and every movement by heart. They wriggled out of their harnesses, laying them on the concrete floor, and took out the specially prepared plastic charges in their mackintosh covers. These, reaching up and over the big circular tubes, they slapped and moulded firmly on to the casting joints of the impeller pumps, which they knew from the Southampton dock engineers could not be replaced in less than a year. Disturbed by two deep muffled thuds overhead which shook them deep below, they were told by Chamberlain far above that it was 'only Captain Donald blowing up the guns'. They worked quickly and confidently. Dockerill was quietly singing 'Blue Birds Over the White Cliffs of Dover' and the other two sergeants chatted casually in broad Norfolk. Their homely, easy voices gave Chant a glow of warmth and affection for these staunch companions, overcoming the pain of his wound and the handicap of his lacerated fingers. He heard one of them say:

'Nearly finished, sir; can I help you?'

'No, thanks, I'm all right.'

The charges laid, out came the ring main. Together they unrolled and laid it out, hands feeling forward to other hands dimly seen in the chequered light. Out next came the cordtex leads to connect each charge to the ring main by a clove hitch. Chant, on No 3 pump, heard successively the reports of his companions:

'No 2 done, sir.'

'No 4 done, sir.'

And finally, with a note of triumphant finality:

'No 1 done, SIR!'

The subsidiary pumps were quickly connected likewise. Finally, out came the two lengths of safety wire, with igniters and detonators already connected, to be crimped on to the ring main.

A hundred and fifty pounds of high explosive was now ready to be detonated at the touch of the duplicated percussion igniters. Three feet of safety fuse gave a delay of ninety seconds, which would give a fit man ample time to run up the stairs and out of the building. It was Chant's duty to fire the charges himself, sending his sergeants up first and being himself last man out. But he was wondering how on earth he was going to get up those forty feet of steep stairs. His knee was now slowing down all his movements. He therefore decided to keep Dockerill with him, sending King and Butler upstairs with instructions to remove Chamberlain to safety and to shout down when the way was clear.

He took one of the igniters and gave the other to Dockerill. Two long minutes passed in the underground darkness. Dockerill continued humming his song. No other sounds were audible and the battle above seemed far away. At last came the expected shout from above and Chant, by pre-arrangement, gave a simple 'one-two-three' to Dockerill. Simultaneously they pulled their igniter pins and the slow fuse began to burn along its three feet passage to the detonator and the cordtex. Subaltern and sergeant turned

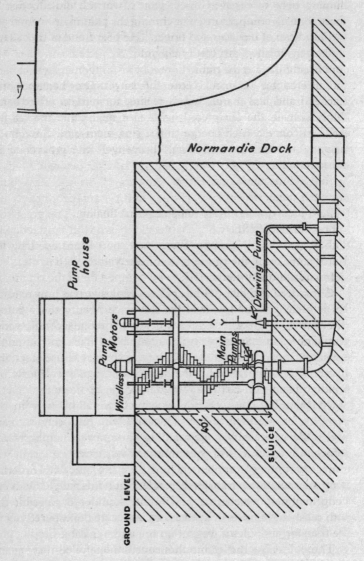

Fig 15. Sectional view of underground pumping system. (By courtesy of Lt.-Col. Chant)

and made for the stairs. With Dockerill leading and Chant clinging tight to his arm, they went up in the dark as fast as possible, Chant hopping two or three steps at a time.

They arrived out into the bright light and the din and Chant ordered his team to take cover behind the concrete anti-blast wall opposite the door of the pump house, but Montgomery was at hand and ordered them at once to cover farther off. They had no sooner reached it than the charges went up, bursting in the confined space below with great violence – 'a great roar of sound that cracked our eardrums', as recorded by Copland, who was passing through not far away – shaking the ground and throwing down a great concrete block upon the very spot where they had lain just before. Clouds of débris billowed out and bright showers of broken glass burst outwards from the windows, glinting in the searchlight beams and falling to the ground in metallic tintinnabulation. The great roar impressed itself on the whole battlefield, heard with satisfaction by both Ryder and Newman, now ashore, and heard even by the motor launches in the agony of their river battle.

It was not quite two o'clock.

Christopher Smalley, fresh at the nearby winding-house, came up at a rolling trot to make his report to Montgomery before withdrawing to his last rendezvous. They exchanged quick con-gratulations and Stuart Chant led his team back to the pump house. They had now to go in again to destroy the motors and electrical gear on the ground floor. Quickly in, they found the building filled with clouds of smoke and dust, the concrete floor caved in, two of the electric motors fallen through it to the pumping chamber far below and the other two lying at crazy angles. It was obvious to them all that the place had already been sufficiently wrecked and that another destructive explosion was unnecessary. Chant contented himself, therefore, with ordering King to smash the transformer pipes and the gauges with his sledgehammer, which that big, broad-shouldered sergeant did with relish and impressive precision, and as the oil poured out of the transformer pipes it was set on fire with tar babies.

Thus, leaving the pump house completely destroyed and burning fiercely, Chant and his sergeants, having accomplished one of the most brilliant and impressive achievements of the raid, set out to withdraw according to plan, supporting between them their wounded companion.

When all was done, Montgomery, having observed a large shed at the side of the pump house, opened the door and threw in an incendiary. There shot up, in the words of Copland, 'a colossal burst of continuous yellow fire', adding yet another to the series of fires that were now raging in the white beams of the searchlights.

Meanwhile Christopher Smalley and his small demolition team had had equal success in their attack upon the southern winding-house close by. Smalley, of the Manchester Regiment, was one of the most distinctive characters among the Charioteers. Somewhat aloof, he was squarely built, had good looks and a ruddy complexion went with his heavy moustache. Like Newman, he habitually adorned his countenance with a pipe. His little team consisted of Sergeant Bright, the miner, Corporal Howard, Bombardier W. Johnson and Corporal E. Johnson.

His was the nearest of the objectives to *Campbeltown*. Within the building he saw the two big wheels by which the caisson was moved and the motors that drove them. On these motors and on the spokes of the wheels he placed his charges, connected all up with cordtex, and, having had permission from Montgomery, pulled his igniters. There was no result. He reported to Montgomery and fresh igniters and safety fuse were fitted. These fired successfully and the whole building and all its machinery went up with a shattering concussion, the bricks and débris showering down upon the motor craft now in the Old Entrance and narrowly missing Ryder as he stood by the caisson watching *Campbeltown* sink.

Leaving it in ruins and blazing fiercely, Smalley went quickly to report to Montgomery, as we have seen, saying to him: 'Bob, I have finished and I'm going to withdraw now.' Returning to his team, he saw at that moment Burt's motor launch in the Old Entrance, disembarking his troops, and he decided to take this opportunity of effecting his withdrawal, instead of going to the Old Mole. He and his team ran to the quayside and embarked, but the boat was heavily engaged by the minesweepers and harbour defence boats in the Submarine Basin. The forward Oerlikon was jammed and Smalley took charge of it in an attempt to free it, but was almost immediately shot dead.

The Gate Crashers

These two teams had been fortunate to meet no enemy resistance and to suffer no casualties while at their work. A different experience awaited those who, with equal dash and spirit, went out to attack the targets at the northern end of the dry dock – the far caisson and its winding-house.

Casualties had begun on board the *Campbeltown*. Etches himself, in control of both attacks, was hit four times, including wounds in both legs, and able to walk only very painfully; he could take no effective part and on Montgomery's orders he withdrew direct to Roy's bridgehead, crawling most of the way on hands and knees. On the other hand, Beattie having laid *Campbeltown* astride the caisson with such skill, there was no need for Burtenshaw's team to attack it and Montgomery accordingly sent them to reinforce Gerard Brett.

Corran Purdon, charged with destroying the winding-house, was another of the 'babes' of the raid. Aged twenty and an Ulsterman, he was the son of Major-General Brooke Purdon, the doctor general. Lightly built, very fair and very good-looking, he had been in the last prewar batch of gentleman cadets at Sandhurst. With others of 'Peachey' Harrison's 12 Commando, he had already taken part in the Lofoten raid.

With young Purdon were four remarkable corporals, also of 12 Commando – Corporal 'Johnny' Johnson, Gordon Highlanders, a tough, sandy-haired, humorous Aberdonian, who was badly wounded in the *Campbeltown* but with extraordinary courage and fortitude carried through his tasks; Corporal Ronald Chung, Royal Engineers, the staunch and redoubtable half Chinese; Corporal Bob Hoyle, Lancashire Fusiliers, a cheerful and good-humoured North Countryman; and Corporal 'Cab' Galloway, a happy and utterly reliable soldier from the South.

To Corran Purdon, Gerard Brett stood in the position of an elder brother. Lean, spectacled, studious, quiet-spoken, having something of the air of a kindly don, the archaeologist came from Cirencester, had taken part in Byzantine excavations and was an assistant curator at the Victoria and Albert Museum in London. Everyone was fond of him.

Brett's team, as might be expected from 12 Commando, had a strong Irish flavour, provided by Sergeant Stewart Deery, the sandy-haired Royal Inniskilling Fusilier and the senior NCO; Corporal Ferguson, Lance-Corporal Lemon, North Irish Horse; and Corporal Joe Molloy, a grand Southern Irishman. Of the others, we have already briefly met Corporal 'Jones the Post', Corporal Wright, the sapper diarist, and Corporal 'Jumbo' Reeves, the humorous ex-RAF pilot. The gallant team was completed by Corporal Chetwynd, Sherwood Foresters, and little Corporal Blount, South Wales Borderers. With only three exceptions, all were to be killed or wounded.

To this band was now added Robert Burtenshaw's team from 5 Commando. His senior NCO, briefly noted already, was Sergeant F. A. Carr, the Regular sapper, an erect and stalwart six feet, dark haired, strong jawed, quietly formidable, a model of devotion and integrity. With him were Sergeants Ide, McKerr and Fergusson, Lance-Corporal Stokes and Private Edwards.

Having got up from their sitting position on the deck of the wardroom, and Galloway having disembarrassed himself of the bookcase that had fallen on top of him when the destroyer rammed, Brett's and Purdon's teams, followed by Burtenshaw's, hitched themselves into their rucksacks, came up into the fury on deck and moved up on to the fo'c'sle. Coming to the smoke-shrouded hole on deck, Corporal Hoyle fell in. His trousers were ripped and burnt off before he was pulled out and he went through all the rest of the action in his shirt-tails, his legs painfully burnt. Passing John Proctor, who waved cheerfully to them, they found Tibbits in the bows, deriding the bullets and standing erect to hold a ladder ready for them.

Behind them came Robert Burtenshaw, the gay and valiant giant, an example of airy unconcern to all who saw him. He was still wearing Beattie's cap, his monocle was in his eye and he was swinging a walking stick. He was passing jestful remarks and humming quietly. With the heavy rucksack on his back, one would have thought that he was off on a walking tour.

Thus on into the seething bows. Their tiny protection squad, under command of the massive Bung Denison, was from the start seriously depleted, for Corporal O'Donnell and Private Mattison had both been seriously wounded in the legs on board ship. Thus Denison led on with only two companions. Behind him the three teams of destroyers scrambled down the shaky ladders, gathered themselves, vowed that they were going to break their own record, swung at a trot around Smalley's winding-house and past Chant's target, their heavy loads jolting on their backs, and so up the west side of the dock – a run of fully five hundred yards. In the dry dock itself, on their right, two large tankers under repair were clearly to be seen.

Not very far beyond the pump house small-arms fire was opened from the roof of a building on the protection squad as it led the way, but Denison and Private Elliott silenced it at once with a grenade and a syringeing from the Tommy-gun. About a hundred yards farther on, from a trench behind a crane that reared its neck high into the moonlight radiance, on the dock side, a sharper fire was opened, wounding Elliott in the leg. Denison ran to the crane, to use it as cover, and, in textbook fashion, shot up the trench by Tommy-gun while his two companions attacked with grenades, executing the little manoeuvre so effectively that when they rushed the trench, they found it full of dead. Denison then doubled forward to his allotted place beyond the caisson, his tiny squad taking up positions to protect as best they could the demolition teams from interference across Bridge M, and the wounded O'Donnell and Mattison gallantly limping up to play their parts.

Behind Denison the demolition teams were thudding up soft-footed. Purdon and his four corporals made for their winding-house on the left. Finding the entrance barred by a heavy metal door Purdon tried unsuccessfully to shoot out the lock, but the broad-shouldered Chung smashed it open with a sledgehammer and they burst in. In no time at all they laid their charges on the spokes of the big driving wheels and on the motors, just as Smalley was doing to the south of them, Johnson, in great pain, fulfilling with fortitude his full part in the team drill. Sledgehammers and insulated axes smashed up the electrical gear. When all was con-nected to the ring main, safety fuse and igniters attached, they withdrew outside, waiting for Brett and Burtenshaw to blow their caisson first. Purdon sent Chung over to report to Brett that he was ready, but the corporal found the caisson under a storm of bullets that rang murderously upon the steel deck, and returned himself wounded.

For the two teams on the caisson were now carrying out one of the most hazardous of all the tasks in the dockyard area, under a violent fire which attacked them simultaneously from several directions, but through which they pressed their purpose with the utmost determination and dash. In the dimly lit and swiftly moving scene it is difficult after the years to perceive the precise details with undeniable certainty, and to make out the identity of each shadowy figure, but the main facts stand out with an eloquence that is clear enough.

As Brett's team, with Burtenshaw's just behind, ran up to the caisson, Brett himself was dropped, hit in both legs and in the right arm. He was carried to the shelter of a wall, whence he helped to direct the operation as best he could from a sitting position. His team swarmed quickly over the caisson and at the eastern end Corporals Wright and Reeves killed with their pistols two Germans who suddenly appeared. When Burtenshaw arrived very soon afterwards he saw Sergeant Deery struggling to open the hatch, or trapdoor, in the middle of the caisson deck. He took charge of both teams and, still in his naval cap, derided the enemy fire with his casual and jaunty air, an inspiration to all who saw his tall, stooping figure striding in the gloom and heard his easy, coaxing voice. From time to time he hummed snatches of that song which tells us that England shall never perish.

In one particular, the caisson was found not to be identical with that of the King George V Dock. At either side of it there were wide, deep scuppers and the whole of the steel surface was decked over with timber, coated with tar and grit. With one important exception, however, the work went forward swiftly. The twelve 18-lb underwater charges were dropped over the northern side and secured by their cords to the handrail. The ring main was run out as the shadowy figures hurried soft-footed from end to end. The cordtex leads from the charges were tied to it with clove hitches. The safety fuses, with their detonators and igniters, were crimped on and laid out in duplicate at the western end.

Sergeant Frank Carr, having seen all this done, sought out

Burtenshaw to report that the underwater charges were ready. He found him with Deery, still vainly trying to open the hatch which gave access to the interior of the caisson, where the wreaths had to be fastened magnetically to the inner walls and floors. Nothing that they could do would move it. Burtenshaw therefore ordered the sergeants to 'clear the deck' while he tried, first with a magnetic clam and then with a wreath, to blow it open. Both attempts failed.

At that moment, aroused perhaps by the explosion itself, there burst upon them a murderous fire from all sides. The six Oerlikons on the towers to their left rear and the guns on the ships in the Penhouet Basin opened up. To their bursts was added a brisk small-arms fire from the nearer of the two tankers in the dry dock immediately below to their right. The explosive bullets and the shot burst and rang on the steel of the caisson with a venomous clangour. Brett was wounded a second time. Burtenshaw, also wounded, ordered the teams to take cover and several of them, including Carr, Lemon and Burtenshaw himself, took refuge in the scuppers under the wooden decking on the dry dock side. From here they returned the fire of the ship in the dock with the only weapons they had – their pistols.

They very soon found, however, that this was no comfortable refuge, for the bullets from the tanker clanged about their ears. Burtenshaw ordered them all out, saying: 'We've got to deal with those chaps.' Out they scrambled, ran down to the dockside and emptied their pistols down upon the tanker. Far more effective, however, was the action of two men from the protection party, who ran down the steeply sloping gangplank and, with their Tommy-guns, silenced the crew with a few devastating bursts.

Sergeant Carr, leaving the dockside after the tanker had been silenced, looked about for the familiar, lanky figure of his well-loved officer, but could not find him. For somewhere in that stark dockyard scene Burtenshaw now lay dead.

While they had been silencing the tanker, a small party of Germans had attempted to attack them from the left rear. Burtenshaw, now also apparently wounded a second time, at once went to meet them, with one or two others. With their pistols alone they scattered the enemy, but the gallant Burtenshaw fell too, full of wounds and, we are told, still murmuring the words of that song which matched so well his gallant spirit. Corporal Blount was killed too.

Of this Carr knew nothing. Finding neither Burtenshaw nor Deery, the tall sergeant instinctively took matters into his own cool and competent hands. He stepped again on the caisson and walked its full length but could see no one alive. He examined the cordtex ring main and the detonators to see if they had been damaged. Some others of the teams made another attempt to open the hatch. Seeing that it was unsuccessful, Carr took the decision that the underwater charges must now be blown. He knew well that, without the wreaths, it was unlikely that the caisson would be completely destroyed, but it would be severely damaged.

He cleared everyone off the caisson, walked back to the western side, took up both igniters, pulled the pins and withdrew. The two feet of safety fuse burnt through in its allotted sixty seconds and the detonating wave shot instantaneously through the whole assembly. A deep, thunderous boom sounded above the raucous din that animated the night, like some huge drum among clashing symbols, and accompanied by a boiling and surge of the disturbed waters.

With the trained coolness of the Royal Engineer, Carr walked back again on to the caisson to inspect the damage. There was little that he expected to observe visually, but above the din he clearly heard water coming through into the dry dock from each end of the caisson. He knew then that the gate had been damaged as much as could be hoped for and that its repair would be long and difficult.

On Brett's orders what was left of the gallant band withdrew, Brett himself being carried by Corporals Wright and Ferguson. Of these parties, Burtenshaw, Sergeants Ide and Beveridge, Corporals Chetwynd, Jones and Blount and Lance-Corporal Stokes were at some time killed and only a few of the remainder escaped without some wound. Thus ended a fine and courageous operation pressed home with great determination and dash and one which, in spite of the clouded evidence in points of detail, ranks high among all the exploits of that night of gallant deeds.

The time had now come for the waiting Purdon and his corporals. About their performance there was no doubt whatever. As soon as the caisson-breakers had withdrawn, Purdon pulled the pins of his igniters. 'It was,' he recorded, 'a memorable sight.

The entire building seemed to rise several feet vertically before it exploded and disintegrated like a collapsed house of cards.'

*

All the commandos' demolition objectives on the machinery of the great Normandie Dock had now been fulfilled with almost complete success in less than half an hour from the moment *Campbeltown* had rammed. Even if the destroyer herself should fail to blow up, it was now impossible to operate either of the caissons and impossible to pump out or refill the dock. The great Forme Ecluse was useless for certainly a year at least, useless to the *Tirpitz*, useless to every kind of ship. It was, indeed, to remain useless until long after the war was over. This brilliant and remarkable feat, carried out at night, under a vicious fire and by a mere handful of men, is unique in military and naval annals. No other example exists of damage so vital and so far-reaching in its results being carried out so swiftly and with such economy of force. A very few men in negligible time had achieved with certainty and precision what the largest bombing raid and the heaviest artillery bombardment might have failed to do. No guess-work, no 'hundred per cent zone', no 'permissible error', no 'near misses' obscured the exactitude of the commandos' attack, for they placed their charges on those small, vital pinpoints which might never have been hit at all by projectiles launched from bombrack or gun.

The achievement was not only the visible record of the daring of the men who performed it; it was also a triumph for the man, now at this moment about to die on the doorstep of fulfilment, who had planned it. It was Pritchard whose imagination, invention and fanatical persistence had built the way to this technical achievement, it was his midnight assiduity that had calculated every charge and written out every item of each man's task and load to the last fusee and it was his patient and meticulous training that had taught each man precisely what to do. In the honours and memorials of the Charioteers his name, denied by death the award of any decoration, stands among the highest in the bright light of its devotion and sacrifice.*

* The award of the DSC to Tibbits was made before it was known that he had been killed.

Having thus completed all their tasks, the commandos of Group Three began their withdrawal according to plan, except for Smalley's team, whom we have already seen taking other means. They were filled with elation at the success of their missions, accomplished against odds. In spite of the quick fury of the awakened opposition, everything was going wonderfully well. Their work was finished and they were now to re-embark for home again. The route for all parties, as we know, lay through Donald Roy's bridgehead at the Old Entrance and so to Newman's headquarters on the other side. Copland had already passed through on his way to organize the re-embarkation at the Old Mole and with his passage occurred a shameful incident of a type of which this book has, happily, to record very few examples.

Crouching at his bridgehead, Roy had observed four figures approaching, darting skilfully from cover to cover and pursued by machine-gun fire from the minesweepers in the basin. A dim blue pinpoint of light appeared and a voice said: 'Copland here.' He answered: 'Roy here; come through.'

Copland was feeling quietly exultant. He had observed most of the dockyard tasks to have been brilliantly accomplished. He said to Roy: 'I must push on now to arrange the re-embarkation.' As he began to move, there was a sharp burst of fire on the bridge and he called out the names of his men in turn. Cheetham did not answer, for he had been wounded at the last gap and was lying forty yards away. Copland said: 'Bring him in, will you, Donald? I must get on.'

Not much relishing the task, The Laird set off alone, found the corporal and supported him back to the bridgehead. There he told Private Gwynne, who had just had a finger shot off, to get the corporal back to the Regimental Aid Post beyond the bridge.

The two soldiers crossed the bridge safely, the corporal supported by the private. There, as they rounded the corner of a building, they ran head-on into a German Tommy-gun patrol. Unable to defend themselves, they were caught and stripped of their possessions. The Germans, adopting a disreputable trick which too many of them practised, ordered the unsuspecting soldiers to run for it, one at a time. Gwynne was the first to go and as he ran the Germans riddled him with bullets in the back. This was the abominable trick of shooting an escaping prisoner.

Cheetham managed by a miracle to dive behind cover and somehow made his way in a shaken condition to Newman's precarious and now threatened headquarters.

Now one by one all the demolition teams came through the bridgehead, darting silently among the shadows, several of them carrying or supporting their wounded comrades, suffering further casualties as they came through, and giving their recognition signals to Roy, passed on, singly, across the fire-swept bridge. Chant, whose party was the first to arrive, found a safe means of crossing by climbing down to the substructure of the bridge and crossing underneath hand-over-hand. Many others followed him.

Chant then led his team to Newman's command post now a very hot spot, with German parties firing into it from only thirty to forty yards away, found Colonel Charles beaming jovially, saluted and said:

'Task completed, sir; pump house destroyed.'

Brett and Purdon, both wounded, came through, with the same reports of success. Etches had crawled through much earlier. Finally there came Montgomery, who had just blown up a railway truck, and who said:

'We're here, sir. All demolition tasks completed. Do I now have to embark, or may I go and look for Bill Pritchard?'

Stanley Day, who was beside Newman, said:

'Embark? Just look in the river!'

16. THE RIVER BATTLE

The spectacle which met all eyes that turned to the river at that moment was one of the utmost desolation. The shining achievements of *Campbeltown* and of the commandos landed from her had found but two imitators among the motor launches that followed astern. From the chapters of success we turn to one in which, with surprise forfeited, failure, and failure of the most agonizing kind, was almost inevitable. Coming up with the utmost dash under a murderous short-range fire from the automatic guns, the little, vulnerable craft met destruction one after another, either as they attempted to put in at their two appointed landing places, or as, frustrated and barred, they made their way out into mid-river. Not all, but sadly too many.

The great arena of light, which had made the Loire like the scene of some vivid tattoo, overlaid with the complex of coloured projectiles darting in every direction, was now punctuated by fiercer orange conflagrations as the motor launches fell victims one by one to the enemy's guns. As they ignited, or blew up in violent explosions, pools of burning petrol spread far and wide, their flames licking the very surface of the water and trapping inexorably the shipwrecked men who were swept into them by the current. From these floating furnaces clouds of black smoke drifted slowly over the water in the almost windless air, disrupting the cold pattern of the searchlights and giving evidence of the cremation of hope and valour. As the watching Frenchman recorded, 'the sky itself seemed to be on fire'.

This spectacle of flame and smoke and shellfire, of burned and drowning men, was, of course, the direct consequence of the enemy's loss of interest in what had been going on in the air. From the moment that the bombing stopped and Mecke made his tactical appreciation, only the grossest negligence by the Germans, or some extraordinary circumstance of good chance, could have saved the little wooden boats from the waiting guns. No one supposed for a moment that motor launches could assault fortified harbours. As soon as they had been spotted one would have thought, with Hughes-Hallett, that their death sentence had been pronounced. That they fought as they did, that some of them landed their troops and that eight out of the seventeen got to sea again past all the cannon to right and left of them – these facts are the measure of the skill and courage of the men who stood on their bridges, who manned their little guns and who drove their highly inflammable engines.

In reading the record of these events in the river, it will not be easy to keep account of time, for much was happening simultaneously both by land and water. The river battle was taking place at the same time as the dockyard battle and while we have been reading of the exploits of Roy and Roderick, of Chant, Smalley, Burtenshaw, Brett and Purdon, we must know that a more deadly battle was proceeding in the river as the launches attempted against heavy odds to put the commando parties ashore.

There are seventeen little ships of whose fate and fortune we have to read, and, since things did not go as they were intended to do, each is a story to itself. These events took place more swiftly than the recording of them and as we read the exploits of each we must carry in the mind's eye the picture of the next one coming up fast astern of her, at less than a minute's interval. Thus the stories crowd into two focal points – the Old Entrance, hard by the caisson that *Campbeltown* has just rammed, where the starboard flotilla of motor launches is due to land the commandos for Newman's Group Two tasks in the centre of the assault area; and the Old Mole, where the port column is to land those for Group One on the left. Sharing in the fortunes and misfortunes of both are those other craft not carrying troops – Curtis's gunboat, which was Ryder's headquarters ship throughout, Boyd's and Irwin's two torpedo-carrying boats in the van, Micky Wynn's tempestuous little torpedo-boat, and the now single spare motor launch of young Sub-Lieutenant Nock in the rear. We shall read first of the affairs of those on the starboard flank and front, bearing in

mind that those on the port hand were taking place simultaneously, and in due course we shall return again to the vivid
stage of the dockyard battle.

In the Old Entrance

After she had sheered off to starboard to make way for
Campbeltown, the gunboat stood off, together with Irwin's ML 7,
to give supporting fire to the destroyer and to the commando
landing. At this stage, Ryder, through the confused complex of
fixed and moving lights, could see only fitfully and imperfectly the
two columns of motor launches coming up at speed astern of
Campbeltown. Very soon he moved into the enclosed water of the
Old Entrance, whence he could see nothing at all. Accordingly he
was quite unaware of most of what is now to be narrated, until
after this phase of the battle was all over.

Let us follow first the fortunes of the starboard column and the
other craft that had business in the Old Entrance.

First Casualty

Leading the starboard column of troop-carrying boats was
Lieutenant-Commander W. L. Stephens, a spirited and charming
Ulsterman of thirty. He was to achieve an honourable notoriety as
an escapist, which cost him imprisonment (with several other
Charioteers) in the grim fastness of Colditz, from which also he
escaped. He was carrying Michael Burn, Tom Peyton and the assault
party that was intended to attack the group of targets at the swing
bridge far away beyond the north end of the Normandie Dock.

First of the motor launches to come to grief, ML 192 was
mortally hit even before Campbeltown rammed. When abeam of
the Old Mole a shell tore a four-foot hole in the engine-room, port
side, threw the port engine completely off its bearings, damaged
the starboard engine also and the Lockheed steering. A sheet of
flame shot straight up into the air and the light craft was flung
hard over to port, out of control. A second shell penetrated the
petrol compartment and a third holed the boat on the waterline
beneath the bridge.

Sheering across the front of the port column, the boat struck the East Jetty, two hundred yards south of the Old Mole on the starboard bow, but bumped off before it was possible to get her troops ashore, the quay here standing fourteen feet above the deck. Stephens gave the order to abandon the burning ship. The wounded were put off on a Carley raft, but the boat herself was carried downstream by the strong current, which that night was to be the cause of many deaths from drowning. All but five of the commandos were lost by gunshot or drowning, including the charming and splendid young Tom Peyton. Of the ship's company, Ordinary Seamen Hallet, Hale and Little and Motor Mechanic Snowball perished.

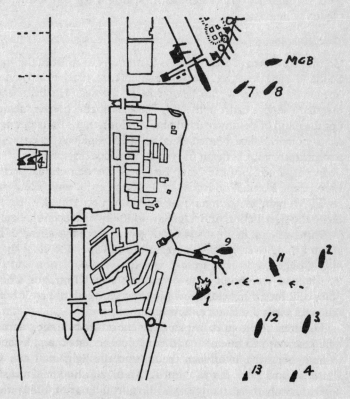

Fig 16. The situation immediately following the ramming at 1.34 a.m.

The only man to escape capture was Michael Burn. Entering the water, he sank like a rock under his heavy load of ammunition, but Lance-Corporal Young, Gordon Highlanders, seized him and towed him to the shore. On the quay the commando party became separated, but Burn quickly recovered and, by an astonishing effort, made his way entirely alone across the whole enemy-occupied dockyard area to his target area three-quarters of a mile away. He found, however, that there was nothing he could do, for the gun towers that he was to attack were unoccupied; he made an attempt to set them on fire, but more he could not do alone. But it was a remarkable effort, exemplifying the nature of commando training. Copland visited him up there and he then made his way back through Roy's bridgehead, dragging a leg but jesting with Chant as he passed.

The Gallant Refusal

Coming up astern of Stephens was Lieutenant E. A. Burt, the young Scotland Yard detective. He wore a small, trim, black beard and was one of those men whose heart was in the sea. He had been a merchant service cadet in the old *Worcester* of affectionate memory, but the hand of destiny had led him into his father's footsteps in the Metropolitan Police. Nonetheless, he had a twinkle in his eye and an adventurous spirit beneath the veneer of police discipline.

In ML 2 (262 of the Navy List) was the demolition party of Lieutenant Mark Woodcock, of 3 Commando, with Lieutenant R. F. Morgan in command of his protection squad, their task being the destruction of Bridge G and the two adjacent lockgates.

Burt came up in great style and, seeing Stephens ahead of him hit and flung over to port, increased to full speed to close up the line. Obliged, however, to take violent avoiding action and dazzled by the searchlights, he overshot his Old Entrance landing place and found himself a few hundred yards up the river before the landmarks disclosed to him his error.

Turning short round, he met Beart, next astern in the starboard column, who had made the same involuntary error, and he spoke to him over the loudhailer and, proceeding, gained the Old Entrance under fire. It was about 1.45 a.m. and Rodier's boat, ML 6, was already there, made fast to the port quarter of *Campbeltown* after having landed her troops. Manoeuvring to avoid the loose ends of the broken torpedo net, Burt successfully landed all his troops on the upstream side of the Old Entrance in accordance with his orders.

The moment they landed, however, the commandos came under a stinging fire from the 20 mm guns of one of the harbour defence ships immediately facing them in the Submarine Basin only one hundred and fifty yards away. They suffered casualties at once, Sergeant Hempstead being mortally wounded in the stomach. From the bridge of the motor launch Burt and Stoker Ball gave them covering fire with their stripped Lewis guns, but it was not enough. Morgan and Woodcock re-embarked, asking Burt to put them ashore on the downstream side. It was at this moment that Smalley and his party, having destroyed their winding-house, ran down and embarked.

As she manoeuvred in the confined space of the Old Entrance for a fresh landing, the motor launch came under fire from the same *Hafenschutzboot* and a minesweeper. The microphone of Burt's loud-hailer was shot out of his hand. Smalley was killed trying to release the forward Oerlikon. Another burst of 20 mm fire struck the after Oerlikon, killing Able Seaman Walker and severely wounding Sub-Lieutenant Hills and Able Seaman Martin. To this stinging 'cannon-fire' the commandos replied as best they could with Bren guns and, while Burt conned the ship, Stoker Ball kept up a vivacious fire with his stripped Lewis from the wing of the bridge; vivacious, because the spirited young fellow, in the midst of the whistling shot and the crackling tracer, was delighting in the battle. 'I never saw a man,' recorded Ted Burt, 'who laughed in action as he did.' When the weapon in his hand was smashed by an explosive bullet, he merely made a salty jest.

Burt withdrew into open water and shaped course downriver under heavy fire, continuing to sustain casualties. He worked up to full speed until nearly abreast of the Old Mole and there he caught sight of Collier's boat, of the port column, disabled and under heavy fire after having skilfully and gallantly landed his commandos. Without hesitation, Burt immediately went to his assistance and Leaney took his boat alongside as coolly as though he were berthing in Weymouth harbour.

There followed one of the many tragic and dramatic moments of the Raid. Dangerously lying stopped in the glare of the searchlights only a cable length off the tip of the bristling mole, the two friends spoke a few hurried words. Tom Collier, who had just given the order to abandon ship, was alone on the bridge of his dying craft, badly wounded, a leg shattered and nearly severed. To Burt's offer to take him off he gave an emphatic refusal. He would not endanger the other ship by another moment's delay. With the end of life immediately before him, he said quietly:

'I've had it, Ted. Get out quickly before the bastards get you too.'

Burt gave the order 'Full ahead together', but the Germans had seen him stop and did not miss their opportunity. Three shells hit the ship in quick succession – on the bridge itself, in the engine-room and aft. The engines, steering gear and telegraphs were put out of action. Five commandos and Stoker Hollands were killed. Mark Woodcock fell, both legs shattered. Ball was hit in both legs also but, without a murmur, hobbled aft in obedience to Burt's order to help Lieutenant E. C. A. Roberts rig the hand-steering gear.

Now out of control, ML 262, as well as Collier's a little way off, drifted out into mid-river and there, at approximately 2.45 a.m., with fourteen or more dead, with most of the others wounded, with the ship on fire amidships and all guns out of action, Burt gave the order to abandon ship.

'In an exemplary manner by both Army and Navy alike,' Burt tells us, all hands slipped over the side into the icy waters. Burt himself put the shattered Woodcock and Hills over the side on a splinter-mat, but both of them tried with their last strength to clamber on board again so that the mat could be used by others. The remaining wounded were put on the Carley rafts, to drift precariously with the current among patches of burning petrol. Burt himself drifted downstream until, by good fortune, he was carried on to Les Morés Tower, where he lost consciousness until he was picked up by the Germans next morning.

Three More

Very much the same anguished fate befell the third of the troop-carrying MLs, commanded by Lieutenant E. H. Beart, a solicitor of about thirty-five or so, tall, fair and a most attractive personality. He had brought a rugger ball with him, hoping for a game on the quay while the commandos were about their business. He had on board Newman's tiny fighting reserve under the splendid and gallant figure of Regimental Sergeant-Major Moss.

We have seen how Beart, following his predecessor, overran the Old Entrance. Turning about, he made into the Old Entrance after Burt and duly landed his commandos, but they also were repulsed and re-embarked. Manoeuvring in the Old Entrance, Beart came under well directed fire. In a few minutes the ship was enveloped in flames and the order to abandon was given, Beart himself being mortally wounded.

The commandos, swimming or on Carley rafts, made for shore in an attempt to carry out their mission. Here it was that Moss, being on a Carley raft, saw a very young soldier in the water. It was Private Diamond. Without hesitation, he slipped off, and ordered Diamond to take his place. He then, with others, towed or pushed the raft towards shore and in doing so was, it seems, shot in the head and never seen again. Out of the eleven commandos on board, only three survived.

Swifter still was the fate of Tillie's ship, No 4 in the column. Burt and Beart having overshot their mark, Tillie was actually the first to shape course correctly and turn in towards the Old Entrance. As he did so, however, he came under heavy and accurate fire. In a moment the boat was a mass of flaming petrol a little astern of *Campbeltown* and after some minutes she blew up, spreading far and wide a fountain of blazing petrol.

Tillie lived, but nearly all other hands on board were lost. Of the seventeen commandos on board only Sergeant Knowles and Lance-Corporal Parkes managed to swim ashore, the remainder being drowned or overcome in the lake of burning petrol that spread over the surface of the water. Among those who perished was Harry Pennington, who thus fulfilled the destiny that he had prophesied for himself.

Already we have seen the first four troop-carrying boats in the starboard column completely destroyed – those of Tillie and Stephens almost instantly. Beart's fairly soon also, Burt's in a long-drawn trial of more than an hour. The fifth, commanded by the gay, handsome and spirited film actor, Lieutenant Leslie

Fenton, was one of the four torpedo MLs and was no less severely handled but yet escaped destruction. He carried the assault party of Captain R. H. Hooper.

Very early in the action both Fenton and Hooper were badly wounded by a direct hit from a shell on the bridge. Obstructed by the movements of ships in trouble ahead of him, including two that crossed his bows sharply from port to starboard, Fenton ordered 'Hard a-starboard', increased speed, made a complete circle and shaped course again for the Old Entrance. He then collapsed and handed over to Sub-Lieutenant N. G. Machin, his first lieutenant, but Machin also was badly hit, the Lockheed steering was knocked out and one engine put out of action. After an attempt had been made to torpedo the *Sperrbrecher*, the three badly wounded officers held a painful conference, decided that they had no other course than to withdraw.

Somewhere about 2.30 a.m., after a long, gallant and bloody fight, in which soldiers and sailors alike had fought magnificently, Fenton began limping painfully downstream on one engine, using hand steering, and, successfully avoiding the fire of the big coast defence guns, gained the open sea.

Mission Accomplished

Lieutenant Mark Rodier, commanding His Majesty's ML 177, was a dark, aquiline, clean-shaven officer of middle height, quiet and unassuming, who spoke several languages and had a taste for classical music. He had under him three other officers, all sub-lieutenants – Frank Arkle, very young, W. J. Heaven, recently joined, and A. J. Toy, the engineer officer of his flotilla. Their ship was another of the four torpedo MLs, armed with a Hotchkiss instead of Oerlikons.

On board they had a particularly stout-hearted detachment of fourteen assault commandos under the command of Troop Sergeant-Major Haines, the short Kent farmer with the big hands and the greater heart who had been ready to tear off his stripes to join the commandos. His tasks were to assist Hooper to silence the suspected waterside guns and then to come into Newman's reserve.

The scene that confronted Rodier's eyes as he followed close astern of Fenton was not one to be faced by the chicken-hearted. To port, to starboard and ahead motor launches were on fire and drifting out of control, for the spectacles that we have seen in the starboard column were being duplicated to port. Already the agonized cries of men trapped in the pools of burning petrol, which were to be one of the memories of that night for British and Germans alike, were beginning to be heard. Wreckage, corpses, flames and drifting palls of smoke were starkly clear in the cold glare of the searchlights. These, the sudden water-spouts of bursting shells and the swift streaks of coloured tracer, 'like red and green stitches on a piece of cloth', threatened the sixth launch with a like fate. Last of the troop-carrying boats in the starboard column, all that had gone before her seemed to have gone only to destruction.

Yet Rodier held firmly on his way. He saw Tillie blow up ahead, Stephens and Platt on fire to port, Fenton sheer away to starboard immediately ahead. Hit several times, but nowhere vitally, he sailed through the maelstrom, past the guns of the Old Mole blazing at him at a hundred yards' range, past the wrecks of his friends, through the stream of projectiles that seemed to bar the way in to the Old Entrance. This he slightly overshot, as Burt and Beart had done, but, quickly discovering his mistake, turned short round, steamed into the Old Entrance, first of the troop-carrying MLs to enter, and came alongside on the southern quay at about 1.40 a.m. He gave Haines the order to disembark and the eager commandos climbed quickly ashore and, in the words of the watching Arkle, 'passed rapidly into the shadows', where we shall meet them again.

As he waited, Rodier saw Burt and Beart come and go and finally Micky Wynn arrive. Then, as we know, he was hailed by Beattie (or by Ryder) and stopped on the port quarter of *Campbeltown* to take off some thirty of her crew. His mission thus ably and coolly accomplished, he made out into midstream at 1.57 a.m. and began his return passage to the sea at fifteen knots with some forty to fifty men crowded into the small craft.

Drawing Fire

One more vessel, victim of sheer misfortune, made for the Old Entrance. This was the spare motor launch, No 16, of Sub-Lieutenant N. R. Nock, youngest of all the ML commanders, very tall, very thin, with a touch of the devil concealed beneath his youthful face.

His main responsibility was to stand by to take off *Campbeltown*'s troops if she should get into trouble; otherwise, he was to man-oeuvre to draw fire, to engage enemy guns and lights and to re-embark troops on the withdrawal. He certainly drew fire, and as he came up last of all he beheld the scenes of destruction almost at their climax. Young Bob Nock rode through it all unharmed, with Petty Officer Hambley a model of coolness at the wheel. Passing the Old Entrance, Nock found a pool of darkness and from there engaged enemy guns and lights with his Oerlikons for some while until he judged it time to make for the Old Entrance to pick up troops. But he found it empty; and the mole likewise. Moving out into the river again, he tried to pick up survivors who were heard crying out in the water on every hand, but caught fire when passing through one of the many pools of blazing petrol. He made downstream at full ahead under cover of smoke but was held in the searchlights and hit repeatedly. Ordinary Seaman Clear, who had been serving the forward Oerlikon almost continuously with great gallantry, was killed; so also were the two junior sub-lieutenants, Spraggon and Vardon-Patten, and Nock himself was wounded.

A little way down the river, under heavy fire, both engines blew up simultaneously, with severe casualties, and it was only through the cool handling of Hambley that the few survivors got away alive.

Newman and Ryder Land

As we have noted, Ryder himself had very little idea of what was happening in those first few fiery moments before he ordered Curtis to take the gunboat into the Old Entrance – and none of what happened in the river in the next hour of anguish and heroism. The dazzle of the searchlights, some fixed and concen-trated on the vital area, others swinging and sweeping, together with the bewildering network of tracers, gave him only a partial and uncertain picture of events as the MLs came up towards him, though supposedly he must have seen Tillie blow up quite close to him. Nor was he able to receive any wireless reports, for the gunboat's aerial had been shot away early and the emergency aerial put out failed of its purpose. Indeed the failure of communications was one of the minor lessons of the operation, as it is of so many others.

To Ryder, therefore, though under considerable strain, there seemed no cause for despondency. The gunboat herself, well handled by Dunstan Curtis, who was feeling tremendously buoyant and uplifted, had behaved perfectly, in spite of the stoppages of the after Rolls gun and the two twin .5s. Able Seaman Savage, at the forward pom-pom, had given a first taste of his mettle and had sent a thrill through the whole little ship when, with cool eye and steady hand, he had silenced the *Sperrbrecher* at close quarters. Then, as the gunboat sheered away ahead of *Campbeltown* and circled, there had come, in Gordon Holman's words, the 'glorious moment' of the destroyer's triumphant crash upon the steel wall of the caisson.

As Curtis brought the gunboat back full circle again towards the Old Entrance, there ensued a sharp controversy on the bridge between Ryder and Newman. To the two friends at the time it seemed hot enough in the tension of the moment, but to us in detachment it does them both some honour rather than otherwise, serving to bring out the identity of character that underlay the different exteriors of the two men. 'It was,' said Newman afterwards, 'the only time that Bob and I have ever had cross words.'

Newman, fully accoutred, was on the bridge of the gunboat, itching to get ashore. His small headquarters staff, which the sailors referred to as his 'bodyguard', stood by on the deck – Stanley Day his adjutant, Sergeant Steele his signal sergeant, trussed up like a chicken in his secret RT set, Terry the War Office representative, Lance-Corporal Harrington, Peter Walker the ex-German specially sent by Mountbatten, and Murdoch and Kelly, the two Tommy-gunners, the last named now in his kilt. Through the din of the mixed orchestra of artillery, the first distinctive notes of Tommy-gun fire ashore, as the men from *Campbeltown* sprang forward to their targets, came meaningly to their attentive ears. The shore battle was on and to them it was a bugle call.

Ryder, on the other hand, watching the fortunes and misfortunes of his little ships as they rode gallantly up, observed that the *Sperrbrecher*, although being roughly handled by every boat that passed her on either hand, had come to life again with plenty of spirit and was beginning to be troublesome; particularly, at that moment, to Fenton. Like the ships within the docks, she was a factor for which they had made no provision. The failure of the gunboat's wireless having left him no means of control, Ryder said to Newman:

'Charles, that ship has got to be sunk. I must find a torpedo ML at once.'

Newman took immediate objection. 'No,' he said. 'You simply must get me ashore first.'

'Not until I have sunk that ship,' Ryder replied.

'Look here, Bob; your job is to get me ashore, and as quickly as possible.'

'It's also my job to sink that ship before she does any more damage.'

'For heaven's sake, Bob, put me ashore first and sink your ship afterwards.'

Ryder gave way with good spirit, for he realized that to Newman it was a matter of honour to be with his men, and in they went, immediately after Rodier. Curtis ran his gunboat safely in to a wooden pier in the Old Entrance, downstream side, past the stern of the destroyer, Leading Seaman McKee bringing her alongside as though he were berthing at Gosport, and the whole of the little ship's company feeling, in the words of their captain, 'on top of the world'. The two leaders, so strong in friendship and courage, not to meet again for some three and a half years, shook hands and wished each other good luck, and Newman's party, we are told by the observant McKee, 'armed to the teeth, sprang over the side and away up the steps like young goats'.

Having ordered Rodier by loudhailer to take off *Campbeltown*'s crew (as Beattie also did), Ryder ordered Curtis to manoeuvre the gunboat alongside the landing steps on the upstream side of the

Old Entrance, bows out. Here, soon afterwards, the remainder of *Campbeltown*'s crew, whom we have already seen scrambling down from the fo'c'sle after the commandos, came running down the steps, carrying or supporting their wounded, and, having given the correct recognition signal as Curtis covered them, were taken on board, crowding it to excess.

About this time Micky Wynn came sailing in with his motor torpedo-boat, last ship of the force. He had had an anxious time coming up the river, for the idiosyncrasies of his craft had required him to move, in the rear of the force, by sudden darts alternating with dangerous stops. However, like Rodier and Nock, he had escaped trouble, except for a small shell that burst inside the engine-room, putting the centre of the five engines out of action, and wounding Lovegrove all down his right leg. Covered with blood and oil, in great pain, weary from lost sleep, but filled with courage and determination, the devoted motor mechanic was at this moment actively repairing the engine, with the help of the two stokers, Simmonds and A. W. Savage.

As he sailed into the Old Entrance, where for a brief space no fewer than five craft were collected, Wynn saw *Campbeltown* securely wedged into the caisson and he knew therefore that he would not be needed for his primary tasks. He came alongside the gunboat, and on Ryder's orders waited.

Ryder meanwhile landed. He had needed to satisfy himself at close quarters that *Campbeltown* was truly rammed and sinking: Wynn might still be needed to torpedo the destroyer if she had not struck properly nor been truly scuttled. He therefore set off along the quay, but he was not alone, for Leading Signalman Pike, having now no task, appointed himself bodyguard, and, picking up a broken bayonet on the quayside, accompanied his commanding officer.

As they hurried along the quay a sharp challenge from a crouching figure with a Tommy-gun halted them abruptly. It was one of Hollywood's protection squad, covering Smalley at his task on the winding-house. Ryder gave the password, which was his own name, and was passed by the sentry. He reached the caisson and hailed *Campbeltown*, but received no answer. He could see the fire burning on the fo'c'sle and there seemed no sign of life on board. He saw Rodier move off from the stern of the ship and he stepped forward and hailed again. The only answer was a burst of fire from behind him which struck the masonry of a small hut close to him. He and Pike dodged quickly into the lee of the hut and from there Ryder watched *Campbeltown* for several minutes. Then to his relief he saw clearly a series of small explosions along her port side and heard others on the starboard. These were the scuttling charges that Hargreaves and White had fired. The destroyer was already clearly sinking at the stern.

Satisfied, he turned to go, full of admiration for Beattie's splendid performance and feeling a moment of exaltation at the accomplishment of his main task. As he turned he was buffeted by the blast of a violent explosion as Smalley's winding-house went up, its débris spattering around him and his escort. A minute later there was a muffled roar and a shuddering of the earth as he saw a great flash from inside the big pump house, with sheets of splintered glass from the windows flashing like heliographs in the searchlight beams. Chant's work. Soon afterwards a like explosion took his eyes to the north as Purdon's winding-hut also went up. Good work, damned good work.

Exhilarated by all this evidence of a brilliant beginning to the operation, he returned with Pike to the gunboat. Wynn, who had been having a quick drink with Curtis on the bridge, was waiting for his orders. Ryder told him to fire his *Scharnhorst* torpedoes at the outer lock gates of the Old Entrance.

'Aye, aye, sir. Anything after that?'

'Yes, come back alongside and take off as many *Campbeltown* ratings as you can. Then straight back to Falmouth on your own at full speed. Make it forty knots no less.'

'Aye, aye, sir.'

Wynn manoeuvred MTB 74 into position and Ryder watched with satisfaction the two torpedoes leap from their tubes through the air like great flying fish, hit the lock gates full pitch and then sink with a splash to the bottom. His centre engine now repaired, Wynn embarked sixteen of *Campbeltown*'s ratings and took his little craft out on her last passage.

The gunboat followed him out not very long afterwards, where she was to witness a scene of a very different colour.

At the Old Mole

While the gallant endeavours of those in the starboard column were thus being extinguished one by one, their fellows in the port column, who were due to land at the Old Mole with the commandos of Group One, were coming up abreast of them with no greater success but with better personal fortune; for five out of the seven were to get safely out to sea and three of them right home to England. Yet the mole was by far the more dangerous of the two landing places.

A small vessel that succeeded in making its way into the Old Entrance enjoyed a certain amount of protection, for it was partially enclosed by quays that stood well above the decks and the quays were not in enemy hands. The mole, however, was entirely exposed to fire and it was itself occupied by the enemy. It stood some twenty-five feet above water level at high tide and the only means of access was by the landing steps on the upstream or northern side of it, or else by the commandos' scaling ladders; on the downstream side there was a dangerous shelving beach.

At the tip of the mole, beside the stumpy lighthouse, a searchlight steadily poured out its beam in prolongation of the structure. Half way along, a 20-mm gun in a very strong concrete emplacement firing through embrasures, defied, otherwise than temporarily, all efforts to silence it by the very light weapons which were all that the Charioteers possessed. This very troublesome gun was Position 63 in the German dispositions. Immediately inland of the base of the mole another 20 mm, Position 62, mounted in or on top of a strong structure covered the deadly area between the mole and the Old Entrance. Landings on the mole were further hindered by parties of the enemy armed with hand-grenades and sub-machine-guns, dropping their grenades or firing their weapons straight down on the deck of any motor launch that attempted to come alongside.

There was therefore exceedingly small hope of any boat getting in, or of any troops being landed, until the enemy positions had been wiped out, though in one instance this was brilliantly achieved. In turn, there was not very much chance of wiping out these positions, or any other positions elsewhere, unless the assault parties of the commandos, powerfully armed for close-quarter fighting, were successfully landed; for the demolition teams, apart from their small protection squads, were armed only with pistols. This condition applied, of course, to both Groups at both landing places, but with far more force at the Old Mole, where the opposition to be overcome was immediately present. As events were to turn out, the loss of Birney's party in the flames of Platt's motor launch was perhaps the most critical of all, for it was Birney's task to attack the guns on the mole that were doing so much damage.

Let us remind ourselves that much of what is now to be recorded was occurring simultaneously with the events of the starboard column and occurring, moreover, more swiftly than we may read it; for the motor launches are fast upon each others' heels. All the landings and the attempts to land were over in a very few minutes. Even making allowance for those who overshot their mark, all such attempts were over within fifteen minutes of *Campbeltown*'s ram at 1.34 a.m.

There is no substance in the criticisms made shortly after the raid, owing to an understandable misreading of early reports, that the motor launches wrongly attempted to land on the southern or downstream side of the mole; all aimed correctly for the upstream side.

The Sergeant-Major's Vision

Ahead of the port column of troop-carrying boats was one of the torpedo motor launches, No 7, commanded by Lieutenant C. S. B. Irwin, a professional Merchant Service seaman, with an Australian Number One, Lieutenant C. W. Wallach, and a New Zealand supernumerary, Sub-Lieutenant G. V. Fisher.

Six minutes after the destroyer had rammed, Irwin sustained a direct hit aft which put the steering gear out of action and damaged the auxiliary steering also. The boat began to drift, an easy target for the enemy, and after some ten minutes Irwin decided that he must withdraw. Successfully running the gauntlet of Dieckmann's heavy guns at the mouth of the estuary, he made good his passage back to the open sea.

A harsher fate befell the leading port motor launch that was carrying troops, No 9. This was commanded by Lieutenant T. D. L. Platt, another experienced Merchant Service seaman, extrovert and breezy. He was carrying the very important assault party, intended for attacking the Old Mole itself, of Captain David Birney, accompanied by Lieutenant W. C. Clibborn, six feet tall, strongly built, very blond, and his dark and athletic troop sergeant-major, Ted Hewett. Below deck were Regimental Quartermaster-Sergeant Seaton and Corporal Crippin, the orderly-room clerk, who had persuaded Newman to let them come at the last minute.

As Platt ran up towards the mole both his Oerlikons were knocked out and their crews, together with some commandos, were killed and Clibborn wounded. He put in on the upstream

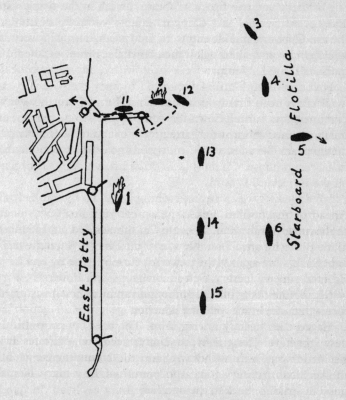

Fig 17. Situation at the Old Mole at about 1.35 a.m.

side of the mole, but stopped somewhat short of the landing steps, apparently aground, and was at once attacked from above by small arms and grenades. Only six commandos were now left who were fit for action, but in spite of this Birney was willing to go in if Platt could land him.

In a fresh attempt Platt went 'Full astern'. He got clear but had no sooner rung 'Full ahead' again than the engine-room received a direct hit and in a moment was a mass of flames. He drifted round to the south of the mole and there he put some of the wounded on a Carley raft and ordered the remaining commandos to swim ashore before giving the order to abandon ship.

Birney ordered a last-minute search of the ship and below deck one of them saw two prostrate figures awash in the rising water. They were Seaton and Crippin, almost certainly dead. Only Birney, Clibborn and Hewett were fit to swim. Throwing away his steel helmet, and standing on the gunwhale, Birney ordered:

'Over the side, you two.'

Had they been a little less prompt to obey Platt's order, they would have seen that help was at hand. Birney, only an average swimmer, was carried down the coast by the strong current and finally reached shore at the extremity of exhaustion. He stumbled up the beach for a few yards, collapsed and died a few hours later in a French house. Clibborn also drifted down and was beached off the Boulevard Wilson.

Now Hewett was a strong swimmer. All his life he had, in a quasi-mystical fashion, linked the act of swimming with the idea of the hope of salvation. The story of the Sea of Galilee held for him a powerful attraction. Now, cast into the icy flood, he had to fight for his life against the powerful current. One by one he got rid of the heavy loads that were weighing him down as he trod water – his sandbag full of Tommy-gun ammunition, his Colt, the hand-grenades in his webbing pouches.

He kept his head, knowing, from the pull of the current, that he might have a long fight, though the shore was not far away. He struck out with all his strength, the cold penetrating him, the smell of drifting smoke and petrol assailing his senses, the missiles striking the water with a hiss about his head. In spite of his strength, he began to fail, his strokes feebler and the water entering his mouth. Very soon only the will for self-preservation kept him above water, but that will alone was not sufficient and he was in the last extremity when there appeared beside him the vision of Christ walking serenely upon the water. He spoke as He had spoken to the disciples, comfortable words that told the faint swimmer that there was nothing to fear. Hewett took the hand that was outstretched to him, as it had been to Peter, and struck out again with fresh strength. In a little while, now in darkness beyond the play of the searchlights, his hands struck a concrete wall. He reached out and grasped some material that he felt on the wall, but it came away in his hand, for it was seaweed. Again he was seized with an access of despair, as he dropped back into the water, but heard himself being told to go on. He grasped again at the wall, and his hand fell upon the rung of an iron ladder.

There, alone with his private thoughts, the troop sergeant-major clung for few moments. Then slowly he began to climb the ladder that went up the face of the quay. He reached the top, exhausted and sodden, and there a group of Germans was waiting for him. They seized him, threw him down on the quay, kicked him brutally, shouting angry imprecations, and drove him away.

The Perilous Rescue

It will suit the sequence of our story, since it concerns Platt's boat also, if we relate at this point the heartening narrative of the second of the torpedo motor launches that had been in the van during the approach. This was His Majesty's ML 160, commanded by Lieutenant Tom, or 'Nero' Boyd, the robust, ruddy Hull trawler owner. Though tactically No 8, he had in fact been in the van of the starboard column, as we have seen, ahead of Stephens. Having no troops, Boyd's business was to be prepared to torpedo any vessel that gave trouble, to give supporting fire to *Campbeltown* with his antique Hotchkiss, to draw fire and look for trouble. Nearly all these he accomplished.

Boyd had with him two officers – Sub-Lieutenant J. A. Tait, a good, sound Scottish officer, and Sub-Lieutenant J. G. Hall, a supernumerary young officer, quiet and reserved. His coxswain was Petty Officer L. S. Lamb, a blond giant of great physical strength, but the hand at the wheel throughout the operation – completely unmoved and serene – was Able Seaman J. Glass. At the 3-pounder Hotchkiss in the bows was Leading Seaman McIver and Petty Officer Motor Mechanic Walker was in charge of the engine-room until he was painfully wounded in the face, when Stoker Petty Officer Rice took over.

We have already seen Boyd's boat giving supporting fire to *Campbeltown* and McIver disabling one of the shore guns immediately to starboard of the destroyer. Taking violent avoiding action against the shellfire, Boyd made off upstream to hunt for two 10,000-ton tankers that were said to be about. He could not find them (for they were actually in the dry dock itself) and accordingly he turned back 'to see what we could do'.

Reaching the heart of the conflict again, he observed a group of 20-mm guns on top of a building inflicting a good deal of damage. Approaching to within two hundred yards of shore, he stopped, and gave it thirty rounds from the Hotchkiss, during which time the ship's company listened delighted as McIver kept saying: 'Och, that's hit the bastards again!'

The place becoming too hot to remain stopped, Boyd moved on downstream and attacked with his torpedoes a target near the avantport, which may have been the *Sperrbrecher*, but she was not sunk. Lamb kept crawling up from the wheelhouse from time to time to see if he was all right, but Tom Boyd indeed was never more so. Finding his steel helmet too heavy, he changed into a very old and very flat cap, known as his 'fighting hat', which his crew preferred to see him wear, as they had a legend that it brought them luck. In this he felt more confident and kept saying: 'By God, we're still alive!'

Turning about, and running short of Hotchkiss ammunition, he fired a few rounds of old-fashioned 'case' shot, which has a shrapnel effect and with which the gun was supplied. The motor launch was now being frequently hit. There was a blinding crash and a cloud of smoke as a shell penetrated the engine-room. The engines cut out, the ship was plunged into darkness and Boyd thought: 'Well, this is it.'

But down below Stoker Petty Officer Rice, realizing that the cut was electrical, searched for the break with a torch, found the battery leads severed, joined them up by placing a jack-knife across and the engines cut in again. Another hit penetrated one of the supplementary deck petrol tanks, but only water came out and the square tank became a round one.

It was about this time that, passing the Old Mole again and looking round upon the lurid and devastating scene, Boyd observed Platt's boat 'smoking like hell and a red glow from the engine-room'. As he approached Platt hailed him and he went in without hesitation to his aid.

With the utmost boldness, Boyd put himself right alongside, between the burning ship and the mole under the very nose of the enemy, and began to take off survivors. Petty Officer Lamb and Able Seaman Lambert, one of Platt's hands, though himself hit, went calmly to and fro between the two ships, carrying off the wounded one after another with flames leaping from the doomed craft. The wounded commandos on the Carley raft were rescued also.

Someone went below to search the ship and there found and rescued two bodies in khaki with the water lapping round them. They were Seaton and Crippin. Last of all came Platt, having examined with Lamb every body that lay on the deck to make sure that none was left who was living. In all some sixteen men in Platt's boat were killed or drowned, of whom about twelve were commandos and among whom were both his junior officers, Lieutenant H. S. Chambers and the Canadian Lieutenant G. MacNaughton Baker.

After this gallant little episode, carried out in the Royal Navy's best tradition, Boyd went astern into midstream and turned to begin his withdrawal. He had proceeded only a very short distance when he heard three men calling out in the water. He hesitated only for an agonizing moment. Then he gave the order to stop ship, himself seized one of the commando boarding ladders, hung it over the port guard rail, ran down it and pulled the men in. No sooner had he ordered full ahead together than the ship was heartily plastered and several of the rescued commandos were severely wounded, one man having 'a splinter through the chest and coming out the other side leaving a hole you could get your hand in', but nonetheless remaining conscious and talking sensibly until he died. Another burst of fire lit a fire astern, and a third hit the engine-room again, but miraculously the boat escaped serious damage to any vital part.

At twenty past two, making only a moderate speed on one engine, but taking violent avoiding action, Nero Boyd proceeded downstream through the bracketing waterspouts of Dieckmann's coast defence guns, successfully making his way to the open sea and so home to England.

Another Landing

As we leave Boyd's eventful little action, we go back again to the movements of the port column and to the quick kaleidoscope of events that was taking place at about 1.36 a.m., there to witness an episode too much like that in which Mark Rodier had distinguished himself.

Next astern of Platt in the port column was ML No 10, commanded by Lieutenant T. A. M. Collier. He was a fair-haired Scottish yachtsman, quiet, unassuming, an attractive personality with a shrewd sense of humour, who had long been fretting to meet the enemy. He carried a particularly important party – Pritchard himself with his squad of four, a demolition party under Lieutenant Philip Walton, whose task was to destroy the bridge and the lock gates at the northern end of the South Entrance, and their protection squad under Lieutenant 'Tiger' Watson, very young and very small, boyish and eager, who owed his nickname to the fond fancy of his parents in his infancy, but who was that night to prove himself a tiger indeed.

As they neared the harbour and battle began, Watson, kneeling at his Bren-gun, spraying the German searchlights and, exasperated at their habit of switching off as soon as he had got their range, was conscious of nothing but exultation. As they passed the *Sperrbrecher* he saw the burning ammunition and heard the screams of their wounded. He heard other screams, however, from Platt's boat also as, accoutred and ready to land, they approached very close to the mole. On the mole itself he saw a party of Germans running landward. 'One couldn't possibly have missed them,' he said, 'but we all assumed that they were surrendering to David

Birney's assault party, especially as they appeared to have their hands up.'

At this moment Collier turned in to port and the thrill of the moment was on them all. Sub-Lieutenant Hampshire and his bow party, however, who were to have removed the port rail to ease the landing of the heavily laden soldiers, lay all dead or wounded. With Platt backing out on fire as he came in, Collier gained the mole by a remarkably fine example of cool and able handling, avoiding Platt on his port hand and bringing his ship neatly to the foot of the long steps that led upwards to the land. Clambering over the rail, Watson's party first, followed by Walton's, followed by Pritchard's, the soldiers were swiftly ashore and running up the steps to enact those vivid events of which we shall read in the next chapter.

Collier, having thus accomplished the first part of his mission, had no more to do until the signal was given for re-embarkation of the commandos. He therefore made out into midstream and manoeuvred under heavy fire for about half an hour, when, perhaps with the intention of awaiting the return of his commandos under the defilade of the quay wall, he swung in again towards the mole. But he was hit again and again and, catching fire near the end of the mole, was obliged to give the order to abandon ship. We have already seen how his friend Ted Burt came in to his assistance, how, wounded very badly, he refused it with Spartan integrity and how, a little distance apart, the two drifted out in flames and presently blew up. Eight of Collier's ship's company were killed.

'Don't Go In'

Despite Collier's success, the Old Mole was from the first a very hot spot. The remaining four motor launches in the port column were coming up fast on each other's heels at less than a minute's interval, but only one of them got close enough to land and all were forced to withdraw.

The one exception was ML 12, immediately astern of Collier, commanded by Lieutenant N. B. H. Wallis, an Australian, very broad-shouldered, deep-chested, dark and very good-looking, a qualified air pilot and accomplished swimmer. His troops were a small demolition party under Captain E. W. Bradley, a very tall young officer who had seen a good deal of service and who carried a cavalry trumpet on his back. With them were Edward Gilling, one of the journalists, who remained on the bridge throughout, and the extra doctor, Captain D. Paton.

Like Collier less than a minute before, Wallis passed Platt backing out from the mole on fire, and as he did so Platt called to him:

'Don't go in! It's impossible to land.'

But Wallis, coming in at eighteen knots, was unable to conform. He succeeded in coming alongside, while Bradley shot down an enemy party attempting to drop grenades on them from above; but, missing the landing step in the confusion, Wallis found it impossible to land his troops at the twenty-five-feet-high quay wall. Backing and making another attempt, he appears to have grounded or struck an underground obstruction. Since the mole was in enemy hands and Bradley's small party was quite unsuitable to fight an opposed landing, the two officers reluctantly decided to abandon the attempt.

Firm and cool throughout, but with agonized self-questioning, Wallis pulled out, sailed over to the eastern bank to engage batteries and searchlights on that side and withdrew downriver at 2.30.

ML 13, commanded by Horlock, who had taken over at sea after the expedition left Falmouth, also failed to get in. Like others, Horlock was blinded by searchlights, overshot his mark and on returning found the fire too hot to attempt a landing.

Henderson, in No 15, also failed, attempting first the Old Mole, where he was covered with spray from near misses by heavy shells, and then the Old Entrance before withdrawing; but after regaining the open sea he was to be involved in a fierce little fight which was a minor epic in itself and which we shall find specially recorded in Chapter 18.

Last of all, in ML 15, came Falconar, whom we have seen embark Briault's commandos while at sea. These were Hodgson's assault party and Barling's medical party. They were out of their proper order, although Falconar had caught up the main force just after making contact with *Sturgeon*.

Falconar also overshot the mole. He went about and was able

to pick out the mole, but by this time he had no guns in action; his after Oerlikon, served with great gallantry by Ordinary Seaman Tew, had had a direct hit, his forward Oerlikon and both Lewis guns were jammed. The gallant Hodgson was dead, killed outright in the approach, and Oughtred and Sergeant Baron badly wounded.

In these circumstances it was useless, he properly decided, to attempt a landing, and he withdrew downriver, still under heavy fire and with the tracers going right through the hull from one side of the ship to the other where Barling was attending the wounded below deck. Before reaching the facilities of a destroyer Oughtred was almost exsanguinated.

All these four boats successfully evaded the fire of the heavy coast defence guns and gained the open sea.

Ryder's Withdrawal

During the greater part of the time that these things were going on Ryder was still on board the little gunboat in the partial shelter of the Old Entrance. The motor launches came and went and last of all Wynn went. The sounds of battle crashed violently on every hand, but the greatest crashes were the welcome roars of our own demolitions and to Ryder's ear each was one more bold entry in the log of success, adding to the triumphant record of Beattie's performance. To him, therefore, it seemed that the night was going well, for within the enclosure of the Old Entrance he could see little of what was occurring outside and the loss of wireless communications prohibited any news reaching him.

Somewhere towards 2.30 a.m., therefore, after having seen Wynn shoot his delayed-action torpedoes and leave for home, he ordered Curtis to take the gunboat out, in order that he might see how things were going at the Old Mole.

The spectacle that was revealed astounded and for a moment dismayed him. 'It was the only time,' observed Dunstan Curtis, 'that I ever saw him momentarily at a loss.' He is said to have ejaculated: 'Good lord! What the hell do we do now?' The scenes that have just been recorded were seen at their culmination. The remains of five motor launches – those of Tillie, Stephens, Platt, Beart and Nock – were burning fiercely and even while he looked a trickle of flame began to spread astern of Wynn. Other boats could be seen withdrawing. The black smoke of the conflagrations, the white smoke-floats of boats making their withdrawals, and the dust of the explosions ashore drifted across the searchlight beams, while the noises of the battles by land and by water made still more uncertain the interpretation of a confused situation.

As he quickly appraised this sinister picture, but still hoping that the mole was in our possession, Ryder observed Collier approaching it for the second time, under heavy fire. He saw Collier's boat hit, burst into flames and begin to drift away, and he saw also Burt come in undaunted to his aid. He therefore ordered Curtis to take the gunboat in immediately to their support.

At once the gunboat herself came under increased fire, from every quarter, but it was at this time that the skill and gallantry of Able Seaman Savage, and his No 2, Able Seaman F. A. Smith, shone at their highest, an inspiration to all. Standing up in the bows at his pom-pom, completely exposed and with no gun shield, the burly, bearded seaman and his shipmate engaged, unmoved by the confusion of tracers that spun round them as in a web. While Curtis closed the mole to within about two hundred and fifty yards, Savage and Smith fought a duel with the specially dangerous gun 63 in the concrete emplacement on the mole itself. So steady was their shooting that they put one or more shells actually within the embrasure of the emplacement. The enemy gun was immediately silenced.

Curtis then directed Savage on to the searchlight that was throwing its beam dead ahead of the mole, but this proved too difficult a target; so also was the gun, silhouetted against the bizarre night skyline, on top of the building just inshore of the mole. A party of Germans was then seen to run down the mole to re-man the gun that had been silenced, but once again Savage, with cool and steady hand, put his little shells right inside.

Meantime the gunboat herself, now the last vessel left afloat on the whole scene, was under fire from all directions, and being repeatedly hit. Those on board her could see the coloured tracers converging upon them like the spokes of a wheel or like some great display of fireworks. With desolation over all the face of the water, there was clearly nothing more that Ryder could do at the mole and he ordered Curtis to return once more to the Old Entrance in an attempt to make contact with Newman ashore and let him know that there were now no craft left to take his commandos home.

On arrival at the Old Entrance, however, he was dismayed to see a strange and uncertain battle going on. Someone had boarded the *Campbeltown* and was manning her Oerlikons. A fierce battle was going on across the Old Entrance, and Ryder clearly observed a figure fire several bursts from one of the destroyer's after band-stands before being shot dead itself. Was this little battle with Roderick's party re-crossing the fo'c'sle? Or were the Germans themselves shooting at each other? Or was it perhaps some small commando party that had got ashore by swimming or by raft and was now bravely playing an impromptu part? For friend and foe were indistinguishable from one another. To Ryder, the only certainty was that the way in to the Old Entrance was now peremptorily barred.

While Savage continued to engage the enemy, pitting his little gun now against the difficult skyline targets beyond the Sub-marine Basin, Ryder looked regretfully round him. Crouching down on the bridge, he held a quick consultation with Green and Curtis, while the boat lay perilously stopped and shielded only by a smoke float.

It went very hard indeed with Ryder to leave Charles Newman and his commandos encircled by enemies ashore. But there seemed nothing more that could be done, and the means of communication were gone. Both points of embarkation were in enemy hands. The melancholy spectacle in the river showed no craft but themselves that were not on fire. The little gunboat was loaded down with wounded. Nearly every seaman had been hit and many of the wounded from *Campbeltown* had been hit a second time. It was scarcely possible to move on deck without treading on them. There was no one left to man even the two Bren-guns mounted aft.

Regretfully, Ryder decided that there was no course open to him but to withdraw. The main purposes of the expedition had been brilliantly achieved. The secondary purposes had failed, but the slaughter of the small boats had been almost inevitable the

moment surprise had been lost. He gave Curtis the order, and
the little gunboat shot off downriver, under the following beams
of the searchlights and the pursuing shells, at twenty-four knots.

The Plan That Went Awry

The outcome of all this sad but gallant effort, therefore, was that
seven motor launches and many brave lives were lost in this river
battle – and more are to be lost before our story is done – and that
only a handful of commandos made a successful landing. Newman's
own headquarters, Haines's party, the party of Pritchard, Watson
and Walton, and the lone Michael Burn – only these got ashore from
the launches and were able to advance, though Burt and Beart had
very creditably landed their men also. The most grievous losses were
those of the vessels carrying the assault troops. Had these got ashore
– the parties of Birney, Hodgson, Burn and Hooper – the results
would almost certainly have been even more brilliant than they were.

Anyone could have foretold that such a fate was almost inevitable if the light wooden launches were to be called upon to
face serious fire from the shore. They were never intended for this
sort of furious purpose. Even so, they stood up wonderfully to the
cannon-fire of Oerlikons and even to the shells of Bofors. At such
short ranges the Germans could scarcely miss. One is not quite
sure how to account for the reports of heavier shellfire in the
vicinity of the harbour, but no doubt this might have come from
No 2 battery of Dieckmann's 280 Battalion at Le Pointeau, which
were 75 mm guns on pedestal mountings with an all-round
traverse. Their range to the Old Mole was less than three miles
and they fired one thousand three hundred rounds that night. The
6.6-inch (17 cm) battery at Pointe de l'Eve, we are told, could
traverse round nearly as far as the *Sperrbrecher*.

One need not be surprised that there was a great deal of heart-
burning and self-questioning among those who were prevented
from attaining their objectives. The commandos, long trained and
eager for operations and specially trained for this one, were highly
tuned and in that state of exaltation which we have noted. All felt
bitterly disappointed and some felt an angry frustration at this
deflation of high hopes. The motor-launch commanders felt no
less keenly what appeared to some of them at the time to be a

failure of their mission. One has but to read these pages, however, and those which follow, to be convinced that St Nazaire provides no instance of any failures, but only of impossibilities.

The contrast with the success of *Campbeltown* and of the commandos landed from her is striking, and one may indeed consider that if, for this dangerous expedition undertaken at their own request, the Admiralty had made the effort to provide a second destroyer, according to the very first plan devised by the COHQ committee, there would likewise have been a still more brilliant result and a smaller loss of gallant lives. Such speculations are by no means idle, for they point a lesson. At the same time, the greater lesson lies in the untimely loss of the bombing support. The tactical principle upon which the whole plan was based was that of surprise. Surprise might conceivably have been obtained if there had been no bombing at all, provided one could legitimately suppose that a first-class enemy was not on the alert in such highly sensitive waters; but it would have been virtually certain if, as planned, the enemy's attention had continued to be distracted by aircraft dropping anything, even, as Haydon had said, soda-water bottles, to mystify and alarm.

With this view the Germans themselves agreed, admitting, as Mecke says, that the air-raid succeeded in distracting attention until that point was reached when its very peculiar nature, and finally the cessation of bombing made it obvious to him that 'some devilry' was afoot calling for vigilance elsewhere than in the sky.

We have already seen that, after intense pressing at the last minute from COHQ, Bomber Command, overcoming some lukewarmness to an operation which heavily taxed their resources, requiring the attack to be sustained for four and a half hours, responded generously enough with sixty-two bombers. We have also seen, however, the inflexible restrictions that were imposed upon pilots, partly as a result of Cabinet directions. It was these restrictions that brought the efforts of pilots to nought and upset the conception and balance of the plan.

Willetts himself flew with the bombers, as did Hughes-Hallett. Sixty-two Wellingtons and Whitleys actually took off from England, all but three reaching the target area. On arrival, however, they found ten-tenths cloud up to eight thousand feet, with

bad icing conditions. In a report and commentary to the Director
of Bombing subsequently Willetts records that, in consequence,
only four aircraft actually bombed, and 'a considerable number of
aircraft were therefore flying over St Nazaire before and during
the operation without actually intervening'.

He observed cogently that 'an important omission from the
plan was the action necessary should aircraft be despatched from
this country which, on arrival, found conditions such that aimed
bombing could not be done'. The target area, he adds, was clearly
disclosed to pilots 'by the flash of flak through the clouds' and he
suggests that the sacrifice of surprise might have been mitigated
had pilots been allowed to bomb on positions so estimated.

Two other facts, however, stand out. First, we know from the
German naval staff's subsequent study of the battle and from
Mecke's action report, that, except for scattered patches, there
was no cloud below three thousand two hundred feet. Second, the
notion of one bomb only per run from a considerable force of
aircraft, which 'pressed their attack with determination', was not
good enough to fool so able and experienced a commander as
Mecke.

Willetts returned sad at heart, and a squadron-leader back in
England next day said, almost in tears: 'If you had only *told* us
what it was all in aid of, we would have come down to nought feet
and given them everything we had.'

This, indeed, was what Newman had asked for, but had been
told that he could not have. But as a final note on this issue there
remains the typical observation made to him by Mr Churchill
when the two met in after years. 'The only person you can blame
for the lack of air support,' said Mr Churchill, 'is me.'

There was still a long road to travel before the true significance
of 'Combined Operations' was to be fully understood and St
Nazaire, both in its glory and its tears, was to provide one of the
clearest fingerposts to the final triumph.

17. THE DOCKYARD BATTLE

That portion of the St Nazaire docks lying between the Old Entrance and the new Southern Entrance, which is to be the scene of the commandos' confused and bitter fighting at close quarters, is divided into two parts. The dividing line is the broad Place de la Vieille Ville, which we shall call Old Town Place. About one hundred and twenty feet wide, it runs almost directly from the Old Mole to the modern town by way of Bridge D, that bridge which is to be the scene of one of our most dramatic and inspiring moments, and which was to be graven in the minds of the commandos ever after as the 'Bridge of Memories'. The breadth and directness of Old Town Place provides a splendid field of fire for any weapons that command it, and a well-placed machine-gun, stoutly manned, can make it impossible for any to traverse its length in daylight.

To the south of Old Town Place lies the Old Town itself, a dense concentration composed mainly of small buildings in narrow streets, but there are also a few larger buildings, such as the power station, to which, with Pritchard, we shall pay a fleeting and fruitless visit.

North of this broad and commanding dividing line lies an assembly of long warehouses and other sheds in parallel rows, with an hydraulic station among them. At the extreme north of this area, close to Roy's Bridge G, lie the offices of the dockyard roads and bridges engineer, which is the building that Newman has selected from air photographs as his battle headquarters.

This area, like all dockyard warehouse areas, is traversed and intersected by a system of railway loops and sidings, as indeed is the whole of the dockyard. On this night numbers of railway

trucks stand on these lines, and they are to afford valuable cover
to the raiding commandos at a vital moment.

*

Charles Newman disembarked from the gunboat in the Old
Entrance somewhere about 1.40 a.m. He was feeling in high
spirits and eager to get ashore. He had just seen Troop Sergeant-
Major Haines disembark from Rodier's boat and the spectacle of
Campbeltown rammed fast into her target, like an arrow in the
gold, was a splendid prologue for the great drama that he saw and
heard unfolding so violently around him. Though he might have
seen Stephens and Tillie hit, he was quite unaware of the full
malevolence of the fortune that was at that moment beginning
to assail the motor launches. The signs were still fair and the call
of the Tommy-guns ashore told Newman that his ardent commandos were about their work.

Preceded by Murdoch and Kelly, his two Tommy-gunners, he
sprang ashore eagerly at the wooden jetty on the south side of the
Old Entrance. The soil of France! For two years he had trained
for such a moment and dreamed of it. As his rubber boots trod
the harsh quayside he tingled with exhilaration. Then he went
forward at a steady double followed by the remainder of his staff.

The brilliant light of the quayside, chequered by the sharp,
black shadows of buildings, gave place gradually to a dimmer
half light, through which they moved apparently unseen by the
enemy, beneath the streams of tracered projectiles that poured
overhead. As he moved up to the building he had selected for
his headquarters, close to Bridge G, Newman could see no sign
of any of his commandos. He expected to see Moss already at
the headquarters, but the heroic figure of the sergeant-major
at just about that moment slipped lifeless from the raft on which
he had given up his position to Private Diamond.

Newman therefore found his headquarters apparently deserted, but on walking round it to find an entrance he bumped
helmets round a corner with a German. It is characteristic of him
that he instinctively said: 'Sorry.' The startled German, for his
part, threw up his hands and began talking volubly. Instantly
Terry, who spoke German, was upon him and Newman laughed

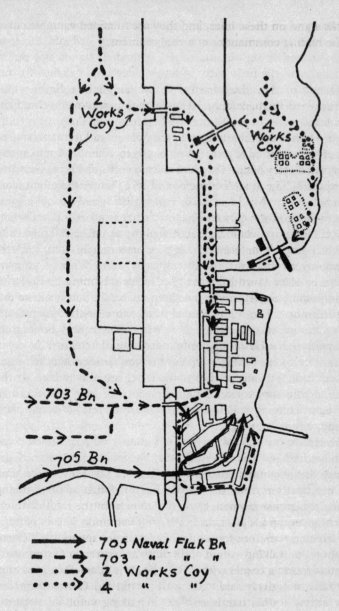

Fig 18. The German counterattack.

ironically when he learned that his chosen headquarters was itself a German headquarters of some sort. Terry ordered the man to go in and bring out the others with their hands up, but at that moment the little party of seven came under dangerous fire from one of the minesweepers in the Submarine Basin which had spotted them, and accordingly they took cover behind the building.

As we have seen in earlier chapters, parties of Germans, roused out of their startled surprise, now began to come alive and spring to arms on every hand. They had reacted very quickly, as Germans always do. The first *Stosstruppen* of 703 Naval Flak Battalion, ordered out by Mecke at 1.20, crossed Bridge D at 1.50, being rapidly joined by others and by the parties from 705 Battalion by way of the bridge just to the south, making a total of 280 men from Mecke's brigade before very long. A detachment from 2 Works Company also arrived, but attempts by other Works Company troops to come down from the north were frustrated by Roderick and the spirited party on the northern caisson. Other detachments were also on the move – those of naval shore establishments, the crews ashore of the tankers *Uckermark*, *Passat* and *Schledstadt*, and perhaps the Harbour Commander's guard company. Many of these were by no means troops of the best quality, Mecke's anti-aircraft troops being no doubt the best, but they added to the considerable superiority of numbers, for not more than 113 of Newman's men were landed effectively, some forty of whom were armed only with pistols.

Except in one instance which will shortly be related, the commandos had not the least difficulty in dealing with any of the troops that they met; what was much more serious to them than the superiority of numbers was the superior weight of fire from the fixed gun positions and from the minesweepers and harbour defence craft, some of them firing from extremely close quarters, to which were quickly added several machine-guns. These weapons, particularly those of the ships in harbour and the hastily mounted machine-guns, very soon began to turn their attention from the motor launches to the little parties of men that they now saw darting about in the searchlight beams or among the shadows of buildings and dumps and railway tracks. Later the quadruple

20 mm beyond the Submarine Basin began to sweep this area with their more venomous fire and occasionally, from some unidentified battery, there came the sharp crump of an airburst shell overhead.

With Moss and his important party missing, Newman was therefore very relieved when his tiny headquarters was augmented by the special task party of Troop Sergeant-Major Haines, which joined him soon after he had taken up his impromptu headquarters. The rugged little sergeant-major, in fact, had arrived before Newman and then moved off for his special task of silencing the guns reported to be on the sea wall between the mole and the Old Entrance. Finding none there, he reported to Newman in accordance with his orders. Standing to attention as on the parade ground, he listened quietly as Newman told him:

'Stay near me in case I want you; because you are the only reserve I have now got.'

He very soon did need him, for fire from one of the 20 mm guns beyond the Submarine Basin and from machine-guns mounted on the roof of the pens began to harass them. Newman called up Haines and said:

'We have simply got to stop these guns. What have you got you can take them on with?'

'I've got a 2-inch mortar, sir. No sights, but it's the only thing we've got.'

With extraordinary unconcern, Haines took forward in his great hands a little 2-inch mortar, sitting it slap in the open near the quayside of the Submarine Basin just beyond the end of one of the warehouses. Here he knelt down and, taking the small bombs that were passed to him by a chain of hands, including Newman's, from behind the cover of the building, dropped them down the barrel of the mortar, to go soaring high into the air and on to the enemy positions only two hundred yards away. With the enemy fire plunging down on the very spot where he knelt, but with unsurpassable coolness, he successfully silenced one position after another, if only temporarily.

There then came against him one of the armed vessels in the basin, the flash of his mortar and the crump of its bombs being only too audaciously apparent. Coming close in, the ship made his position a veritable death trap. Quite unperturbed, however, Haines leaped over to a Bren-gun that some fallen comrade had left, and although the fire from the ship's machine-guns was cascading in the very place where he was now lying, he sent a series of bursts so devastating and so well directed that the ship ceased fire and sheered away.

All this time Newman was quite in ignorance of the progress of the battle elsewhere, for, as we know, he never succeeded in establishing wireless communication with Ryder, though the 38 set on the gunboat had its own independent rod aerial. Sergeant Steel opened up his own set immediately in the shelter of Newman's headquarter building, and almost at once heard Lance-Corporal Fyfe, Copland's signaller in the Normandie Dock area. But Newman was not interested in Copland. He kept anxiously asking: 'Have you got the boat yet?' But Steele, swinging his dial from time to time, chanted 'Newman calling Ryder – Newman calling Ryder' for over an hour without any effect, till at length there was disclosed a situation in which wireless could only too clearly have no value.

The Captain and the Corporals

The silence of the radio, however, was not matched by the din and clamour all around, and very soon sounds of fresh Tommy-gun fire on his left told Newman that something was afoot there also.

This was the party successfully landed with skill and daring at the Old Mole by Collier's ML 11, containing Philip Walton's team for destroying Bridge D, Watson's protection squad and Pritchard's demolition control team. Pritchard's tasks were to control the timings of the demolitions, to help where necessary and to attack targets of opportunity.

With Watson's squad leading, followed by Walton's, followed by Pritchard's, this little band ran quickly up the steps to the landward end of the mole. Watson had orders that if his was the only squad to gain the mole he was to attack and hold it himself. He could probably have done so, had he not been led to believe that Birney had already arrived. As it was, he stopped to examine and empty his Tommy-gun into what appeared to be a new gun position at the top of the steps, until the cry came up from Pritchard in the rear:

'What are you up to, Tiger? Get on!'

Without more ado, the three parties made straight for Bridge D, but very soon came under fire. In commando fashion they did not wait for each other's support, but made straight for their objectives independently. Pritchard, passing two bodies dead or wounded on the ground, reached Bridge D the first, having probably taken a different route from Watson and Walton and perhaps having seen the trouble into which they both ran.

Pritchard's party consisted of four corporals – I. L. Maclagan, a Royal Engineer Territorial of slight stature who was an apprenticed civil engineer of Carnoustie, J. Deans and H. Shipton, all of 9 Commando, and S. Chetwynd, of 12 Commando. Approaching the lock of the Southern Entrance, they beheld before them the steel latticework swing bridge which was Walton's objective, looming in the half darkness ahead of them like the ribs of some giant skeleton. There was no cover at all on the bare and open quay, except for a small concrete hut, about ten feet square, a few yards from the bridge. To this Pritchard and his corporals sprinted, dumping their rucksacks on its sheltered side – four men alone in the half light with the enemy just across the bridge and all behind them also. Pritchard, looking round at once for prey, saw two ships berthed alongside each other against the quay of the Submarine Basin, forty yards to his right, and in a moment of inspired daring he whispered to Maclagan:

'Mac, I'm going to sink those two ships. Get out two 5-lb charges.'

Under full observation from an enemy scarcely sixty yards away, the two men ran to the quayside, jumped on to the nearer ship, crossed to the second and coolly lowered the charges between the two ships, three feet below water. They tied them to the rail of the ship, pulled the igniter pins and hurried back to the shelter of the hut.

There Pritchard gave instructions to the other three corporals, in the absence of Watson's party, to 'do what you can' to the swing bridge, while he and Maclagan went round to visit, as he hoped, the other demolition parties in that area. He lingered a moment, however, listening for what he hoped for, and before they separated smiled happily as the charges between the two ships blew up with a muffled roar, followed by a violent and prolonged hissing which told convincingly that the charges had been accurately laid against the ships' boiler-rooms. When Newman passed there nearly two hours later he found the two ships sunk. They were the tugs *Champion* and *Pornic*.

Having accomplished this daring impromptu act, Pritchard and Maclagan, the tall Welshman and the smaller Scot, set out at a trot towards the South Entrance, going boldly and silently along the open lock side, in the half light from the spill of the searchlight beams and from the moon that shone through the high cloud. But they passed in turn one lock gate after another, and the farther bridge likewise, disappointed to find no demolition parties yet arrived. At the most southerly gate they turned left to visit the power station that operated all these southern lock gates, close by on the edge of the Old Town. They could hear the tread of leather-soled boots, that signal which always gave notice to commandos of the presence of an enemy near at hand, but they saw no one.

At the power station Pritchard therefore decided that he must go back to find out what was happening. Together with his corporal, he turned about left-handed and began trotting across the Old Town, making for Bridge D again, Maclagan on Pritchard's left. They passed through a labyrinth of small buildings, making their way through back yards and narrow streets.

They were nearly half way across the Old Town when, at a sudden corner in the half light, Pritchard ran straight into a German. The end came swiftly. At one second they met and in the next Pritchard had fallen backwards, possibly bayoneted, for no shot was fired by either. Maclagan took a quick pace forward and riddled the German with his Tommy-gun.

He then dropped down on his knees beside his leader. Pritchard was breathing terribly heavily and for a few moments could not speak. Then he said:

'That you, Mac? Don't stop for me. Go straight back and report to HQ. That's an order.' So far as we know, he never spoke again.

This order the corporal was desperately unwilling to obey, but the tall, strapping Welshman was far too great a weight for his

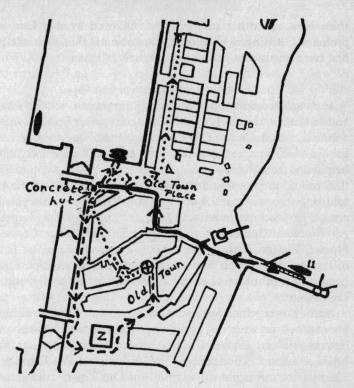

Fig 19. Pritchard's party. Thick line shows probable route of party; broken line, Pritchard and Maclagan; dotted line, Maclagan alone. Cross within circle is where Pritchard believed killed. Z, the power station.

smaller frame. He resolved therefore to return to the concrete hut, send one of his comrades to headquarters, and bring the others to Pritchard's assistance.

He made his way back alone through the eerie, hostile streets and reached the concrete hut safely, but all that there was to be seen was a dead body. It was that of Philip Walton.

Still quite alone, therefore, in the heart of enemy territory, Maclagan, in a remarkable example of cool and steady bearing, continued on his way, across the dangerous and exposed Old Town Place, through the rows of warehouses and so to Newman's battle headquarters. There he asked for help to bring Pritchard in, but was told it was out of the question. At some time or other Corporal Deans and Corporal Chetwynd were also killed, Maclagan and Shipton being the only survivors of Pritchard's party.

Tiger's Teeth

Watson's tiny squad comprised young Sergeant Wickson, steady and reliable, Lance-Corporal Grief, an irrepressible, sharp-featured, ribald Cockney, the sturdy Private Davidson and the good-looking Private Lawson, with a frank and open face, curly hair and a staunch heart.

Coming up immediately behind them was Philip Walton, the schoolmaster, quiet and wiry, with his demolition team for the critical Bridge D, consisting of Sergeant Dick Bradley, Sergeant Alf Searson, Corporal George Wheeler and Lance-Corporal Homer. Watson, with boyish eagerness, set off at a smart pace, too smart, indeed, for Walton's heavily laden demolition team, from whom they soon became separated. At the first group of buildings after passing the landward end of the mole, Watson saw in the half light what appeared to be a group of French civilians. He shouted to them, as he had been instructed: 'Dedans vite' (Inside quickly), and fired a burst from his Tommy-gun over their heads as he ran. They disappeared, and he saw also a group of German soldiers running away into the Old Town – the second group that he had already seen to run away.

Full of confidence, therefore, he doubled along the broad open space of Old Town Place, but had gone only about one hundred and fifty yards before he met some Germans who did not run away. He called to them: 'Hände hoch!' (Hands up!) But they answered him with a grenade and a similar summons. Himself a little way in front of his squad, he therefore dropped to the ground to engage them, his orders having been to keep the enemy occupied while the demolition team went on, then to disengage and join up again.

Disengagement became difficult, however, when a machine-gun opened up on him from a rooftop to his left. He was almost stunned by a grenade that fell and burst beside him. With a metallic clang a litter tin attached to a lamp-post just above his head was riddled with bullets. Another bullet or other projectile burst open his haversack of grenades and the movement of scrabbling about to pick them up drew fresh fire. From an emplacement beyond Bridge D another machine-gun began spraying the area at random. Watson therefore lay low for a minute till the shooting stopped, then rose quickly and darted back several yards to rejoin his squad, who had taken cover behind a railway truck and who would have shot him but for his blue pinpoint torch.

Watson was upset to find the demolition party here also, but without Walton; they had seen him fall while running across Old Town Place, but in fact, unknown to all, Walton was with great daring making his way to the bridge alone, there to die in an heroic attempt to lay his charges single-handed at point-blank range. The subsequent study of the battle by the German naval staff reveals that German troops found charges actually laid on this bridge, though whether by Walton or by one of Pritchard's corporals who was killed we know not.

To Watson's urgent enquiries, Corporal Wheeler replied that they had been unable to cross the road and that he thought Walton must have been killed. Watson shouted for his friend, who had been to him as an elder brother, without result and turned to question Sergeant Bradley, when the sergeant was shot through the lung by the rooftop machine-gun. While bending down to administer morphia, Watson himself was wounded in the buttock. Bradley was dragged under better cover, but before long he was shot again.

To Watson the check that he had suffered was merely a fresh spur and goad, quickening his purpose and sharpening his temper. Some reinforcement was clearly necessary for his tiny squad, but when he raised his Very-light pistol to fire the required signal it was shot out of his hand. He therefore sent Wheeler to run to Newman's HQ with the request for help. Determined to maintain his purpose he then attempted a new approach, moving half right through the sheds and warehouses north of him towards the Submarine Basin, closely accompanied by Private Lawson. He had nearly reached the quayside when he heard German voices at the end of an alley between the warehouse, and, instead of ignoring them, he hurled a grenade.

He was answered by a violent burst of machine-gun fire, which enveloped him in clouds of dust from shattered bricks at head level from the wall alongside him and from cement stored in the warehouse. This brusque stoppage came from one of the ships of 16 Minesweeper Flotilla still berthed at the quayside only a few yards from him; he saw her outline clearly, heard her engine-room telegraph and heard the orders from her bridge. He also saw some cement bags lying in the road and thought in the half light that they were his comrades. His calls to them brought no answer and the way ahead was blocked by wire. Frustrated a second time, he made his way back through the shadows to Newman's HQ, accompanied by the bewildered but staunch and obedient Lawson and pursued by the ship's malevolent machine-gun.

Among all the wrathful clamour and the darting tracer Watson found Newman – who was not yet aware of the failure of the Old Mole landings – jovial, kind and reassuring.

'Hard luck, Tiger,' he said. 'You've done jolly well. I can let you have a couple more Tommy-gunners. Go back and have another shot.'

Not much relishing this order, but determined to do his damnedest, the little officer, still accompanied by the faithful Lawson, retraced his steps. 'I was convinced,' he said, 'that it meant certain death, but orders were orders.' He made contact again with Sergeant Wickson and the remainder of the party and they turned about. His blood was up. He was damned well going for it bald-headed now. Observing one man straggling, he shouted at him angrily:

'Do you want to live for ever?'

The effect of this startling challenge (to be attributed in the London Press later to someone else) was magical and by the time that they had all reassembled on the dangerous edge of Old Town Place, they had all become charged with the same burning ardour. They were at a point close to where they had left Sergeant Bradley, of whom they could see no sign. What they did see on that spot was a party of Germans standing easy, and these they wiped out at a few yards' range.

While they were bracing themselves for the new effort, a runner arrived from headquarters cancelling the order and instructing them to assemble with the other parties, for it must have been about now that Newman had seen Maclagan, had learnt from him

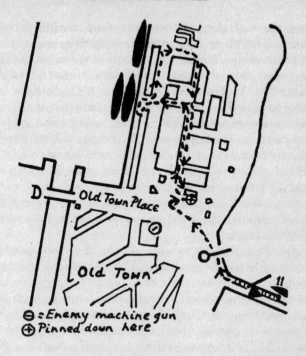

Fig 20. Watson's route.

that none of the demolition teams for the Southern Entrance had
yet arrived and had begun to realize accordingly that these targets
might be beyond accomplishment. Watson complied with mixed
feelings, for from now till the painful end he was in an angry
mood, burning to have it out with the enemy in atonement for the
failure of his mission; but he had done better than he knew, for his
spirited little fight had created a valuable diversion, distracting
enemy attention from what was now a more vital area and keeping
at bay superior forces that would otherwise have been a danger to
the remainder of Newman's troops, who were now beginning
stealthily to muster together.

The Happy Soldier

The sounds of Watson's little fight had told Newman that some
at least of his troops had landed at the Old Mole and were about

their business. He had no reason yet to suppose that the mole was not in our hands or that anything on the left wing of the battle had gone seriously wrong. On the contrary, sounds of a different sort began more definitely to tell him a story of resounding success. One by one the explosions on his right flank and rear began to tell their tale. He heard Purdon's and Smalley's winding-houses go up, Chant's deep underground explosion in the pump house, shaking the earth, and the dull thud and boom of the northern caisson's underwater burst. He saw the tall flames leap into the sky and heard the débris of all these destructions clattering around. He felt tremendously exhilarated and began to crack jokes with his staff. On the left, however, no such detonations interrupted the unceasing crash and clatter of guns and machine-guns.

Apart from those who were already in his designated head-quarters, parties of the enemy in this confused situation were extremely close to Newman's small team. One party was no more than twenty yards away, occasionally lobbing grenades, and small-arms fire seemed to be coming from every direction, besides the vicious air crumps from some unidentified battery from time to time. But no man was ever further from losing his nerve than Charles Newman. His easy and unruffled disposition and his jovial manner were an inspiration in a situation in which excite-ment and uncertainty might have unsteadied the best of troops. Mindful of the need of being personally out in the open with his men, he abandoned the idea of occupying his proposed head-quarter house, and after some grenades had been thrown into it, took up a fresh position behind a shed near the quay (where Haines had fired his mortar), from which he could check the demolition parties as they came in and direct them, as he hoped, to the determined point of re-embarkation on the Old Mole.

One by one these parties began to come in, the young officers in charge of each – all of them wounded, though Montgomery only slightly – reporting personally to Colonel Charles. All those who could do so stood up and saluted as though on parade. Tremendously pleased with them all, Newman rewarded them with his genial smile – the smile that they were always so glad to see – and said:

'Well done, old boy. Better move along now towards the mole and wait for Major Bill.'

Copland came in very soon after, giving Newman the good news from the Normandie Dock area, and the less promising news of Burn's lone arrival far away at Bridge M. The time had therefore come to fire the rain rockets that were the signal for the withdrawal, but there were no rockets, for they had all been lost when Regimental Sergeant-Major Moss had gone down in the river. Newman therefore called upon Lance-Corporal Harrington to go out and take verbal withdrawal orders to Roderick, a quarter of a mile away and to Roy. This hazardous order Harrington acknowledged with a salute and, as upon an exercise, set out alone at the double with complete composure. He crossed Roy's fireswept bridge after due challenge and reply, and swung to the right to traverse the dangerous no-man's-land beyond which lay the *Campbeltown* on her altar of sacrifice. On the way across the intimidating scene he was fortunate enough to meet Roderick, who, as we have seen, had already begun his withdrawal. The gallant lance-corporal returned, passed the order to Roy also and reported back to his CO with another parade ground salute.

'When the situation is uncertain or confused, collect your forces.' By the time that Roderick and Roy had completed their withdrawals, this maxim was being complied with. Newman and his commandos, now reduced by fatal casualties and by the re-embarkation of Smalley's party to something just under a hundred, of whom many were wounded, had collected loosely together in the warehouse area. Newman now knew that the main purpose of the expedition, as Haydon had set it out, had been achieved. The situation on the left was dubious, but, so far, no more than that. The general impression on his buoyant mind, therefore, was that the operation was developing favourably. Of the fate of the motor launches he had little or no knowledge, for where he stood the warehouses and railway trucks acted as a baffle to any view of the river.

Thus when Copland said that he would push along to organize the re-embarkation, for which the parties from the north were now ready, Newman said: 'I'll come with you, Bill.'

Together they made their way south-eastward through the

ranked warehouses, keeping to the selvedge of black shadow that bordered the buildings under the contrasting harsh, white beams. Emerging from the buildings to a line of railway trucks, they had their first glimpse of the river north of the mole and were all brought up standing by the menacing spectacle that confronted their astonished gaze.

Struck with consternation, Newman exclaimed involuntarily: 'Good heavens, Bill! Surely those aren't ours!'

Nothing, in the recorded words of Copland, more exactly resembled a scene from the *Inferno*. The very river itself was on fire. Close in to the mole the hulks of burnt-out motor launches still glowed red on the water, while in the night beyond, seemingly suspended in the air, there blazed a sea of burning petrol which had spread outwards and outwards from each burning ship or had been splayed far and wide like so many fountains of fire as other craft blew up. The flames leapt and flickered from the very water. From this floating furnace a pall of black smoke, frustrating the glare of the searchlights, rolled indolently towards the north-west in the almost still air, mingled with the dissolving white clouds from the withdrawal smoke of the escaping launches. From out this curtain of smoke there shot towards the watching officers, like sudden meteorites in the night sky, the burning trails of cannon-fire from the batteries at Mindin Point beyond. In all this forbidding scene there was no sign of life, nor did it seem possible that there could be life; nor was there any sign of movement, except the leaping flames and the slowly drifting smoke. And on the Old Mole itself the still-glaring searchlight at its tip and the emplaced gun half way along its length, firing far downstream on some target that they could not see, betrayed to the watching officers in whose hands the pier still remained.

For a moment they both gazed in silence, the import of the scene only too apparent. Then, with a little, wry laugh, Newman said:

'Well, Bill, there goes our transport!'

Gone were the hopes of a safe return to their native land. What now? It was characteristic of them both that they accepted the harsh prospect not with mere resignation, still less with despair or with backward-looking thoughts or recriminations, but with a cheerful equanimity which made a call for positive action.

The first requirement was to rally, consolidate and organize for the new situation. The disposition of the parties that were now coming in was confused, the various little bodies grouped loosely together, independently returning fire from enemies only a few yards away as the *Stosstruppen* and others hurried over the bridges of the Southern Entrance and began to probe forward, penetrating the warehouse area. Against such thrusts, tentative and inexperienced though they were, those commandos who were armed with pistols only were ill equipped, and the numerous wounded were an impediment. Copland set briskly to work to re-form the little force, choosing as the rallying ground the loop in the railway one hundred and fifty yards north of the Old Mole, where there was some field of fire and where a few railway trucks gave a little protection. Using the well-armed assault troops to form protective screens, he put out Roy on the southern flank, whence increasing fire was every minute being directed from the Old Town, and Haines to the west, where stood the ranks of warehouses.

Here at this rallying point an extraordinary situation existed. Until the commandos were re-formed, both sides were in considerable confusion. Often only a few yards from each other, friend was not instinctively distinguishable from foe. The winking blue torches, the white webbing and the occasional kilt proved their value but were not infallible, as Sergeant Searson found. The tread of boots and the shouted orders likewise gave clear indication of German presence, but no one knew who was on the other side of a building nor who had thrown a grenade. In Newman's words, the enemy 'were shooting at us round corners'. The gaunt dockyard reverberated to the bursts of Tommy- and Bren-gun, the explosions of hand-grenades, the crack of rifle and pistol and the answering fire of the enemy, echoing among the warehouses and accented by the cries of the wounded of both sides. A post only twenty-five yards away bothered Newman himself until Stanley Day threw them a grenade, saying: 'That's all right now, Colonel.' Perhaps it was this post that had just killed Private Kelly, Newman's gallant Tommy-gunner, who fell at his colonel's side, shot between the eyes.

Steadily augmented in numbers, the Germans were now on all

sides of them, except to the north, probing forward with caution, but were kept firmly at bay by spirited and well-directed fire from troops far more highly trained in the use of infantry close-quarters weapons at night.

Virtually surrounded and their means of withdrawal gone, the commandos nonetheless, now and throughout the tempestuous final hour, never ceased to enjoy a sense of complete superiority over the enemy. They had no sense at all of being cornered or of being at the last ditch or of being in a desperate strait. They intended to retain the initiative as long as possible. Had they not, with the single exception of the party for Bridge D, successfully done what they had come to do? Thus in this most nerve-testing of situations – an infantry close-quarters fight by night – we hear them still laughing and cracking jokes and occasionally cursing each other, taking no notice of all the noise about them, infected by the gaiety of their Colonel Charles. For Newman radiated confidence. His buoyant spirit, his air of cheerful unconcern, his hearty laugh and his friendly word for every man communicated themselves to all.

Newman himself, with the responsibility for men's lives on his shoulders, alone had a moment's doubt. They had, he reflected, accomplished the major part of their mission. They could do no more. Though the idea of giving themselves up was entirely re-pugnant to him, he knew that there could be no dishonour now in doing so. To satisfy his mind, he sought a second opinion, calling Bill Copland into a short conference. Did Copland think, he asked, that they ought 'to call it a day'?

'Certainly not, Colonel,' replied the old warrior of the First World War, who was as cool and unexcited as though on church parade. 'We'll fight our way out.'

Nothing pleased Newman more. He made a quick plan to divide his force up into groups of about twenty, fight their way out of the dockyard, through the town, into the open country beyond and try to make their way in pairs to Spain and thence to Gibraltar. A thousand miles or more, but others had done it. A courageous decision indeed, and one that may well serve as a classic example of the soldierly spirit and of the will of men who are dedicated to fight.

He quietly told Copland and Day his plan, a grenade exploding at their feet as they talked. Copland then moved off to divide the force into detachments of twenty and brought the group leaders to Newman for their orders. Newman's own words vividly illustrate this moment. 'The scene at the Old Mole,' he said, 'is hard to describe. There were flames and smoke everywhere. Some wounded Germans were screaming down an alley and small-arms fire was coming from all the buildings around us. Our own chaps were forming a perimeter round the Old Mole; some railway trucks gave them cover and from behind these they were coolly returning the fire with ever-decreasing ammunition. When the group leaders came up to me for my orders, they saluted and grinned. I told them that, as usual, there was no transport to take us home, and that we should fight our way into the town and from there to open country. No one seemed at all surprised.'

Their shortest route into the town was by Old Town Place and Bridge D, two hundred yards away, but this broad, open approach was so covered by enemy fire that it would be rash to attempt it. The route decided upon, therefore, was through the area of sheds and warehouses to the north of them, and thence back along the quayside of the Submarine Basin, which Watson had already attempted, this route being chosen because by any other they would have to pass between warehouses with the enemy on both sides of them, for the whole of the warehouse area was now alive with Germans. It was a run of some six hundred and fifty yards, which would have to be undertaken by the wounded also.

Quickly and efficiently Copland marshalled the force into their groups, his tall, erect grey-haired figure perfectly cool and collected, a steadying force among all these ardent young men. Making a final round of the positions, accompanied by Private Fahy, he found a party of Germans trying to break through a weak point, and saw them scatter with casualties as Fahy opened up on them with his Tommy-gun.

Then, when all was ready, Copland reported to his colonel.

Breakout

Some time after 3 a.m. this extraordinary column, encumbered with wounded, short of ammunition, with little to hope for but a faint chance of vagrant freedom, began its inspired and defiant dash straight through the serried rows of buildings thronged with enemies firing from every window and lying in wait at a few yards' range at every corner. Little finesse was possible now. Like an old-time garrison sallying out to cut their way through a besieging army, they moved forward at the double with spirits high. They were fewer than a hundred now, a third of them armed with pistols only and nearly one man in three wounded. Burn and a small squad were placed in the van, followed by Roy leading the strongly armed assault and protection parties of Roderick, Watson and Denison; behind these came the more vulnerable demolition teams, while the rearguard was in the sure and strong hands of Troop Sergeant-Major Haines.

They moved by bounds, keeping to the shadowed ways at the edges of the long warehouses and halting from time to time to squat in some dark patch and collect together – sometimes to rush some open stretch by parties under covering fire, or to overcome some point of enemy resistance or to give time for the straggling wounded to catch up. These, obedient to the precept that the lame must not impede operations, fell out to await the inevitable when they could no longer keep up. Gerard Brett, with manifold wounds, could move no further than the first twenty or thirty yards and, giving his Colt to a man who had lost his own, he sank down in a warehouse.

Thus, in good order and with unbroken ranks, the little company fought their way forward at Newman's command of 'Get on, lads! Get on!' Nearly all the searchlights were out now, but the fires still glowed and leapt on the tortured water behind them as the lost launches burned low and on the twisted wreckage by the great dock, while the bright moon overhead, gleaming through the clouds, suffused all the scene with a dim radiance which gave to all objects a phantom substance. No guns any longer spoke on the river front and all sound was concentrated in the crackle and rattle of rifle and machine-gun fire, the sharp bursts of grenades and the shouts of voices. Throughout the whole route, from concealed positions a few yards away in the dark, a ragged fire, now feeble, now bursting into an angry challenge, was sprayed upon the silent footed column as it swept along, an eerie but inspiring spectacle of defiant men cornered but not defeated, isolated but strong in their fellowship, victorious in spirit.

Stumbling through a bomb crater made that night by the RAF, they ran the gauntlet through the warehouse roads, turning left, right and left again, and reaching the approach to the old headquarters building. Contact with Burn had somehow been lost at the first or second turn and Donald Roy was now in the van, in high spirits, bearing a charmed life, an inspiration to all. Somewhere about the old headquarters he was held up by heavy fire, and here again the sturdy figure of Troop Sergeant-Major Haines comes boldly to the front. Summoned by Copland, he stood to attention in the midst of the battle as Copland ordered him forward to reinforce Roy and 'crash on with all speed'. As upon an exercise, Copland asked him:

'Any questions, Sergeant-Major?'

And as upon an exercise, 'and he the perfect student', came the steady, quiet answer:

'None, sir.'

What he and Roy did we do not quite know, but soon the column was on the move again. The Laird quickened his pace, a tall, splendid figure in his kilt, a grenade in either hand, striding now along in the middle of the road, contemptuous of the enemy. Had he not seen them run away from their guns on the pumphouse roof? Now as he doubled along another party, lurking in an alley, also fled as he passed. As he led, Day and Haines served as whips to the field under Copland's cool mastership, running up and down the column, regardless of fire, 'as though on the rugger field', to bid Roy slow down or quicken up, to urge forward any stragglers and to keep the column closed up. Somewhere always in the van was to be seen the inspiring figure of Newman, still jovial, still cracking jokes, never taking cover, always on his feet and directing fire or calling out: 'Keep going, lads!'

Reaching the Submarine Basin, the commandos swung boldly left handed along the quay. An hour earlier this route would have been impossible, but the minesweepers had now moved from their berths at the quayside and, appreciating that the attack might be directed against the submarines, had taken up positions in front of the pens. In their place, however, the commandos met the fire of the dangerous guns across the water on their right, while on their left small-arms fire assaulted them at a few yards range from the sheds. Halted by one troublesome party, Copland took a squad right into the shed to silence them.

Watson, his blood still up, trying to rush a rifleman who was firing at close range from round a corner, was hit in the left arm, the bullet shattering the humerus. He sank to the ground and prepared to shoot it out with his Colt, but Roderick appeared, killed the German, administered morphia to Watson and began to carry him, but Tiger called in pain to put him down. Hopwood, staunchest of friends, was there, too, and together they put him down at the side of the road, spent in body but still aggressive in spirit. Very quietly, ignoring the boy's cry of 'Hoppy, what the hell are you doing with my gun?' Hopwood slipped his Colt off its lanyard, apprehending well from his angry mood that he would otherwise sell his life dearly, rather than submit to capture.

All down the line many other vivid or touching incidents were occurring, too numerous to tell. Roy, meanwhile, was sweeping along to the southern extremity of the Submarine Basin, fretted only by the cracks in his ear of Newman's pistol fired over his shoulder and to all else unconcerned. At the end of the quay came the most dangerous place of all – the wide, open stretch of Old Town Place, which, turning right, they must cross before reaching Bridge D. At Newman's order they halted accordingly in the pale moon shadows aslant the buildings on their left hand, while Newman himself, accompanied by Roy and Haines, darted across the open space for a quick reconnaissance from the buildings opposite. Immediately they came under fire from a machine-gun in a pill-box beyond the Southern Entrance, commanding the open way by which they must all go.

There lay the girdered Bridge D, gaunt and ghostly in the curious light. It was barely seventy yards away. Beyond it the German machine-guns looked down from roof and window. Astride it on the far side, and stretching along the quayside, lay a line of enemy riflemen, last remaining elements of the German naval troops.

No means of indirect approach to the bridge was at hand, no cover to make use of against the cocked and loaded weapons, no opportunity for finesse. Very coolly Haines, at his own suggestion, sited a Bren-gun to give a little covering fire. Then Newman called to his waiting soldiers:

'Away you go, lads!'

Without hesitation the commandos went for it, moving at a steady double as a hurricane of fire burst upon them from beyond the bridge. The astonished Germans, quite in the dark about the purposes of all these confounding occurrences, shot high and wide, as they had done all that night. A violent storm of bullets swept over the commandos' heads; others struck the steel girders of the bridge like hammers ringing on an anvil and, as the bullets ricochetted away, their tracers shot like sparks in all directions.

Disdainful of it all, Donald Roy made on right in the middle of the road, a splendid and inspiring figure, Newman now beside him. Close behind him were Sergeant Rennie, Denison, Montgomery and Haines. They saw the German riflemen athwart the bridge scramble to their feet and retire. They passed the ships that Pritchard had sunk, passed Philip Walton's dead body and swept superbly over the Bridge of Memories, their rubber boots thudding on the hollow road while the bullets rang and sparked on the steelwork or whistled overhead into the night. They were a smaller party now, their route marked by a sprinkling of their dead and wounded, but marked too by the bodies of their enemies. To all those who took part it was the most inspiring moment of the night, like a charge of olden times across fire-swept ground right into the heart of the enemy. In the stirring pages of British history there have been many glorious charges, many heroic assaults on battlemented walls and ramparts deemed impregnable, but, on its smaller scale and in its more modest intent, the break out of the commandos at St Nazaire ranks high among them as a manifestation of soldierly purpose and of the will and determination to defy odds. If its purpose was not to defeat an enemy army, but to fight through it to the green fields beyond, it was nonetheless splendid in its indomitable spirit. The clerks and bakers, the lawyers and engineers, the plumbers and farmers, the students and postmen who made up Charles Newman's tiny army showed in this brave hour the mettle of their pasture and the worth of their breeding.

As they reached the end of the bridge Sergeant Rennie fell, shot in the knee. A German grenade hit Corran Purdon in leg and shoulder, bowling him over on top of Day. At that moment Copland went straight for the pill-box, emptying his magazine into the slit and others followed his example. Roy, seeing a German run out from behind it, attacked him with a grenade. He ran to a roadside pit with Denison, Haines and a sergeant to attack with fire another machine-gun in action from a window a little way up the street. A motorcycle combination, carrying machine-gunners, came suddenly from round a corner at a crossroads. Every commando in sight opened fire and the Germans, riddled with bullets, crashed into a café wall. Further up the road what

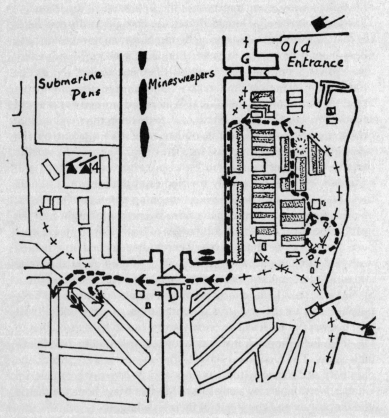

Fig 21. The commandos break out. Dotted ring shows the re-organization area. Rail lines shown in part only.

appeared to be an armoured car drove up very fast, spitting out fire at random in every direction and taking station at a crossroads a hundred and fifty yards ahead, thus barring further progress by that route.

So, about a hundred yards beyond the bridge, ended the commandos' dockyard battle. For the motorcycle combination and the armoured vehicle gave notice of the arrival of the first troops of the German Army. They were units of 679 Infantry Brigade, a partially motorized formation, consisting of one or more infantry companies, half a company of machine-gunners, two companies of 559 Construction Battalion and probably a unit of the 333 Division's artillery regiment. The brigade commander himself arrived in the town about this time and took over command of the operations at 4.30 a.m. These troops had arrived too late to mar the splendour of the commandos' break out from the dockyard, but just in the nick of time to stop them from getting any further. Had they been fifteen minutes later, all the commandos who were fit enough would have made their way through the town and into the marsh country beyond, for, once over the bridge, there were no more naval troops to oppose them.

It is not often that victory is followed by surrender, but St Nazaire was without question a resounding victory for the little combined force of Ryder and Newman, a victory out of all proportion to their numbers and a victory of which the complete fulfilment was yet to come. The splendour of their achievement was for long to be veiled by obscurities due to the loss of the men who were responsible for them, by the reluctance of the British authorities to make claims of which they had not the most positive proof and by the jibes and belittlements of the German propaganda machine. To the Germans of the superior staffs, as we shall presently see, the import of the achievement was evident. To the German troops on the spot it was an act 'brave but mad', but the occurrences of the next few hours were to show that it was an act far from mad but still very brave.

'I cannot pick out,' wrote Newman afterwards, 'all the chaps who made the breakout and the crossing possible, but outstanding among them was Troop Sergeant-Major Haines, who was superb. He alone knocked out several pockets of enemy with Tommy-gun and Bren-gun fire. He always seemed to have a fresh weapon in his hands. Captain Roy's leadership and coolness also stands out, and Major Copland's constant efforts to hold the parties together, and Stanley Day, my adjutant, dashing about as if he were on the rugger ground.'

Capture

Immediately after having crossed the bridge, the little force, deflected by the armoured car, turned left and soon broke up into separate parties. Copland, finding a lorry parked at the roadside, seized the heaven-sent opportunity for escape, but inside the cab the only switch he found to work was the one for the headlights, which illuminated Denison, who gave vent to the familiar wartime cry: 'Put out those bloody lights!'

From this point all becomes confused as the small parties of commandos, with no maps and not knowing which direction to take, made their way through the streets, sticking close to the shadows of walls. All over the town the Germans were now rushing in reinforcements, uncertain what was afoot, believing that the raid was the spearhead of an invasion. Armoured cars or machine-guns were being posted at every road intersection. Newman himself squeezed into a doorway to avoid an armoured car that shot past. Everywhere the Germans were shooting promiscuously at any object that moved, frequently firing at each other, as the watching commandos, trained in all the skills of street fighting by night, observed several times.

To avoid all these patrols and pickets, now being augmented each minute, the British began to forsake the streets, and to engage in what they were afterwards to term the 'St Nazaire Obstacle Race', clambering over walls, passing through one back-yard after another, even going through houses from front to back. Private Hannon dropped over a wall into a chicken-run, awakening the startled fowls to a premature reveille. Newman also dropped into a chicken-run and, going head first through a window, entered a parlour with the breakfast things already laid out on a blue check cloth, and so passed through the house to the front door.

By now, however, time was running out. It was somewhere

about 4 am and only two hours of darkness remained in which to find lying-up places for the day. Ammunition was very short and, with every street corner now picketed by the enemy and every street swept by fire, effective progress became difficult. Worst of all was the condition of the wounded. By now about three men out of every four had been hit. All but a few had kept up with astonishing fortitude, but were now weak from loss of blood and fatigue. Etches and many others were nearly done. Here and there small parties, becoming broken off from their main groups, began to seek shelter in cellars and outhouses.

Michael Burn and Rifleman Bushe were surprisingly caught in the boiler-room of a ship in the docks. Very few of them had any luck.

Donald Roy, at the head of a party, seeking water for the wounded who were with him, called at a building which unfortunately turned out to be a police station, and the police, after stalling him, had a squad of German bayonets round in a few minutes, for the French police, under orders to collaborate with the invaders, were nearly as dangerous to escapers as the Germans themselves.

Newman himself, with about fifteen others, found refuge in a large cellar equipped as an air-raid shelter, with eighteen palliasses. Of them all, only himself, Copland, Day and Steele were unwounded. Steele was posted as lookout near the head of the stairs and wounds were dressed as far as possible. Here Newman intended to stay until night, when they would set out in pairs for the open country. 'But I also decided,' he said, 'that if we were found in the cellar I should surrender, as the wounded were in a pretty bad way and a single grenade flung down the stairs would see the lot off.'

They were indeed discovered, the commander of 679 Brigade having ordered a systematic search. Newman himself at once dashed upstairs and offered surrender. Roughly handled, the party was frog-marched across the road and taken into the house immediately across the road, which turned out, to the amusement of the unquenchable Newman, to be the German headquarters. Under heavy guard, they were stripped of their weapons and interrogated by a German officer without much success.

While this was going on one of the commandos had some occasion to take out his fighting knife, which they all wore strapped to their legs inside their trousers and which, as we have noted earlier, they scarcely thought of as weapons, the British instinct (and, one thinks, the German too) being averse to the use of the knife as a soldier's weapon. The interrogating officer, who was what Newman called an office type, observed this action and flew into a rage. Why had they not surrendered all their weapons? They were then all stripped naked under the muzzles of Tommy-guns and lined up against a wall. 'I really thought,' said Newman, 'that that was going to be the end of things.' At that moment, however, another German officer appeared who was not an office type, and he quietly gave orders for the prisoners to resume their clothes.

Back in the dockyard Chant lay by the quay, unable to rise. Wounded a second time in the legs, he had been bowled over in the dockyard battle. Sergeant Butler and Private Brown, of the Argylls, had come to his aid and carried him onward as far as the Submarine Basin, but there he had bidden them leave him. He lay in the weird half light looking straight across to the submarine pens and watching the Germans moving about and manning their weapons on the housetops. A dazed young soldier whom he did not know came and sat down beside him.

There they were found in the morning by a German patrol, who came up to them, Tommy-guns levelled, and, in that particularly harsh and grating German manner, shouted: *'Herauf! Herauf!'* (Get up! Get up!). The young soldier, prompted by Chant, obeyed and was immediately shot dead. They turned to Chant and again ordered *'Herauf! Herauf!'* Chant, mad with anger but helpless, pointed to his injured leg. One of the Germans then noticed the stars on his shoulder, and said *'Offizier'*. They searched him, taking all his personal possessions, and carried him to a café at a corner of Old Town Place, where Gerard Brett and several other wounded or dying prisoners already lay.

Not far from here Roderick, Hopwood, Sergeant Searson and one or two others, all wounded before or during the breakout (Roderick had been hit a second time), were lying up in a warehouse stored with bags of cement. They all managed to climb to the top of a pile of bags high off the ground and for some hours they avoided capture, watching the German search parties at work.

It was not until 10.30 in the morning that a German, on a higher level than they, looking out from a shed across the dock road, saw, through a bomb-splinter hole in the wall of their warehouse, the bandaged and bloody head of one of the commandos. In next to no time the place was alive with Germans. The wounded men were roughly manhandled to the ground, searched, lined up against a wall, and, like Newman's party, thought that 'they had had it'. Again, however, some responsible German intervened and instead of being shot they were hustled off to a ship in the Submarine Basin before rejoining their comrades in captivity.

Thus, little by little, what was left of the commandos began to come together again. 'It was just like a reunion,' Newman recorded. 'In spite of personal misfortunes our spirits were high. We never gave in to the Jerries. We all felt that a good job of work had been done, and as each newcomer arrived we pieced the story together. What we were all waiting for, and straining our ears to hear, was the big bang of *Campbeltown* going up in the air.'

Not all, however, could maintain this high note. Many were wounded very grievously. And among these prostrate forms there was to be exhibited again those callous instincts in the German character which Hitler so designedly fostered. Wherever the wounded lay the camera-mad Germans gathered round, clicking from all angles and stepping over bodies to take close-ups of the most spectacular and gruesome hurts. Private McCormack, grievously wounded in the head, lay in an open space in St Nazaire town, a piteous spectacle with his head between his kilted legs, dying. The Germans gathered round him in crowds, jeering and laughing, while their gloating cameras clicked, and so successfully indecent was one of these ghoulish pictures that it was published throughout Europe in the German armed forces magazine as a whole-page picture with the derisory title 'Picture of a British Commando', to feed a gross taste and a hungry arrogance.

18. NOT THE SIX HUNDRED

While the commandos were fighting their dockyard battle and gallantly trying to effect their withdrawal by land, the little motor craft of Ryder's force, or what was left of them, had begun their withdrawal by sea. For some of them the fighting had by no means been ended, and the tally of their losses was to be further increased.

Seven of the seventeen craft we have already seen in flames in the immediate neighbourhood of the docks – those of Stephens, Platt, Burt, Beart, Tillie, Collier and Nock. The remaining ten, which include Curtis's gunboat and 'Wynn's Weapons', have begun their homeward journeys, setting course at full speed for the open sea. There, we may remind ourselves, they are to make rendezvous at Point Y, twenty-five sea miles from St Nazaire, with their escorting destroyers *Tynedale* and *Atherstone*, with whom they parted company at 8 p.m. It was intended that, having assembled at Point Y, the force should be well on its way home before first light, which was at 5.48 a.m.

Tweedie and Jenks, commanding *Tynedale* and *Atherstone* respectively, had passed an anxious night, having had no news at all of what was happening in the river. All that they had heard on the air, picked up between 2.18 and 3.25, were the 'leaving' signals wirelessed by five only of the MLs. Their anxiety had been added to by the knowledge that the five small German destroyers of the 5th Torpedo Boat Flotilla, which had left St Nazaire early that night as a result of the signal from U 593, were somewhere in the vicinity and might be encountered at any minute.

While the destroyers waited, the ten remaining motor craft, passing beyond range of the small, rapid-firing flak guns in the harbour area, came under fire from the heavier and more dangerous guns of the coastwise batteries that armed those jaws of death. With the exception of the 75 mm battery at Pointe de l'Eve, which was not manned, all these batteries engaged them hotly, even the big 9.5-inch guns on railway mountings at La Baule. The 6.6-inch battery at Pointe de l'Eve fired no fewer than four hundred rounds that night, mostly in this withdrawal phase, their shells of about a hundred and ten pounds splashing up great fountains of water as they detonated on the surface. Yet all but two of the withdrawing craft successfully ran the gauntlet.

The first of the unfortunate two was Mark Rodier.

Death of Rodier

Having with skill and coolness accomplished his mission of landing the assault party of Troop Sergeant-Major Haines in the Old Entrance and having taken on board Sam Beattie and some thirty or more of the *Campbeltown*'s crew, Rodier set off down the river at three minutes to two. As he emerged again into the blinding arena of searchlights, the enemy guns turned upon him again, but Rodier, unperturbed, successfully took avoiding action.

Beattie joined him on the little bridge and suggested to him a course to steer. They began a light-hearted discussion on trivial subjects, such as the schools they had been to. Off the tip of the East Jetty some 'floating shapes' were seen, and, thinking it a pity to take home his torpedoes, Rodier fired them, but with uncertain result. Then, at full speed and making white smoke astern with his chlorosulphonic acid equipment, he passed successfully out of reach of the dangerous rapid-firing short range weapons in the harbour area. The boat was embarrassingly crowded but Winthrop, *Campbeltown*'s doctor, helped by Hargreaves, the torpedo-gunner, continued to dress and attend to the wounded both above and below deck.

Very soon, however, they were picked up again by the searchlights lower down the river and came under fire from Dieckmann's dangerous 75 mm and 6.6-inch guns. Rodier took evasive action as he was straddled with increasing accuracy. The end came after they had gone some three miles. A shell from the 75 mm guns at Le Pointeau on the eastern shore hit the boat on the port side of the engine-room, lifting one engine bodily on top of the other and stopping both. Toy, the Flotilla Engineering Officer, went below at once. Beattie left the bridge and went down also. He had no sooner left than another shell hit the bridge direct. Rodier was mortally wounded and died a few minutes afterwards. The same shell wounded Frank Arkle.

The engine-room was now on fire, burning fiercely, and the sprayer mechanism for fire-fighting had also been put out of action. Toy, who had come up momentarily, at once returned to the blazing compartment but was never seen again. Locke, *Campbeltown*'s Warrant Engineer, was able partially to repair the extinguisher mechanism. The flames amidships divided the crowded ship into two, but the ship's company continued to fight the fire for some three hours by whatever means were available. At length, when all means had failed and the fire had spread throughout the boat, the order to abandon ship was given at about 5 a.m. One Carley raft had been damaged, but a few of the wounded ratings were got away on the other, and the remainder of those alive entered the icy water, in which they remained for four and a half hours, many of them succumbing to the ordeal.

All *Campbeltown*'s officers were lost except Beattie and Locke, among those who perished being the brilliant and devoted Tibbits, to whose skill and resourcefulness the epic success of the Raid was so much due and whose work was so soon to be triumphantly fulfilled. Salter, one of the stewards of *Campbeltown*, was terribly burned about the head as he was caught in a pool of blazing petrol. Petty Officer Stocker, Chief Boatswain's Mate of the destroyer, was carried out to sea, apparently with some others, and, with some taste of poetic irony, found refuge on the wreck of the *Lancastria*. At 9.30 a.m. the survivors were picked up by a German patrol trawler.

The End of 'Wynn's Weapons'

Some twenty minutes or more after Rodier had left the Old Entrance, Wynn also left. After having fired his delayed-action torpedoes into the outer lock gates of that entrance, he had stood by for further orders from Ryder and had been a witness of the little fight between Savage and the Old Mole pillbox. Like Rodier's ML, the MTB was very overcrowded, carrying, in addition to her own small crew of ten, some sixteen hands she had taken from the

Campbeltown and the ten others that she had stopped to rescue from the water on her way in. The gallant Lovegrove, enduring his wounds with fortitude, had restored to life the damaged centre engine and the little torpedo-boat shot off at high speed, making smoke to cover her withdrawal.

She had now no weapons but her speed and a few light machine-guns. After going only a few hundred yards she was hit in the stern and a small fire resulted, but, under the impetus of her five engines, she was soon racing over the Loire at forty knots, her forefoot high out of the water, her stern settled down into the froth of her yeasty wake, and throwing out high on either hand great wings of flying spray. At such speed she was a very difficult target for any gun to hit and as she flew down the river she had no need to resort to the tricks of evasive action. Very soon the searchlights and the guns gave up the hunt and in a minute she was racing ahead through the grey dark, the open sea only a few miles away.

With a clear course before her, nothing seemed able to stay the utmost gallop of her 3600 horses. Spurred up to forty-four knots, she flashed through six long sea miles in nine minutes. The rendezvous with the Wrens drew nearer at every beat of her racing engines.

But the course was not clear. Directly ahead of her in the grey pallor of the night, there appeared the forms of two men on a Carley raft. Impossible to avoid cutting right through them or capsizing them by the boat's violent wash. It was typical of Micky Wynn and all those who served under him that he did not hesitate a moment. Operating the engine-room telegraph himself, he pulled the lever immediately to 'Stop' and then to 'Slow astern'.

With her extraordinary knack of pulling up within a few yards, the MTB stopped right alongside the raft. Within a matter of seconds, before the shipwrecked men could be hauled on board, she was brilliantly illuminated by a searchlight. In another few seconds she was struck amidships by a heavy shell and Wynn was blown unconscious from the bridge into the charthouse. For some minutes he lay there and when he began to recover consciousness, his senses were dimly aware that all the world was red. Instinctively he reached his hand up for the methyl bromide fire extinguisher and at the same moment he became aware of a dim figure struggling to make its way to him through the enveloping red clouds. It was Lovegrove.

The boat was on fire from stem to stern, the petrol-red flames roaring fiercely and the boat's timbers crackling like the fire of innumerable rifles. All hands had abandoned ship. Lovegrove, however, looking about for his young captain, could not see him. In pain from his own wounds, and tired from lack of sleep he went back to look for him without a moment's hesitation. Fighting his way through the flames, he saw the recumbent figure in the charthouse, with the left eye hanging out of its socket. He ran in, lifted Wynn to his feet, half carried him up on deck and then, putting his arms round him, pulled him into the water and swam with him to a Carley float. There he supported him for nearly twelve hours, lashing him to the float or holding on to him himself in one of the bravest individual acts of the whole Raid.

Through his blurred vision Wynn could see that some thirty men were crowding round the raft as it was carried downstream, either on it or clinging on to its life-lines or to each other. The water was bitterly cold, and one by one, as their strength failed, men let go their grasp and slipped from life into death, drifting off with the swift current of the Loire. One of these was the New Zealander Arthur O'Connor, Wynn's Number One and his dear friend. As the night wore on he heard O'Connor call out to him:

'Goodbye, Mick, I'm leaving you now.'

Wynn called back to him: 'Don't be a bloody fool, Arthur. Hang on!'

But all the answer he got from the night was:

'It's lovely, Mick. I am going. Cheerio.'

The night wore on, growing more densely dark before dawn, and as the first pallid hues of the day then began to suffuse the water's face the survivors on the raft realized that they had been carried out to sea. They observed that only four of them were left – Wynn, Lovegrove, Petty Officer Robert Ward, the coxswain, and Stoker William Savage. Lovegrove and Savage therefore climbed up on the raft and between them they pulled up Wynn. Then they tried to get Ward, but he would not come. He made a last gallant effort to swim with them, pushing the raft in front of him, but after a little while suddenly sank beneath the water.

A little while before, Able Seaman Leonard Denison, one of the most resourceful of hands, had successfully swum out to some concrete structure in the river mouth, although wounded, and found safety there. All the rest of the thirty-six souls on the little boat were lost.

The long morning of Saturday, the 28th, dragged on as the raft drifted in the currents, but the indomitable Lovegrove remained full of spirit to the end, and when at long last a German gunboat appeared at two o'clock in the afternoon and approached them he actually drew his revolver and only with the greatest difficulty was restrained by Wynn from using it against the Germans. No doubt they were all three by now somewhat delirious. Taken on board by the Germans, they were kindly and generously treated by a chivalrous captain, whose final act before landing them earned Wynn's lasting gratitude. Knowing that, once ashore, officers and men would be permanently separated, he allowed them some little time together in private in the enjoyment of those bonds that tied them so closely together.

The Last Fight

In personnel, the losses of Rodier's and Wynn's boats were the most grievous of all, for they accounted for at least sixty per cent of the naval fatal casualties. But the account is nearly closed. Only one more fee has to be paid before the full tally of the profit and the losses can be assessed. Nine craft have now been lost, but, of these, three have accomplished their missions in full. The astonishing circumstances in which the tenth met her end deserve that we should look at her more closely.

His Majesty's ML 306 was commanded by Lieutenant Ian B. Henderson, RNVR, who in peace was an underwriting member of Lloyds. He had a young wife and small family to whom he was devoted. He was fair-complexioned, but premature baldness made him seem older than his thirty years. He had a deep love of the sea and in particular was devoted to his ship, for whose well-being he was as solicitous as a trainer is of his racehorse.

Number One to Henderson was Sub-Lieutenant P. J. C. Dark, very young, very tall, very dark. He was a student of both anthropology and art. The supernumerary officer carried especially for this expedition was Sub-Lieutenant P. W. Landy, a stocky, wiry and athletic Australian. The Coxswain was Leading Seaman W. G. Sargent, young, quiet, good-looking and an aspirant for the Fleet Air Arm. The engines were in the care of Petty Officer Motor Mechanic A. L. Bennett, with Stokers E. A. Butcher and A. Ritchie, but at action stations Ritchie was as an ammunition number on deck. The telegraphist was a New Zealander, R. H. Newman, and among the others of the little ship's company we shall see a good deal was Able Seaman A. V. Alder, a little fellow of no heroic form or figure but who was to behave with singular pluck and devotion.

The commandos whom Ian Henderson was carrying were a demolition party under Lieutenant R. O. C. Swayne, of the Herefordshire Regiment and 1 Commando, and their protection squad under Lieutenant J. Vanderwerve of 2 Commando. Ronnie, or 'Roc' Swayne was an officer of tall and athletic physique, black-haired and black-browed, with strong and characterful features. He had played rugger for Oxford, but missed his Blue, and been a member of the University Air Squadron until he was badly concussed in a crash. He was an old hand at the commando game, having taken part in the very first little try-out raid on the French coast in June 1940, his patrol being the first to inflict German casualties, and in the semi-abortive raid on the Channel Isles the next month.

Johnny Vanderwerve was another dark-haired young officer, with a healthy sallow complexion, and a quiet charm of de-meanour. Although otherwise a good athlete, he could not swim – probably the only officer in the Commando Brigade with this shortcoming, and one which was to prove fatal to him.

Of the non-commissioned ranks, the most outstanding – and, indeed, one of the most remarkable characters in the whole of our story – was Sergeant Tom Durrant, that swarthy, intense Royal Engineer in whom there glowed secret fires that must one day burst into flame. We have met him already in an earlier chapter, have noted the strength of character and of purpose that marked him, have remarked upon his soldierly integrity and have observed that as he was a loyal friend so also was he an enemy to be feared. We are now about to see him winning the first

Victoria Cross in history awarded to a soldier in a naval engagement.

The remainder of this demolition team from 1 Commando consisted of Sergeant Chappell, Corporals Salisbury, Evans and Llewellyn and Privates Bishop, Tomblin and Hopkins – all first-rate, hand-picked men, a well-knit and eager unit with a strong Welsh and West of England flavour. Remember that these men had no personal weapons but their Colts. In his more strongly armed protection squad Vanderwerve counted Sergeant Gallagher, Private Eckmann and two other ranks.

Such was the ship's company, naval and military, that ML 306 carried up the estuary of the Loire. They numbered twenty-eight souls – fourteen naval and fourteen commandos. We have already, in Chapter 16, momentarily seen Henderson take her up in the port column in all the blaze of the searchlights in an attempt to land at the Old Mole. Circling, he attempted the Old Entrance also, but so heavy and continuous was the flow of tracer across it that it seemed to Swayne as though 'the way was being barred by lighted chains'. The boat was hit several times by 20 mm fire and her decks were splashed with spray from larger shell bursts that narrowly missed her. Philip Dark was slightly wounded in the leg and Durrant was slightly wounded also. Regretfully, Henderson set course for Point Y at eighteen knots under cover of white smoke.

Swayne, standing on the bridge beside him, very bitter at this letdown of tuned-up hopes, felt nonetheless bound to accept his decision absolutely. But he had to face a very obvious feeling of resentment among his troops. Durrant was cold and sullen and all the team very grumbly, saying to each other: 'What have we come here for?' It was the measure of their spirit, if not of their judgement.

As they entered the arcs of fire of Dieckmann's coast defence batteries lower down the estuary, they were engaged continuously by heavy pieces and drenched with spray from water-bursts of near misses. But they successfully evaded it all by frequent changes of course and speed which taxed the promptitude of Leading Seaman Sargent at the wheel and Petty Officer Bennett in the engine-room. Thus they made their way safely out to sea.

They were much ahead of time for the rendezvous at Y with *Tynedale* and *Atherstone* and reduced speed to three-quarters and then to slow. 'We were,' said Stoker Butcher afterwards, 'a bit early, worse luck.' Henderson therefore said to Philip Dark, who had been clearing up the ship and whose injured leg was now stiffening up:

'There's no point in hanging about here; we might get caught by a German patrol any minute. I shall go on to the next rendezvous. You'd better go below and rest your leg.'

And when Dark offered to relieve him on the bridge he answered: 'Oh no; I can go on for days at this sort of thing.'

Dark accordingly went down into the little wardroom, lay down on a couch and took his boots off. He was never to put them on again.

A little before 5.30 in the morning, when forty-five miles out to sea, while it was still very dark, and with a light sea mist resting on the water, Dark was summoned urgently to the bridge. He went instantly, in his sea stockings. He was followed closely by Swayne, who was, however, merely taking up some bully-beef sandwiches to the naval officers on the bridge. He found Henderson and Dark puzzled by some white streaks on the water that could be faintly seen some little distance off ahead. His flippant suggestion that they might be caused by a large fish was not well received and he went below again. The commandos and hands below were drinking cocoa and eating sandwiches. All seemed set fair for England.

A minute later Dark came down and asked Swayne to return to the bridge at once, very quietly. Swayne was still eating a sandwich. When he arrived on the bridge Henderson said nothing but handed him his night glasses and pointed ahead. Swayne put up the glasses and there, fine on the port bow, he saw the outlines, faint, but distinct, of three or more German destroyers, coming towards them on a nearly parallel course. His sandwich turned to dust in his mouth.

'Those,' said Henderson, 'are some of your fish.'

They were, in fact, the five ships of Schmidt's 5th TBD Flotilla, which, as we know, had put to sea the evening before on orders from Naval Group Command West as the result of the report from U 593. Schmidt had put out his paravanes to search for the suspected mines and was about a hundred miles out to sea when he was astonished to receive the wireless signal 'Enemy landing at St Nazaire'. He was ordered to return at once and to endeavour to intercept the raiding craft as they withdrew or their escorts.

Henderson immediately stopped ship and asked Swayne to bring his men and Vanderwerve's to action stations as quietly as possible. No talking. Swayne went below and passed the order to Vanderwerve and Durrant. The sergeant merely nodded and had the men moving swiftly and silently at once, collecting their arms. Swayne went back to the bridge and watched the German ships looming larger and larger.

'What will you do?' he asked Henderson in a whisper.

'Keep as quiet as possible and hope they won't see us,' Henderson answered.

'And if they do see us?'

'We shall have to fight, of course.'

Fight! A featherweight launch against a steel ship of eight hundred tons. A handful of machine-guns against high explosive of three 4.1-inch guns, three 20 mms and two Hotchkiss. A speed twice their own. Yet they would fight. Of course. No other choice was thought of. Quietly the word was passed along the little deck.

It was very cold. Cold enough to shiver a little in the early March morning. A bright phosphorescence lit the disturbed waters at bow and stern as the German ships came on. Another minute and they were right on the port beam, barely a hundred yards away, menacingly large.

In the motor launch hands could even hear the German voices. Every man followed the enemy shapes intently, his weapon ready. The forward Oerlikon was still jammed, but the after gun stood ready, manned by Ordinary Seaman Garner and Batteson and controlled by Pat Landy, wearing a white submarine frock. Amidships, between the bridge and the mast, Able Seaman Alder manned the little twin Lewis guns on their high, exposed anti-aircraft mounting. Just abaft the mast, among the commandos, Sergeants Durrant and Chappell, the sandy-haired Corporal Evans and Corporals Llewellyn and Salisbury were manning the four Bren-guns, crouching low behind the deck petrol-tanks. Manning Tommy-guns were Vanderwerve, Sergeant Gallagher and the remainder of their squad. Down in the engine-room Bennett and Butcher, having no idea what was afoot, stood by attentively with their engines stopped.

The German ships appeared quite blind to the presence of the little motor launch. Two of them passed ghostlike into the night behind them, the silence broken only by the German voices and the swish of the bright bow waves. The third ship, which we now know to have been the *Jaguar*, came abeam and began to pass likewise. The little group on the bridge of the ML held their breath, scarcely believing their luck.

On board the *Jaguar*, meanwhile, the short, stocky, dark-featured person of Kapitänleutnant F. K. Paul reported by radio to Schmidt, in *Seeadler*, that he had observed a shadow on his port hand. Schmidt did not at first credit him, but when Paul repeated his suspicion, ordered him to investigate.

Thus, when the German was on his extreme port quarter, Henderson observed him to swing out of line and begin to come round astern. The next moment the black shroud of night was violently ripped apart by the white blaze of *Jaguar*'s main port searchlight. The solitary motor launch stood instantaneously revealed, illuminated with so fierce a glare that all on board her felt as though suddenly stripped naked. Above them the White Ensign hung clearly displayed.

Henderson immediately ordered: 'Slow ahead together.'

Almost simultaneously the two ships opened fire on each other, and in the very first burst the German's searchlight was put out, the tinkling of the shattered glass clearly audible on the ML. There was a moment or two's darkness before he switched on a second searchlight, the fusillade continuing meantime. The German did not bring his main 4-inch armament to bear for such apparently easy meat, but his heavy machine-guns soon caused casualties on Henderson's exposed deck and tore through his wooden hull. Paul counted upon an obvious surrender in such a hopeless case and he was eager to capture a prize rather than to sink.

Continuing her circular movement, *Jaguar* came up on Henderson's starboard hand at a range of only a hundred yards, still keeping the ML fully illuminated and under fire. A burst hit a small group of soldiers amidships, wounding several of them and kindling a small fire on the bridge. When nearly full on Henderson's starboard beam, she bore round still harder to port, closing the ML bows-on. Henderson, seeing her bows suddenly looming high and near, realized that she was bearing down to ram. He ordered 'Hard a-port!' in the nick of time. Sargent swung the wheel over. The *Jaguar*, instead of ramming, struck the ML a glancing blow that caused no material damage, but it rocked the little craft so violently that Vanderwerve, who had just been wounded in the head while blazing away with a Tommy-gun, was thrown overboard together with Ordinary Seaman Rees and two others; Vanderwerve was never seen again and Rees, sucked underwater, had his toes taken off by the propellers.

As they recovered from the impact, hands on the motor launch saw the bows of the destroyer 'poised above us like a huge carving-knife', in Sergeant Chappell's words. The fo'c'sle rails were crowded with Germans shouting excitedly and pouring down a shower of small-arms fire. The motor launch replied instantly, every small weapon blazing upwards. The German's attempt to ram had the effect of further stimulating the vigorous and combative spirit with which every man was filled that March morning – it was 'bloody sauce', it was like a foul at football, and they settled their weapons more grimly to their shoulders, Durrant tense, tight-lipped, and already wounded again, Alder cool and quiet, Evans angry, cursing the Germans aloud with the volatile ardour of his race. Ammunition ran low and hands repeatedly went below for replenishment. Every minute added to their casualties. Vanderwerve, Llewellyn and Tomblin were dead, Durrant, Bishop, Hopkins, Chappell and several others wounded, but not a man was dismayed.

After the attempt at ramming, the *Jaguar*, apprehending from the movement at the ML's after Oerlikon that Henderson might drop a depth-charge at these close quarters, sheered sharply off to starboard and then began again to circle the motor launch. 'I was,' said Paul, 'very angry.' When the range had opened to about fifty yards, enabling his guns to depress on to the ML, he opened fire again, now using his Hotchkiss guns as well as his 20 mms. A shell burst in the wheelhouse, wounding Sargent at the wheel, and he staggered up to the bridge, clutching his stomach. Another knocked out the only remaining Oerlikon, killing Garner and wounding Sergeant Gallagher at his Tommy-gun. Landy, perhaps somewhat earlier, was shot in the back by a bullet. Alder was badly hit at his twin Lewis abaft the bridge and Durrant, though now wounded a third time, stepped over, stood up and, calling for more ammunition, took over. Down in the engine-room Bennett said to Butcher: 'I had better go up and see what's happening'; but on reaching the deck he was at once mortally wounded in the stomach and head.

Henderson, admirably cool and possessed, watched the *Jaguar* continue her circling movement and come round on his port hand. Philip Dark was beside him on the bridge and the wounded Sargent lay in pain at their feet. When square on his port beam, the destroyer, according to British reports, fired her 4.1-inch armament. The shell hit the bridge direct, mortally wounding Henderson, killing Sargent and miraculously missing Dark but throwing him unconscious into the starboard corner.

There was a moment's deathly hush. Swayne, the only officer of either Service left unhurt, coming up from below at that moment with ammunition, looked around upon a scene of desolation and menace. The ship reeked of high explosive. The deck was covered with prostrate forms and by the pallid light of approaching dawn he saw the dark bulk of the bigger ship closing in upon them again in a tighter circle for the destruction of its now immobile and helpless prey.

It looked, thought Swayne, as though they were nearly finished. The German certainly thought so. He hailed them in English, calling upon them to surrender and shouting: 'Stop shooting! Don't shoot!'

Immediately everything came to life again. Durrant, shot through with manifold wounds, opened fire once more with his twin Lewis, followed by Evans. The Welshman was shouting angry abuse at the Germans as fire was resumed. Stoker Butcher, having come up after the order to stop engines, was immediately hit in the leg. The enemy ship was now barely thirty yards away. Seeing no other course to take, Swayne started along the deck, scrambling over the crowded prostrate forms to get out the small dinghy which Henderson had managed to retain. He passed Durrant, covered in blood but still standing up to his Lewis, gripping it with what little life and strength remained to him. He struggled aft to the dinghy and began to unship the gear that was stowed in it, but found it full of holes. *Jaguar* now came virtually right alongside, only a few yards away, and Paul, high on his bridge, again called down to them to surrender.

He was answered by the heroic Durrant. Lying half collapsed across his gun, the dying sergeant fired a burst straight up at the German bridge. It ripped across the small navigational table within an inch of the German captain.

Disconcerted and astonished, *Jaguar* went astern. At such close quarters she could not depress her guns down on to the ML; but when the range had opened far enough, she resumed firing

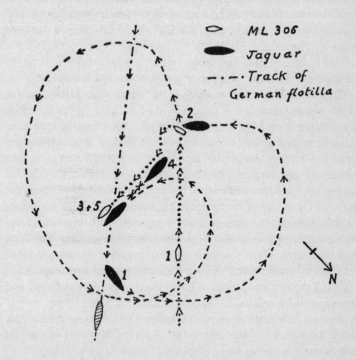

Fig 22. Probable course of the action between ML 306 and *Jaguar*. 1, on sighting; 2, on attempt to ram; 3, summons to surrender; 4, *Jaguar* goes astern; 4, final positions.

and went ahead again. Once more Durrant was hit. His body was riddled with bullets – hit in both arms, both legs, stomach, chest and head. In terrible agony, he collapsed on deck.

It was time to stop, Swayne decided. There were no longer any means of continuing the fight. Out of twenty-eight all hands of both Services, not fewer than twenty were dead or wounded. Dark had recovered consciousness, but he was very shaken and his face was covered with blood from small wounds in the nose and forehead. It was now daylight and the destroyer was alongside, towering over them. Swayne, standing up by the dinghy, called out in English, and then in French: 'I'm afraid we can't go on.'

There was a moment's dead silence. The German commander looked down in astonishment upon the shattered boat, its deck covered with blood and litter and carpeted with dead and wounded men. Fearing that the British might 'play a Richard Grenville', he said in English:

'You must not play any funny tricks.'

Swayne answered: 'No, I give you my word of honour.'

Thus ended this astonishing fight, which the gallant motor launch had sustained, it is said, nearly a full hour – from the pitch dark of soon after 5.30 to the daylight of 6.30. Leaving their dead where they had fallen, her survivors climbed or were carried on board the enemy destroyer. Ian Henderson, still just alive but completely unconscious, was brought up with them. Like Wynn and his companions, they were fortunate enough to fall into the hands of Germans of honourable behaviour in the old tradition. Kapitänleutnant Paul treated them not only with humanity, but also, one is happy to record, with consideration and chivalry. The wardroom and officers' cabins were given over to the wounded and officers' sheets were torn up for extra wound dressings.

Tom Durrant was dying. 'The amount of pain he suffered and bore so well,' Dark said, 'was incredible for any human being.' Because of a wound deep in the belly, Dark had to refuse him water, for which he was crying out. Bennett also was dying and Able Seaman Sparkes had compound fractures of both legs.

Paul, who spoke fairly good English, invited Swayne to his cabin for a drink, and when Swayne refused, said: 'I don't want to question you.' Thinking that it might be best not to offend an enemy obviously so well disposed, Swayne agreed. When they had gone to his cabin the German said:

'I wanted to compliment you on your brave fight. You had no chance, of course. Besides, I knew you would need a drink.'

It was clear to Swayne that here, at least, was one German who regretted the war. It was a pity, he said to his prisoner, that the Germans and the British should be fighting each other. Swayne could not help thinking that Paul could have blown the motor launch out of the water any time he liked with his heavier guns; had he, Swayne wondered, been actuated by feelings of humanity? Or had he been lured by this rare chance of capturing a British ship – an achievement of very singular triumph for any antagonist of the Royal Navy? That, we know today, was in fact Paul's motive. Well, he had had to fight damned hard for it. The German naval staff's *Operation und Taktik* states that *Jaguar* had sustained a 'bad hit' on No 1 gun, at which the ready-use ammunition had exploded; but this Paul declares to be erroneous.

Dark, still in his sea stockings, was also well received by the first lieutenant, Oberleutnant Heilig, who invited him into his cabin to wash the blood from his face and to have a drink. They conversed in French. Afterwards, as he had had a year's medical training and as the German ship carried no doctor, Dark was asked to treat the German wounded, 'after you have seen to your own'. There were few medical supplies and no morphia, but fortunately the British officers carried morphine ampoules. Assisted by the German first-aid hand, Dark therefore did what little he could, and he put a tourniquet on Ordinary Seaman Shephard's shattered leg. He noticed the German upper deck soiled with blood, especially below the bridge, and he treated four of their wounded before a new excitement distracted the attention of all as the German crew were ordered again to action stations.

Swayne had been given licence by Paul to be on the upper deck for a short time and it was with mixed feelings that, at a little after 6.30 a.m., he saw the silhouette of HMS *Tynedale* on the horizon. By such a narrow margin had ML 306 failed to reach the safety of her protection. The motor launch, which had been made fast, was now cast off. Swayne wondered what it would feel like to be shot up by one's own friends and thought what a strange paradox it would be to cheer on the shelling of oneself. Hopefully he asked Paul if he intended to fight; but the German said no, he was fast enough to make port. Unfortunately, he was right. Separated from the rest of his flotilla, he did not engage in the brief action that had just taken place between *Tynedale* and Schmidt's leading ships.

Thus, bearing the bodies of Ian Henderson and Tom Durrant, feeling a little flat as they looked upon the sad relics of their friends in the estuary and wondering what they might have done that they did not do, the survivors sailed once more up the Loire and came at last to St Nazaire, anchoring not far from *Campbeltown*. There, as they went over the side under guard, Paul paid them the signal honour of calling his ship's company to attention and himself coming to the salute to a gallant foe.

About a week later a German officer called on Newman in the prison camp at Rennes and said that he wished to bring to his notice the gallant conduct of a sergeant in a captured motor boat, 'as you may wish to recommend him for a high award'.*

'I Don't Call That Failure'

The tally of losses is complete. Except for a few 'write-offs', there is nothing more to enter on the debit side. Ryder, whom we have left a long time ago in the harbour area, had no knowledge at all of these last three entries but had already seen and heard enough to have grounds for qualified satisfaction.

The gunboat left the Old Entrance, a little before 3 a.m. It was high time she did so. The only one of the raiding craft now left in the harbour area, every German gun was waiting for her. Only by a miracle had she so far escaped any vital damage, for she was riddled with holes, littered with débris, laden down with wounded men in every inch of her space, her decks slippery with blood. Dropping a smoke-float, Curtis ordered full speed ahead and

* The above account is compiled mainly from the narratives and personal interrogations of Swayne, Dark and Paul, together with several other testimonies. While differences on some points of detail persist, the main features of the action have been reconciled. Paul does not agree that at any time he used his 4.1-inch guns. He also thinks that the relative positions of the two ships at the moment of ramming were slightly different from those on the sketch.

quickly worked up to twenty-four knots on his three engines, those on the bridge noting with satisfaction that the enemy at once opened fire on the flames and sparks emitted by the float.

On ordering Sub-Lieutenant Worsley to check the guns' ammunition and their readiness for action on the withdrawal, Curtis was distressed to learn that the gallant Able Seaman Savage and Able Seaman F. A. Smith lay dead at the forward pom-pom that they had served so well and so fearlessly. At what precise stage they were killed is uncertain, but the burly bearded figure and his shipmate had that night, in their exposed position, given a stirring example of the devotion that inspires those who serve the Royal Navy's guns, whether they be 16-inch giants or midgets of uncertain vintage.

The pom-pom, now the gunboat's only weapon, was taken over by Able Seaman A. Sadler and Ordinary Seaman H. A. Boswell. As the gunboat sped out, searchlights and guns from both sides of the river concentrated on her, and to their elusive flashes the two seamen replied with spirit. Though the group of officers assembled round Ryder on the little bridge remained miraculously unhurt, every single seaman on the gunboat had by this time been wounded and many of *Campbeltown*'s wounded on board her had been hit again. It was scarcely possible to move anywhere without treading on the prostrate forms, and below decks there was, in Curtis's words, 'a gristly mess of groaning men'. Even to Ryder the ship was 'a shambles'. In these conditions Curtis ordered Leading Seaman McKee, the coxswain, to help Worsley with the casualties, while he himself and Ryder personally took alternate tricks at the wheel. There was little that could be done beyond first aid, the administration of morphia and some attempt at making men comfortable in the cramped quarters. No lights could be allowed below deck because of the innumerable holes in the ship's hull, and the first aid party worked as best they could by the light of torches. To this work CERA Howard also gave his hand, together with Gordon Holman, who, his journalist's task forgotten, was throughout a conspicuous example of calm and comforting devotion. His touching description of the fortitude of these young sailors glows warmly in his book *Commando Attack*.

By speed, smoke and the tactics of evasion, the gunboat successfully sped through the storm of fire from the flak batteries in the harbour area. With equal skill and luck, she also avoided the more dangerous fire of the big guns in the estuary, the fountains of water from their shell bursts spraying her decks as she slipped between them. Gaining the open sea, she fought her last engagement; one of the German patrol boats at the mouth of the estuary attacked her out of the dark, sending a burst through her deck petrol tanks. Every man held his breath, waiting for the sheet of flame, but although the tank was full no harm ensued. Sadler and Boswell then put the enemy ship to flight by superior gunnery, with a fire burning on his deck.

Rendezvous Y was reached at 4.30 a.m., but, like Henderson, Ryder decided that it was unwise to loiter, and he ordered Curtis to proceed on course. At daybreak they sighted the badly damaged Fenton (No 5) and immediately afterwards Falconar (No 15). At almost the same moment they were cheered by sighting *Tynedale* and *Atherstone*.

The two destroyers had just come from a brief encounter with the four leading ships of Schmidt's flotilla. The British destroyers had been patrolling on a south-westerly course parallel with the withdrawal route from Y, five miles apart, and looking out for the returning motor launches, when, at 6.29 a.m., the enemy ships had been sighted in line ahead to the westward by *Tynedale*. She altered to southward to close *Atherstone* and protect the MLs, and the enemy altered to starboard. Six minutes later *Tynedale* came under the concentrated fire of the enemy and a running action ensued for nine minutes, both sides scoring hits. *Tynedale* then made smoke and the enemy did not press the action.

The two British destroyers were now therefore in company with the gunboat and the three MLs. Fenton's was in a sinking condition and she was accordingly abandoned, her crew and her commandos (Hooper's party) being taken on board by *Atherstone*. At the same time the wounded from Platt's and Falconar's boats were transferred to *Tynedale*. For Ryder it was time to say goodbye to the gallant little gunboat which, under her courageous young captain, had taken him on his memorable exploit and which, surely under the hand of Providence, had been the beneficiary of what Holman aptly described as 'the miracle of getting out'. As Ryder and his small headquarters staff returned to *Atherstone*, he saw the gunboat covered with scars – one engine badly damaged, water coming through the many wounds in her hull, her pumps out of action, an improvised chain of buckets struggling to keep down the level of rising water, the petrol running out of the deck tanks that had just been hit, her speed reduced to ten knots and her decks crowded with the patient human wreckage of the battle. For these also it was time to say goodbye and to be taken to the comfort and attention of the destroyer, but the task was accomplished only with great difficulty and distress, for the injured lay closely packed together and men were slipping on blood as they attempted to move.

As Bob Ryder quitted for ever the gunboat's bloody deck and climbed to *Atherstone*'s bridge, he realized that he was completely exhausted physically and emotionally and was beginning to feel that flat reaction which is quite commonly experienced by men who have come out of a harrowing action, even when the results are known to have been achieved. Though he had not seen *Campbeltown* actually blow up, he knew that the demolitions of the pump house and winding gears were of themselves sufficient to immobilize the Normandie Dock for a long time to come. He knew, however, that the assault on the Old Mole had been a failure, and he felt very distressed at having been obliged to leave Charles Newman and his commandos to their fate.

It was in this mood that Ryder mounted to *Atherstone*'s bridge, to be greeted by Robin Jenks, her commanding officer, who gave him a chair and ordered coffee. Jenks had naturally been on tiptoe to learn the fortunes of the expedition and had suffered acute disappointment when an officer from a motor launch that had had a very rough time had given him a pessimistic report, saying that no boats could get in and that no objectives could have been gained. Jenks, therefore, observing Ryder's silence and fatigue, and fearing the worst, observed a solicitous silence also. After a time, however, he could stand the uncertainty no longer and said to Ryder:

'I'm sorry it was a failure, sir.'

Ryder, without any change of expression, answered with a quiet incisiveness:

'Well, I personally saw *Campbeltown* firmly wedged in the lock gates and her fuses fired – objective No 1. I was nearly killed by a piece of masonry from the pumping-station blown up by the commandos – objective No 2. I saw Wynn fire his torpedoes at the foot of the old lock gates – objective No 3. I don't see why you should call that a failure.'

In the fine spring morning the remnant of the force moved on at a painful eight knots, slowed down by the damaged craft. At 8 o'clock a Heinkel 115 dropped out of the sky, but the pilot would not face the formidable concentration of fire from the force and contented himself with sinking Fenton's waterlogged wreck, now some distance away. A little later the appearance of a Beaufighter from 19 Group Coastal Command cheered them all and when a Junkers 88 also appeared the British pilot attacked it with such ferocity that he rammed the German in the air and the two went locked to death. Twenty-two sorties were to be flown that Saturday from St Eval and Praedannock by Beaufighters, Blenheims and Hudsons of 19 Group, under Air Vice-Marshal Geoffrey Bromet, and in the numerous air encounters that took place five enemy aircraft were shot down for the loss of two of our own.

Soon afterwards, with still further relief, they sighted the two additional destroyers that Forbes had sent to their support – the *Cleveland* and the *Brocklesby*. Command then passed from Ryder to Commander G. B. Sayer (*Cleveland*), who was Ryder's senior. He decided, both on grounds of safety and in the interest of the wounded, many of whom would die unless hurried to hospital, that the three motor craft that were holding them back so seriously, though seaworthy enough to get back at their own speed, must be scuttled. Thus the motor launches of Irwin and Falconar and Curtis's stalwart little gunboat, which with such daring had led into the jaws of death the 'noble six hundred' of this seaborne Light Brigade and upon whose deck the death of Able Seaman Savage had epitomized the heroism and self-sacrifice of the men of 'our light Coastal Forces', passed quietly to an honourable sleep.

It was a sad moment for Dunstan Curtis and for all that very gallant little ship's company, who looked forward with seamanlike pride to taking their ship home; but it was as well that this step was taken, for, unknown to Ryder and his friends, a hundred German aircraft were then bombing up at Rennes to attack the remnants of the audacious force that had set the German High Command by the ears. After *Brocklesby* had shot down a Junkers 88, the destroyers' twenty-five knots took them safely home at last as a bright moon rode high on that memorable Saturday night.

Meanwhile, unknown at first to Ryder, three other motor launches, having failed to make contact with the destroyers at Rendezvous Y, were making their way home alone in accordance with orders. These were the boats of Boyd, Wallis and Horlock. This little force, pushing far out to the westward and thence north up the meridian of eight degrees west, made a most creditable passage, shooting down on the way a Heinkel 111 by the combined fire of their Oerlikons (thus making a total of seven enemy aircraft shot down as an extra dividend for the operation) and seeing off a Blohm & Voss seaplane. These three boats, together with Briault's, which we have seen return much earlier on account of engine defects, were the only ones to return home out of the eighteen small motor craft that had set sail from Falmouth two and a half days before.

> They that had fought so well
> Came thro' the jaws of Death,
> Out of the mouth of Hell,
> All that was left of them,
>   Left of six hundred.

19. HAVOC

Hopeful though Ryder was as he sailed home that fine March morning, and reasonably confident that the grand design of the Charioteers had been accomplished, he could enjoy no certainty for quite a long time to come. Indeed, the results had still not been fully accomplished, and it is in keeping with the temper of the whole enterprise that that which had been put in train with such daring should, like yeast within the oven door, be pursuing its stealthy purpose unseen and unheard. If, in the manner of their coming, the Charioteers did not win the surprise that they had wished for, they certainly accomplished it in dramatic fashion after their exit. It was one of the kinder ironies of chance that only those who were left behind in captivity were to be the delighted witnesses of the fulfilment of their work.

While Ryder and his companions were sailing home, while Wynn and Lovegrove and Stoker William Savage were drifting out to sea on their Carley float, while Beattie and the survivors of Rodier's unhappy boat were immersed in the bitter waters, an air of crisis hung over St Nazaire, undispelled by the Saturday's early morning light. The Germans were ill at ease, having no idea of the purpose of the raid, nor of what was in store. There in the stark light they now saw *Campbeltown* securely jammed into the gate of the big lock. There for all to see were the demolished pump house and winding gears. These three small sunken ships, wrecked guns, the burnt-out Forge de l'Ouest and some seventy-six corpses were the visible evidence of the havoc so far.

Nor did the shooting stop when Newman's men at last surrendered. Desultory shots cracked and flicked and ricocheted about the town. Here and there the patriot French had begun to take out their few hidden arms, believing that the British invasion had begun. The sight of the old familiar khaki, not seen since that sad day in 1940 when France had fallen, aroused long-nourished hopes. 'The inhabitants,' wrote Monsieur Grimaud, one of the assistant mayors, reporting officially on behalf of the absent mayor, 'coming out of their shelters realized the incredible events that had just taken place.' Philip Walton's body was particularly noted, 'close to one of the gates of the South Entrance that he proposed to blow up'. Parties of British prisoners were seen. Here and there the Nazairiens began making Mr Churchill's V sign, to be instantly suppressed whenever observed by the Germans. The *patron* of the Old Town café where Chant and Brett had lain, coming out to wave and shout his good wishes as the British wounded were carried away, was immediately hustled inside by the Germans.

German Army troops continued to pour in, mingling with the bluejackets and white moleskin trousers of the seagoing sailors on the town side of the docks and with Mecke's field-grey naval units beyond. What all these troops were does not clearly appear from the available German documents, but maps show a continuous girdle of troop positions all round the town and Burhenne declares, somewhat improbably, that no fewer than six thousand troops arrived on the east side of the river, where he was stationed. Other troops of 333 Division were also hastily re-deployed in various areas. The town of St Nazaire itself was placed in a state of siege, all exits being closed, tram and train services stopped, crossroads picketed by machine-guns, and the docks sealed off to the French except for a few specialist workmen. The infantry brigade instituted an intensive house-to-house search of the town to ferret out any hidden commandos who, for a long time, were believed, by reason of the continued desultory firing, to be still lurking in concealment with the connivance of the French. Meanwhile, from the beaches and from the sea, the naval forces were collecting in the living and the dead from the wrecked motor launches, and as the bright March sun rose higher it appeared to the Germans that the situation was under control.

As one may suppose, the Germans lost no time in boarding *Campbeltown*. A group of very senior officers and many technical specialists, to the number of about thirty, climbed on board by the ladders that the commandos had left and carried out an examination. It is said that the Admiral-Superintendent of the Dockyard himself arrived and, immediately suspecting the existence of an explosive charge, ordered a search to be made; but none was found, so shrewdly had it been concealed in its steel and concrete jacket. On being so informed, he said, we are told: 'Well, the British must be very stupid if they think we can't deal with this.' For the problem of disengaging the destroyer from the caisson was not one of serious engineering difficulty. It was apparent that she would sink in the lock entrance if simply towed out, and the methods to be adopted for getting her clear without immobilizing the dock for longer than necessary were being discussed. The acting Harbour Commander also visited the ship, but neither he nor the Admiral-Superintendent stayed very long. Mecke also came, driving up from his headquarters at St Marc, and he took some photographs.

But these were by no means the only visitors. Orders had been given for a cordon to be placed round the dock, but either the order was never carried out or the cordon was ignored. For the word very quickly flew that here were plenty of cigarettes and chocolates to be had for the taking and a throng of curious sightseers of all sorts began to arrive by car and on foot – the submarine commanders, the gun position officers, officers of the naval shore staff and so on. And their lady friends. Looking for souvenirs, they roamed the gristly and littered upper deck from the shattered bows, where the displaced 12-pounder stood precariously by the big hole in the fo'c'sle, on past the tangles of twisted metal, underneath the band-stands where the Oerlikons had been so bravely served, and so down the steep incline towards the sunken stern, where the falling tide lapped quietly on the quarter-deck. They penetrated to the darker chaos below, where the officers' sherry lay spilled and wasted in the wardroom, where the butter was plastered on the mirrors, where the broken glass, the cigarettes, the clothing and the little personal things littered the cabins and the messdecks and where the inert corpses indifferently lay.

While this tour of his ship was being made Beattie, black-bearded, blanketed and barefoot, was brought ashore in St Nazaire with the other survivors of Rodier's boat. It was probably some time after 10 o'clock and he was disappointed to see

Campbeltown still intact on the caisson. The latest possible computed time for Tibbits's fuses to act was 9.30. What had gone wrong? He supposed that the Germans had discovered the arrangements and found some way of disarming the fuses, though he thought that Tibbits had provided against that contingency also. He had no opportunity, however, to stand and stare and was hurried on, very cold, to some German office, where he was taken for interrogation by a pleasant-mannered German Intelligence officer, who spoke English well. The Intelligence officer got nothing out of Beattie, but he was persuasively talkative, and he remarked:

'Your people obviously did not know what a hefty thing that lock gate is. It was really useless trying to smash it with a flimsy destroyer.'

At that precise moment the glass from the window crashed to the floor, as the room, and indeed, the whole town was shaken by a thunderous explosion sustained for several seconds – 'an explosion,' in the words of Monsieur Grimaud, 'of an unbelievable violence.'

'That, I hope, is the proof,' observe Beattie dryly as the vibrations began to abate, 'that we did not underestimate the strength of the gate.'

The interrogation was brought to an abrupt close.

This heartening evidence of their success was heard, or even seen, by nearly all the Charioteers who had now been swept up. It was witnessed by the survivors of ML 306 while the *Jaguar* was at anchor only two and a half cables away. A German doctor had come on board and was supervising the transfer of the wounded to a lighter alongside. Philip Dark was being mildly interrogated by Kapitänleutnant Jacobson, of the *Iltis*, who had an English wife. Using a fat, seven-langauge dictionary, Jacobson was discussing with him the details of the action. Dark was dizzy with fatigue and hunger and everything continued to smell of charred cordite. The German said:

'What a mad thing your raid was!'

'What raid?' parried Dark.

At that moment, to quote Dark's prison diary, 'there was an almighty explosion. The ship shuddered from stem to stern. The

German captain leaped from his chair and rushed outside. There were harsh, strident shouts from the Germans (our first introduction to this particular kind of noise) and, sitting in the cabin peacefully by myself, I seemed to be surrounded on all sides by complete pandemonium.' Fragments of steel débris splashed into the water around the ship. Others of ML 306 who were on deck at the time, including Pat Landy, Ordinary Seaman Batteson and Stoker Ritchie, were actual spectators of the event in similarly dramatic circumstances, for, a bare moment before, a German petty officer had said to them in English: 'That is one ship you will never use again!'

Newman and those with him also heard the stirring sound. They were still at the headquarters where they had been taken after capture and as the great roar went up, Newman tells us, 'the place shook like an earthquake and all the Jerries rushed to the doors pell-mell. It was jolly nearly a panic. We, of course, knew what it was all about and, as we sat about on the floor, we burst into laughter.' Now more than ever did they know that their mission had been accomplished.

The time, as nearly as can be judged, was 10.35 a.m.; not earlier. Between them, Beattie and Tibbits had done better than either could know. *Campbeltown* erupted with an enormous flash and a titanic column of black smoke. Under the impact of this violent blast, reinforced by the hammer-blow of the inrushing sea, the great one-hundred-and-sixty-ton caisson burst open inwards. The sea poured like a tidal wave into the empty dock. The northern caisson, the inner face of which had not been destroyed by Brett and Burtenshaw, held, but the two tankers that lay inside the dock – *Schledstadt* and *Passat* – were flung against the dock walls and damaged and the sunken stern half of HMS *Campbeltown*, cut off as by a giant saw, was swept inside by the force of the flood. Of the rest of her nothing remained but the fragments that were flung far and wide.

Nor was this all that was thus blown into mutilated fragments. All the Germans on board the destroyer – men and women – went with her. So, too, did large numbers of those who clustered about her on land, shocked and dismembered by the violence of that blast of death. Fragments of their limbs and entrails were blown far and wide to litter the dockyard in gruesome refuse, to hang obscenely upon wires and rails and to adhere like plaster to the walls of buildings. It was two days before these horrible relics were cleared away and more than a week before Burhenne's adjutant had discovered to what now disintegrated bodies had once belonged the wrecked and empty cars that lay unclaimed in the desolation of the docks.

No reliable death-roll has been published. Normally reliable French sources gave sixty officers and three hundred and twenty men as 'conservative' figures. The German naval staff's *Operation und Taktik* says 'about a hundred', but this is both too round and too small a figure. Captain Mecke gives 'a hundred and twenty or so'. Ordinary Seaman Batteson and Stoker Ritchie, watching from the *Jaguar*, say that there were at least one hundred and fifty on the upper deck alone, besides those shocking relics that the German divers subsequently discovered below deck in the undamaged after portion. Paul, *Jaguar*'s captain, also tells us 'at least a hundred and fifty'. But it does not matter; *Campbeltown*'s mission was not to destroy lives.

How shall one explain the fact that this explosion took place so long after the extreme limit of time expected of its fuses? Not one fuse, but at least three. Under normal functioning, they should have burnt through at 7 a.m. Even under the extreme expected tolerance, they should have acted by 9 a.m. When they did act, they were nearly four hours overdue.

There persists a belief in St Nazaire that a British officer, either voluntarily or involuntarily, went back on board and, in a deed of self-immolation, re-fired the quiescent charge. Workmen are said to have seen one or more go on board. The finger of surmise points at once to Pritchard. He understood the charging and fusing of the explosive ship. He had the professional competence.

Did Pritchard die in the Old Town where Maclagan saw him fall? No shot was fired and the corporal did not know by what weapon he had been struck. Had he only been very badly winded? Or had the wound been not a fatal one?

If there is any truth in the legend, it would, of course, explain the delayed explosion; but it is a legend not easy to sustain. For Bill Pritchard lies buried in the cemetery at Escoublac. Had anyone else gone back on board the destroyer, it is difficult to explain how,

without the requisite gear, which he is unlikely to have carried, and
in the presence of the Germans, he could have fired the great charge.
It was recognized that these fuses were of an experimental and
uncertain nature in regard to their timing and we can do no more
than suppose that some unknown factor of temperature, moisture or
material led to an excessive delay in the action of the acid on the
copper. Yet it remains very odd that all the fuses should have been
so long delayed without failing altogether, and even a man so little
given to fanciful speculation as Hughes-Hallet thinks that 'some
hero' may have gone back on board and immolated himself.

An alternative interpretation of this persistent French legend is
that some one or two British officers, on being ordered or invited
by the Germans to go on board, did so in order to encourage the
belief that the destroyer was not armed with a deadly charge. That
is entirely possible, but there is no positive evidence.

Whatever may be the truth in this matter, nothing detracts
from the brilliance of the demolition plans conceived and carried
out by Nigel Tibbits, which so conclusively prevented the enemy,
for all the remaining years of the war, from using against our most
vital convoy route the most dangerous ship that they possessed.
And to the memory of Pritchard we owe a like acknowledgment
for those acts of demolition against the operating machinery
which would have put the big dock out of action for at least a year
even if *Campbeltown* had never blown up.

*

'It was from this moment,' said Monsieur Grimaud in his report
to Paris, 'that a state of tension became apparent between the
Germans, unnerved by the surprise of the night and the explosion
of the morning, and the population, who had now recovered from
their astonishment and were becoming ironically amused at the
events which were unfolding themselves before them like a surprising motion picture.'

The great, black cloud of *Campbeltown*'s explosion, drawing all
eyes to the sky, dissipated idly in the hush of astonishment that
followed, while fragments of metal clattered down on roof and
road over a radius of a mile. It was a very severe shock to the
Germans. Men ran to the scene, to stand horror-stricken not only

at the towering column of smoke, the shattered gate, the swirling waters, the crashing ships, but also at the spectacle of human flesh and bones showered over all the devastated scene.

Gradually the Germans' discipline and order re-established itself, but their unease showed itself in a tightening of their grip. Scattered shooting was still going on, believed by the Germans to be coming from commandos not yet discovered, and the bullets were still whistling about the streets, and in the country also, when Newman and his friends were lorried off to La Baule. At late as 6 o'clock that evening Dieckmann, driving back to his coast defence guns after a visit to Admiral Lindenau's headquarters in Nantes, was shot at as he passed through St Nazaire.

By Sunday a superficial calm was restored but with no easing of the tension. On Monday the French workmen were permitted to return to the docks and there saw, to their astonishment, but scarcely concealed satisfaction, the evidence of the carnage from *Campbeltown*'s explosion still, after two days, polluting the ground and buildings. Groups of Germans, in an apparently dazed manner, were shovelling up the human refuse and scattering sand as upon the floor of a butcher's shop.

The episode, however, except for the terrific row, the reprimands and the military inquisitions, now appeared to be over. But at about 4 o'clock that Monday afternoon another heavy explosion shook the surroundings and threw the whole place once more into confusion and consternation. In a great shower of smoke and water the outer gate of the Old Entrance blew up, as one of Wynn's torpedoes exploded.

A new anger seized the Germans, an anger the more dangerous because they were completely mystified. What was this big charge that had gone up under water, and who the devil had placed it there? It was two and a half days since all the British had been rounded up. The Germans began to look still more sourly upon the French. Had the inhabitants been conniving with the British in these acts of destruction? A search of all houses and an examination of identity cards were set on foot. Orders were issued to the mayor that all cafés must be shut at 9 p.m. Patrols were sent out through the streets, where the French were gathering in small groups and discussing with animation the extraordinary events.

They were very well aware of the dangerous temper of the
Germans. The threatening looks and the peremptory commands
told their own story. The news that a furious Hitler had ordered
an immediately inquiry on the spot had already set the Germans
on edge. Like the Charioteers' fuses, a corrosive acid was inexorably at work, ready at the appointed moment to release the
springs of an emotional explosion.

An hour later the second of Wynn's torpedoes blew up.

The acid had done its work. The spring leapt into action.
Tumult burst into flames throughout the dockyard. A group of
French workmen, fearful of German suspicions and reprisals,
threw down their tools and ran for Bridge M at the northern end
of the Submarine Basin. There they were met by German troops,
who, supposing this to be an organized rising, opened fire on
them, driving them to take refuge in trenches and shelters where
they remained far into the night. The fever spread quickly all
through the port, as everywhere the Germans began to fire upon
bewildered parties of Frenchmen.

It is very unusual for German troops to lose their heads, but they
did so on this occasion. The mysteriousness of these events, the
troubled and uncertain atmosphere, the renewal of shooting by a
few Frenchmen, to whom every explosion was a new song of hope,
the kindling of fires in the Old Town and in the Loire and Penhoët
docks threw them into a state of angry bewilderment. Unnerved
and acting on sudden impulse, on what official orders we know
not, they began, with the fall of night, to shoot in every direction,
shooting at any sign of movement, imagining British commandos
about to spring on them from every shadow. Inevitably German
soon began to shoot German in the confusion of the night, each
thus believing that he was being attacked by an enemy. Sohler,
hurrying in by car from La Baule to ensure the safety of his
submarines from the reported civilian rising, was repeatedly fired
at on his way and the officer accompanying him wounded.

At 8.30 p.m. squalls of musketry, machine-gun fire and even
grenades broke out in the neighbourhood of the Boulevard de
l'Océan. The streets were filled with troops and naval ratings,
circulating in small parties, seemingly under no orders, engaging
each other and the French. They emptied their magazines into

houses and into the hospital. They opened fire on passengers arriving at the railway station from Nantes. They fired at every head that appeared at a window and at the reflections of the flashes of their own rifles.

No doubt there has been some exaggeration of the events of this night of terror. Mecke tells us that he ordered his own troops to shoot only if definitely attacked. But certain facts are clear and official casualty lists speak for themselves. Thus Louis Potin, a Passive Defence worker, coming out of his waterside house at Penhoët in his white helmet to bring aid to the wounded, was killed; his five-year-old son was riddled with bullets on the doorstep and his eight-year-old daughter wounded while inside the house. Near by a father, taking his two children by the hand to go to a shelter, was shot down from fifty paces behind by a kneeling sailor, 'like a deer in the forest'. In the rue du Bois Savary, one of the main streets of the town, a woman approaching her window to close the shutters was killed by a grenade. At a corner of the rue Villès-Martin, a cyclist coming from his garden with a basket of vegetables, was riddled by a fusillade.

Before midnight this panic shooting had died down in the main town, but new outbursts began in the Old Town and at Penhoët. A chance bullet, breaking the high tension electric cables, plunged the whole town in darkness. The water supply stopped also; and these occurrences served only to give further emphasis to the enemy's conviction that a concerted rising was taking place.

It was upon the Old Town that the German hand fell heaviest. After their search parties had combed the houses, the inhabitants were thrown out without notice, locked up in the German block-houses, to be thence conveyed, to the number of one thousand five hundred, to the prison camp at Savenay, while their houses were ransacked. At about 11 o'clock a fog mercifully descended and silence gradually returned, but during that night sixteen French men, women and children, from the ages of five to seventy-six, were killed and twenty-six wounded.

A little after midnight squads of the *Feldgendarmerie* entered the houses of the mayor and the four assistant mayors and, standing over them with sub-machine-guns as they dressed, carried them off under Leutnant Mayer to the Collège de Saint-Louis, where the office of the military administration was installed. Here, after having passed through a labyrinth of darkened corridors, they were brought into a very large room lit only by a few twisted red candles of the sort habitually used for upright pianos. In this sombre and disquieting atmosphere, they found themselves in front of a cold and forbidding Prussian colonel who had arrived that evening from Army headquarters at Angers – very tall and very thin, high-coloured, grey-haired, his legs encased in gaiters so tight as to accentuate his thinness. He spoke to the Frenchmen very fast in a harsh and menacing tone, charging them that the civilian population had been attacking the Germans and threatening them that if these acts continued tomorrow one-tenth of the persons in the quarter responsible would be shot without hearing.

As a result of this savage threat, the unfortunate officials spent the rest of the night preparing a proclamation to the town, turning printers out of their beds, searching for bill-posters, and directing where the posters should be displayed so that they could not be defaced by the public. The proclamation was read next morning by a stupefied populace who, in the words of Monsieur Grimaud, looked upon it 'as a vicious revenge for the reverse to German arms that the landing of the British commandos constituted'. The mayoral authorities stoutly denied that any citizens had attacked the Germans, but there is small reason to doubt that many patriotic Frenchmen, convinced that deliverance by their allies was at hand, brought out such weapons as they may have managed to hide and set fire to installations in the docks.

Throughout France the impact of the news of the Raid was immense. In spite of the mendacious accounts circulated by the Nazis and their Vichy lackeys, the hearts of all loyal Frenchmen rejoiced in the shining prowess of the deed and saw in it the first hope that the long night would have an end. And in St Nazaire itself a lamp was lit which still shines with even more brilliance than the glare of the searchlights in which so many gallant men lost their lives.

★

In the German hierarchy there was a terrific row. Hitler was extremely angry. What enraged him as much as the loss of the

Normandie Dock was that British forces had succeeded in penetrating German defences and actually landing on territory that he held. To him that was always a particular affront. The very day after the Raid he took the extraordinary step of ordering Field-Marshal von Rundstedt, Commander-in-Chief of all German forces in western Europe, to conduct a personal inquiry immediately. This von Rundstedt accordingly did at St Nazaire on 31 March, while the terrors of the night before still held the population in a grip of fear as they read the menacing proclamations and as the German troops patrolled the streets and swept civilians away to prison camps.

Von Rundstedt reported that there was no fault to find with the German conduct of the action and that no blame could be assigned to anyone for the British landing. But Hitler was far from satisfied. He demanded a head on a charger and would not let the matter rest. On his orders General Jodl, Director of Operations of the supreme command of all the armed forces, visited von Rundstedt three days later 'to examine further the failure to repel the enemy' and the inquiry, under pressure, very soon shaped itself into one of those violent quarrels between the Army and the Navy which are so familiar a picture in German military archives. Hitler declared that the measures taken to detect Ryder's force at sea were quite inadequate and critical interest became focused at once on that crucial encounter between Ryder and U 593, when, as we have seen, the Naval Group Command West had been misled by Ryder's change of course and by the submarine's faulty report, into thinking that the British force was merely returning from laying mines or else was on its way to Gibraltar. It was this assumption that led Group Command West to order 5 TBD Flotilla to sea to make an exploratory sweep. 'An imminent attack from the sea on a port of the French west coast was never anticipated.'

This probing into naval affairs, or the manner in which it was done, lit the fires of wrath in Grand Admiral Raeder, the Commander-in-Chief. There seemed to be no one at Hitler's headquarters, he complained, in a position to present a correct picture of events and as a result the army officers of Supreme Command had formed a judgment wholly false and detrimental to the Navy. In very much sharper terms Raeder wrote personally to Field-Marshal Keitel:

> I have heard with the greatest displeasure of your signal to C-in-C
> West on the subject of the St Nazaire enquiry and the question-
> naire that has been drafted at your express wish. I have not been
> informed at any stage of the proceeding, although the greater part
> of the questions are within my province and are my personal
> responsibility. You have not once informed me of the instructions
> you were issuing. This procedure is against all military custom. I
> must therefore insist on an explanation and apology from you.

As far as official records go, he does not seem to have received that
apology.

In the official report the factors contributing to the successful
British penetration of the Loire were set out as:

Failure to anticipate the repetition of small raids such as that
on Zeebrugge.

The diversionary bombing raid (which did at first divert
attention).

The incorrect conclusion drawn from the report of U 593.

Lack of aerial reconnaissance.

Inadequate patrolling of the estuary and the absence of wireless
on the patrol boats.

The existence of only one naval radar station, which had been
diverted to an anti-aircraft rôle.

Examining the British plan and performance, the Germans
acknowledged that the principle of a diversionary air attack was
sound. Mecke (who was awarded the Knight's Cross by Hitler)
stated in his report that had the RAF been able to continue
bombing he had little doubt but that the raiders would have
penetrated entirely unobserved. It was admitted that the chief
object of the Raid had been achieved and it was described as an
operation cleverly planned to the last detail and boldly carried out.
The failure of the subsidiary objects was attributed to the half
measures adopted by the British, 'who always fight shy of shed-
ding blood even when the target is important enough to justify it'.
Had the operation been planned on the larger scale of Zeebrugge,
employing more men and larger ships capable of withstanding
heavy AA fire with equanimity, the Raid would without doubt
have been a complete success in all its objectives. These tactical
criticisms, however, were based on an entire misconception of the

very factors that had confronted Forbes – lack of suitable ships and the difficulty of an undetected approach.

Such were the views of Germans at higher levels who knew the true facts and who could assess them objectively. Very different was the torrent of lies poured out to the world by the Nazi propaganda machine. We need not study them here in all their nauseating untruthfulness, but it is proper to note that, in the absence of any immediate and conclusive evidence of the achievements, no firm and convincing claims could at that time be made in the British announcements; so that for a very long time, even indeed until today, it was believed by a great many people, and by many people who ought to have known better, that this 'deed of glory intimately involved in high strategy' was 'a bit of a flop'.

20. THE CAPTIVE AND THE FREE

Of all these later happenings most of the captured Charioteers knew nothing until years afterwards. As they gradually came together in small parties on that Saturday morning, some very roughly handled, others treated decently, they greeted each other with the utmost cheerfulness. Exhausted, bedraggled, hatless, uniforms torn and stained, shoulder-straps ripped off by Germans rapacious for souvenirs to give colour to their boasts, limping, supporting one another, they had nonetheless not lost their spirit and they met again with smiles, excepting only the more desperately wounded.

As the commandos of the dockyard battle were gradually gleaned by the Germans, a still larger harvest was being gathered in from the sea. Gunshot, drowned or burned to death in the cruel petrol fires, the dead were brought in for burial. All down the estuary others were rescued, or washed ashore, miraculously alive after long immersion. Some of these, including Beattie and Burt, were stripped of their wet clothing and rubbed down, but provided with nothing more than a blanket to wrap around themselves and in this exiguous cover, barefoot, they were required to endure the long day and journey before them. These parties from the sea – soldiers and sailors – were brought ashore at various places, but, by some time about midday, nearly all had been collected in La Baule, the wounded and the able separately. Here there were more 'reunions' of men who in adversity lost none of their high morale, for they knew that, although they were prisoners, they had won a victory. The echoes of *Campbeltown*'s explosion still rang in their ears. Memorable of the many vivid incidents of that day was the moment when, to Newman and the others already assembled at La Baule, there came in the tall, slim figure of Sam Beattie, black-bearded, blanketed, barefoot and chilled to the bone, yet still with a broad grin and a hearty laugh.

There now began for the Charioteers a long trek to the trying and squalid life of a prisoner of war. But, so long as they were together, they were no ordinary prisoners. For a long time they were specially guarded and kept separate from all others. So important were they considered that a few days later Hitler sent his own interpreter, the celebrated Dr Schmidt, to interrogate them. Not the least memorable feature of their captivity was what Copland called 'the absolutely marvellous spirit which bound both the Royal Navy and the commandos together'. This fusion of feeling had its roots not only in the usual British aptitude for making the best of things, but, even more surely, in the knowledge that they had all been companions in a momentous enterprise which was peculiarly and utterly their own. There grew up a terrific pride in their brotherhood one with another in one of the most daring of exploits, a pride which was shown not least in their high bearing and continued good discipline as prisoners.

As far as can be gathered from the scattered and inexact records, a total of about two hundred, perhaps a few more, were taken prisoner. The dead have in all official accounts been reported as 144, but in point of fact they reached a total of 169 – a proportion of more than one man in four of all the 611 who sailed (not 640 as officially recorded). This was an extremely high proportion of fatal casualties for any operation; yet, in the harsh accountancy of war, a low price for the high results achieved. By far the greater number – probably more than three-quarters – were killed in the river battle and the withdrawal. The commando losses amounted to 64 and the naval losses to 105, fully two-thirds of the naval losses being accounted for in the two sinkings of the crowded boats of Rodier and Wynn during the withdrawal.

The enemy casualties, as given by the German naval staff, amounted to 42 killed, plus the hundred or more (almost certainly far more) admitted as blown up in the *Campbeltown*, and 127 wounded. To these are to be added a few army losses. According to Mecke, all the German losses, except for a few wounded and except for the deaths incurred in *Campbeltown*'s explosion, were inflicted by the commandos ashore, but this is not easy to accept.

If the German figures are accepted, the losses in men were thus pretty much the same on both sides, although the losses of an assaulting force are usually expected to be the higher. It is not, however, by such figures that the merits and value of the action are to be measured; though we may note as a matter of interest that the British losses at St Nazaire were proportionately more than twice as heavy as those in the Zeebrugge Raid.*

At La Baule the captive Charioteers came together in two main parties. The able and the slightly wounded were lorried away to the large Brittany town of Rennes, where they were shut up in a prison camp of unspeakable filthiness (Stalag 133) used for French colonial prisoners of war. The main body of the wounded, to the number of about ninety, were taken to the German naval hospital that had been established in the *de luxe* Hermitage Hotel at La Baule. The conditions for the British wounded, however, were anything but *de luxe*. Their beds were the floor. The place was crammed with the British and German wounded, the medical staff inadequate for the emergency and, as was not uncommon in German hospitals, poorly supplied with anaesthetics. All but the most severe operations – even the removal of Wynn's eye – were carried out without anaesthesia. All the time, day and night, German Tommy-gunners paraded up and down between the rows of prostrate forms. They even followed the stretcher cases up to the operating theatre and when the patient revived after his ordeal there was the Tommy-gunner still.

On Wednesday – four days after the Raid – there took place a ceremonial burial of the dead of both sides, organized by the Germans with honourable decorum. The British were invited to send a party and all who were able to walk turned out in the best shape they could. From the pile of clothes, which had been taken away from them, the least spoilt items were picked out. The sailors borrowed razors from the commandos. All hatless, and most without jackets, a party of some twenty paraded under Hopwood, and marched as smartly as they were able into a field at Escoublac, adjacent to La Baule. For a brief space all hostilities were forgotten

---

* At Zeebrugge the fatal casualties numbered 195 out of a total of 1784 officers and men in the assaulting forces.

in an act of mutual homage and respect. The Germans provided a generous wreath. The British dead lay in a long trench in a double row of coffins, and beside this common grave stood one more coffin, covered with the Union Flag. The German coffins were similarly disposed. Services were then conducted by Protestant and Roman Catholic chaplains, but unfortunately the British were not able to understand a word. Six British sailors and soldiers then advanced and lowered into the grave the remaining coffin. Hopwood let fall the wreath and three volleys of musketry were fired. 'It was,' Dark recorded, 'all extremely impressive and our hearts were filled with twisted and unintelligible emotions.'

This field of graves was the beginning of a cemetery which during the next three years was to be much expanded by British dead, particularly of the Royal Air Force, and there it still is.

As they became well enough, the wounded were moved on, also to Rennes, and were put into St Vincent's Hospital, a very stark, bare and cheerless hospital for French colonial troops, where they received devoted care from the French doctors, ill-provided though they were with the barest necessities, and from the cheerful, friendly, smiling, warm-hearted native orderlies – Senegalese, Moroccans, Cambodians and others – all themselves prisoners. Thence all but a few were moved on into Germany, to a prison camp at Westertimke, near Bremen, known as Marlag-Milag; until, the Germans deciding to break them up, officers and men, navy and army were sent away to separate camps.

There we must leave the main body of these gallant gentlemen, continually plotting their escapes, often succeeding, but nearly always being caught again. The more persistent escapists were sent off to the notorious punishment castle of Colditz – Stephens, Purdon, Wynn and Morgan. Michael Burn was sent there, too. Even from there, however, Stephens escaped successfully at last, in company with the very gallant Major Ronnie Littledale, of the 60th Rifles, who was later killed in the Normandy campaign. Disguised as French workmen, they escaped from the formidable prison under cover of music from the camp band, made their way to Switzerland and crossed the border near Singen, existing for the last two days on apples, and evading by the skin of their teeth the German sentry on the very edge of the frontier.

Even more remarkable, perhaps, was the successful escape made by Sergeants Alf Searson and Dick Bradley, old friends of 2 Commando and members of Walton's demolition squad, and Private Jimmy Brown, of 5 Commando, one of the most resourceful and quick-witted of all the Charioteers. All had made several attempts before, learning by experience the tricks of the trade, and they were fortunate to have in the robust and resolute Bradley a man who spoke good enough German. On their third attempt Searson and Bradley had come within an ace of success, reaching the Swiss frontier where the Rhine joins it, but at the very last moment had stumbled into a German frontier patrol hut. Nonetheless, Searson was already thinking about the next attempt, for, as they waited for an escort to take them away, he carefully studied the frontier and noted the dispositions and movements of the German sentries.

The last time they were joined by the irrepressible Brown, blond and sturdy, friend of previous attempts. They had now been moved to a camp at Gross-Zeidel, far away in the south-west corner of Poland, six hundred miles from Switzerland, but they set out again undaunted on Trafalgar Day 1943, making designedly for the very spot where they had before been. Going openly by train the greater part of the way, they survived extraordinary encounters, boldly asking the way of a German sentry, who challenged them on the roadside at midnight, coolly going back for an English novel which Bradley had left at the office of a burgomaster where they had bluffed their way out after arrest on suspicion, giving deliberately stupid answers to a German sergeant-major who took them for recruits. Finally, on 25 October, crossing a ploughed field in stockinged feet, creeping from shadow to shadow, they slipped across the frontier at the very spot where they had been captured last time.

To escape is honourable and the duty of all prisoners of war. To avoid capture and to fight again is still more honourable. Not all who landed at St Nazaire fell into enemy hands. Five commandos, by their own determination and wit, by a great deal of luck and through the generous help of patriot Frenchmen given at peril of their own lives, succeeded in avoiding capture and in obeying Newman's order to make their way to far distant Gibraltar.

These remarkable achievements were carried out by three separate groups, and two of them originated from the cellar of a bombed shop in St Nazaire, where a particularly gallant and resolute party of six men had concealed themselves. These were Troop Sergeant-Major Haines, Sergeant Challington (Camerons), Lance-Corporal Howarth (Grenadier Guards), Corporal Wright, the RE diarist, Corporal Douglas (Liverpool Scottish), and Private Harding (Gloucesters). All but Douglas and Harding were pretty sharply wounded, Wright bleeding profusely from a calf partly shot away, but that did not lessen their determination to seek freedom. Taking up a posture of defence, they stayed in the cellar all that Saturday, in considerable pain and with very little to eat, and narrowly escaping discovery as a German search party went through the ruins overhead. By good fortune some civilian trousers and a jacket were found for Challington, who had no hope of escape in the kilt, and a jacket for Haines.

Haines decided that that night they should make their way out in pairs, but Wright, knowing that he would seriously hold back other people and that he was too badly injured to go alone, walked out after dark and gave himself up. Haines and Challington, both with leg wounds, set off painfully together, the first to leave, and succeeded in making their way into the country but had the bad luck to run into a party of Germans.

Howarth, who had been with Roderick's assault party and twice hit, was the next to leave. Going alone and reaching open country, he was befriended by a French family who gave him a bath and put him to bed, and a day or two later an English-speaking schoolmaster, Monsieur Barratte, at great personal risk, took him to his own house in St Nazaire and afterwards accompanied him by train as far as Bordeaux. Going on from there alone into unoccupied France, Howarth fell into the hands of the Vichy police and spent eight months in confinement before he made his escape.

Last to leave the cellar were Douglas and Harding, who had both been members of Haines's own assault party. Still in uniform, they rolled up their battledress trousers, opened the collars of their blouses and sailed safely through the Germans at the street barriers put up at the entrances to the town, Douglas painfully aware of the corporal's stripes on his sleeve. Marching by night, they reached La Roche Bernard, where, near the end of their tether, they barely escaped capture by a German flak battery. Chance led them to a kindly French butcher and he in turn passed them to an American lady, who gave them clothes, money and bicycles. Making their way to Loches, they were befriended by a French lawyer, who provided them with faked papers and, together with his wife, took them all the way to Marseilles, where an escape organization took charge of them.

*

Perhaps the most colourful of the evaders' experiences, however, was that which befell Corporal George Wheeler and Lance-Corporal R. Sims, who had nothing to do with Haines's party. Wheeler, slender, wiry, spectacled, dark-haired, an honours degree man in economics, has already been briefly seen with Philip Walton's demolition team. He could speak schoolboy French. Sims, a totally different character, well set up, robust, of simple character, was a young Canadian who was a Regular soldier in the Somerset Light Infantry. These two took refuge together in a small cavity beneath a house in St Nazaire just as day was breaking on Saturday.

That night, just before midnight, when all was quiet, they crept out into the moonlight, noiseless in their rubber-soled boots and reached the outskirts of the town. There they passed a dance café where the Germans were noisily celebrating. Regretting having left their grenades behind, they fingered their Colts, sorely tempted to break up the party, but thought better of it.

Just before daylight, they reached the little village of L'Immaculée Conception and lay up in a haystack, where they were discovered by Monsieur Guillaume Francis, who, astonished and alarmed though he was, took them to his house, and together with friends whom he summoned, generously provided them out of their little store with food and two hundred and fifty francs each and clothed them with old 'Sunday best' black jackets, green with antiquity, and pinstripe trousers, but no civilian boots. He took away their pistols. 'Not safe for you, my friends,' he said, 'but might be useful to me one day.'

The two men went on that night but, bedevilled by the uncertainty of where to go and by the lack of a map, went to and fro for two nights, still only a very little way out of St Nazaire, trying to find a way round the marsh that stretched for thirty square miles inland from the town. At the little village of St André des Eaux, however, they were given a calendar map issued by a firm of agricultural implement manufacturers; these were issued separately for each district, showing every lane and cart-track. 'After that,' Wheeler said, 'it was easy. Wherever we went, all we had to do was to ask for the PTT calendar.'

Receiving much contrary advice on the best direction to take, they knew, however, that they must avoid Germans and large towns and travel by remote byways. Finally they made their way round the north of the big marsh and struck east, never certain whether it was best to march by night or by day, sleeping in hayricks, barns or open woods, incongruous figures in their black suits and commando boots, often very hungry, often generously fed, experiencing the oddest encounters and many close shaves, frequently wet to the skin but always determined to press on. To Wheeler, one of their greatest dangers was Sims's passion for smoking; he thought nothing of accosting a startled Frenchman on a lonely road to ask for a cigarette.

Not all the French were friendly; some hostile, some frightened, many highly suspicious of the identities of these shabby and weather-soiled apparitions. It was as well for the refugees' peace of mind that they did not know that the Germans were on their trail and had circulated descriptions emphasizing their boots and Wheeler's spectacles. Except for these few instances, however, the two young soldiers found that the words '*évadés de St Nazaire*' were a magic password to the hearts of Frenchmen; for everywhere the news of the great deed had brought hope and rejoicing.

To their surprise, they crossed the Loire without being challenged at a bridge seven miles from Angers. They were getting very footsore as they pressed on through the drenching rain over a country well trodden by English armies of old and through antique places haunted by ghosts of French kings. At the tiny village of Pouant a very pro-British farmer wept when they left. The most serious of all obstacles was before them – the Line of Demarcation between occupied and unoccupied France, under strong surveillance by German guards; but for this obstacle they were to have help of a most unexpected kind.

Having learnt that the Line of Demarcation in this area was the River Creuse, they were taken by a Frenchwoman to the house of a gamekeeper in the Forêt de Guerches, a mile and a half from the river. Here the Frenchwoman and the gamekeeper's two daughters, pretty and vivacious, held a feminine council of war and made a plan, based, as all good plans should be, on accurate knowledge of the enemy's movements and habits. The French here knew that all the German cyclist patrols on the riverside roads came in to change guard on the bridge at Leugny at midday.

In accordance with the feminine staff plan, the two girls, carrying towels, left on their bicycles the next morning at 11.30, followed by the two soldiers. They met on the riverside road. All was clear; the last German patrol had passed.

'Take off your jackets,' the girls said, 'and give them to us.'

They did so and the girls turned left and rode away to Leugny, a quarter of a mile away, while the soldiers watched from the screen of roadside trees. After a minute or two they saw the girls dismount by the sentry with a great flurry of skirts and begin talking to him.

This was their cue. Wheeler and Sims crossed the road and waded into the river, ice-cold from the winter snows. Looking to their left they saw the French girls still flirting with the sentry. Scrambling out on the far bank they hurried to conceal themselves among the trees and no sooner had they done so than the girls, with a great business of flying skirts, displays of leg and waves of the arm, mounted unsteadily and rode across the bridge.

In a few minutes the spirited and resourceful girls rode up, restored to them their dry jackets and gave them the towels, with which the men dried themselves as best they could, and waved them a cheerful goodbye.

We cannot stay too long to follow this adventurous and well-contrived evasion of the two commandos. The worst was over. The next day – 14 April – after having marched about two hundred and fifty miles – they arrived at Azay-le-Ferron and were welcomed with open arms, as though they were their own sons, by Monsieur Maurice Génichon and his wife at their fine, small château. Their rags were stripped off, good clothes and shoes given them; a hot bath was followed by a memorable dinner that ended with green Chartreuse and then real beds in private suites, the enjoyment of the warm hospitality of Monsieur and Madame Génichon enhanced by their excellent English.

Next morning, overcoming with the utmost difficulty a nervous reluctance to travelling openly in public transport, they were put on a bus to Châteauroux by Monsieur Génichon, fell in by chance with a sterling and resourceful Belgian youth named Gilbert Mahun, who was himself trying to get to England, travelled with him by train down to Toulouse, and there, once more by fortunate chance, met Monsieur Pierre Uhlmann and his American wife and through their agency were put in touch with an escape organization which took them, with many a near squeak, over the Pyrenees and thence to Gibraltar.

Regaining England, Wheeler, Sims, Douglas, Harding and Howarth rejoined their units and fought again in the great campaigns that led at last to victory.

*

The last scene of all is fittingly presented by Micky Wynn. Repatriated on medical grounds, he was barred by the rules of war from bearing arms again against the Germans, but he was determined to fulfil one ambition. At the time when our armies were sweeping victoriously into Germany he persuaded the Admiralty to send him on a mission for the rehabilitation of released naval prisoners of war. He insinuated himself into the area of the Canadian Army, made contact with the Guards' Armoured Division and, wearing the White Ensign, rode in a leading tank into the Marlag-Milag prison camp, to release his gallant shipmate, Bill Lovegrove.

APPENDICES

A. The Fallen

All due care has been taken to ensure that this list (as well as those following) is accurate and complete, but exactitude is not entirely certain in one or two instances. No official composite list seems to have been published. Substantially, the list of those killed and died of wounds is that on the St Nazaire Memorial, with corrections and additions.

Private D. **Aird**, 2 Commando
Able Seaman Alfred **Baker**, *Campbeltown*
Lieutenant G. **MacNaughton Baker**, ML 447
Sub-Lieutenant K. **Bachelor**, ML 268
Leading Seaman R. J. **Bailey**, *Campbeltown*
Stoker E. C. **Barber**, ML 457
Ordinary Seaman Leonard **Barber**, ML 298
Ordinary Seaman A. **Bartlett**, ML 267
Lieutenant E. H. **Beart**, ML 267
Ordinary Seaman G. **Bell**, ML 267
Petty Officer Motor Mechanic A. L. **Bennett**, ML 306
Leading Stoker W. H. **Berry**, *Campbeltown*
Ordinary Seaman A. T. **Bett**, *Campbeltown*
Lance-Sergeant R. **Beveridge**, 5 Commando
Captain D. L. **Birney**, 2 Commando
Corporal A. **Blount**, 12 Commando
Petty Officer H. P. **Booth**, *Campbeltown*
Lance-Corporal R. **Borgman**, 4 Commando
Able Seaman H. E. **Bott**, *Campbeltown*
Able Seaman D. F. **Bowman**, *Campbeltown*
Telegraphist David **Bowyer**, MTB 74
Private J. D. **Boyce**, 3 Commando
Able Seaman George **Brearley**, ML 457
Leading Stoker W. C. **Brenton**, *Campbeltown*
Stoker David **Broome**, ML 447
Able Seaman John **Brown**, ML 177

Lance-Corporal E. **Bryan**, 2 Commando
Lance-Corporal L. **Burgess**, 9 Commando
Lance-Corporal R. E. D. **Burns**, 2 Commando
Lieutenant R. J. G. **Burtenshaw**, 5 Commando
Lieutenant H. S. **Chambers**, ML 447
Corporal S. E. **Chetwynd**, 12 Commando
Leading Stoker E. J. **Chick**, ML 267
Ordinary Seaman Douglas **Clear**, ML 298
Lieutenant T. A. M. **Collier**, ML 457
Lance-Corporal J. **Coughlan**, 2 Commando
Sapper G. **Coulson**, 4 Commando
Private H. **Cunningham**, 2 Commando
Corporal J. **Deans**, 9 Commando
Private T. **Diamond**, 2 Commando
Ordinary Seaman L. S. **Dickson**, ML 457
Able Seaman Edwin **Dodd**, ML 298
Lance-Corporal I. **Donaldson**, 2 Commando
Able Seaman H. G. **Drapper**, ML 447
Lance-Corporal R. **Duncan**, 9 Commando
Sergeant Thomas **Durrant**, VC, 1 Commando
Sergeant L. F. **Eldridge**, 2 Commando
Able Seaman Thomas **Findlay**, *Campbeltown*
Able Seaman W. R. **Findley**, *Campbeltown*
Corporal N. **Fisher**, 2 Commando
Ordinary Seaman T. N. **Garner**, ML 306
Sub-Lieutenant D. A. **Garnham**, ML 268
Lance-Corporal A. E. **Garratt**, 2 Commando
Lance-Sergeant W. **Gibson**, 2 Commando
Able Seaman S. W. **Giles**, *Campbeltown*
Private G. **Goss**, 2 Commando
Lieutenant C. H. C. **Gough**, *Campbeltown*
Petty Officer Motor Mechanic R. G. **Gough**, ML 262
Private W. E. **Grose**, 2 Commando
Private J. **Gwynne**, 2 Commando
Ordinary Signalman A. E. **Hale**, ML 192
Ordinary Seaman G. H. **Hallett**, ML 192
Sub-Lieutenant K. G. **Hampshire**, ML 457
Able Seaman Eric **Hargreaves**, MTB 74
Gunner (T) H. **Hargreaves**, *Campbeltown*
Lance-Sergeant P. **Harkness**, 2 Commando
Lance-Sergeant M. **Harrison**, 2 Commando
Lance-Corporal W. **Hay**, 2 Commando
Lance-Corporal W. B. **Heather**, 2 Commando
Sergeant S. **Hempstead**, 2 Commando
Lieutenant I. B. H. **Henderson**, ML 306

Ordinary Seaman John **Hextall**, ML 177
Sub-Lieutenant K. I. **Hills**, ML 262
Stoker Petty Officer R. J. **Hodder**, *Campbeltown*
Captain E. S. **Hodgson**, 2 Commando
Stoker F. R. W. **Holland**, ML 262
Petty Officer Motor Mechanic Albert **Howard**, ML 268
Able Seaman Victor **Howard**, *Campbeltown*
Lance-Corporal G. H. **Hudson**, 2 Commando
Sergeant G. **Ide**, 5 Commando
Sergeant R. **Jameson**, 9 Commando
Lieutenant M. **Jenkins**, 2 Commando
Telegraphist A. H. **Jones**, *Campbeltown*
Able Seaman G. J. **Jones**, ML 262
Corporal H. H. **Jones**, 12 Commando
Private J. **Kelly**, 2 Commando
Leading Seaman L. **Kemp**, *Campbeltown*
Leading Motor Mechanic E. E. **Kenningham**, ML 267
Leading Seaman K. C. **Kirkup**, ML 268
Able Seaman John **Leech**, ML 267
Private G. **Lewis**, 2 Commando
Able Seaman C. W. **Liddel**, MTB 74
Ordinary Seaman H. W. **Little**, ML 192
Corporal F. **Llewellyn**, 1 Commando
Petty Officer Steward Albert **Love**, *Campbeltown*
Private A. **Lucy**, 2 Commando
Chief Motor Mechanic E. B. **Marsden**, ML 298
Able Seaman W. J. **Martin**, ML 262
Lance-Corporal H. **Mather**, 2 Commando
Stoker J. R. **Mathers**, ML 298
Leading Seaman Peter **Mawby**, *Campbeltown*
Private G. **Maylott**, 2 Commando
Private J. **McCormack**, 2 Commando
Leading Seaman S. **McKeown**, ML 262
Able Seaman Joseph **Miller**, *Campbeltown*
Able Seaman A. **Milner**, ML 298
Motor Mechanic Peter **Mooney**, ML 457
Regimental Sergeant-Major A. **Moss**, 2 Commando
Private A. W. **Neal**, 2 Commando
Able Seaman H. E. **Nelson**, *Campbeltown*
Engine-Room Artificer R. R. **Nelson**, *Campbeltown*
Able Seaman J. A. **Nicholson**, ML 268
Sub-Lieutenant A. F. **O'Connor**, MTB 74
Stoker William **Oliphant**, ML 267
Leading Seaman S. J. **Onsorge**, ML 457
Motor Mechanic T. G. **Parker**, ML 447

Able Seaman Joseph **Parsons**, ML 457

Lance-Corporal K. **Patterson**, 2 Commando

Lieutenant H. **Pennington**, 4 Commando

Lieutenant T. G. P. **Peyton**, 2 Commando

Leading Seaman K. K. S. **Pitt**, ML 177

Captain W. H. **Pritchard**, MC, Special Service Brigade

Stoker Petty Officer J. W. **Purver**, *Campbeltown*

Leading Seaman Montagu **Rakusen**, ML 268

Chief Motor Mechanic R. **Ramsey**, ML 296

Leading Stoker J. B. **Reville**, *Campbeltown*

Private T. **Roach**, 2 Commando

Guardsman S. **Robinson**, 2 Commando

Lieutenant M. F. **Rodier**, ML 177

Able Seaman Allenby **Rollin**, *Campbeltown*

Petty Officer Motor Mechanic S. W. **Roots**, ML 267

Ordinary Seaman A. **Ross**, *Campbeltown*

Leading Seaman W. G. **Sargent**, ML 306

Able Seaman W. A. **Savage**, VC, MGB 314

Petty Officer Telegraphist H. B. **Scott**, *Campbeltown*

Private J. **Shenton**, 9 Commando

Able Seaman Albert **Sheppard**, ML 267

Leading Stoker Harold **Simmonds**, MTB 74

Lieutenant C. J. **Smalley**, 5 Commando

Able Seaman James **Smith**, *Campbeltown*

Able Seaman John W. **Smith**, ML 268

Stoker L. C. **Smith**, ML 298

Motor Mechanic G. **Snowball**, ML 192

Lance-Corporal W. **Spaul**, 2 Commando

Sub-Lieutenant A. **Spraggon**, ML 298

Ordinary Telegraphist D. M. **Steel**, ML 267

Able Seaman A. R. **Stephens**, MGB 314

Lance-Corporal G. **Stokes**, 5 Commando

Ordinary Seaman Gilbert **Swann**, ML 298

Sergeant G. **Taylor**, 2 Commando

Lieutenant N. T. B. **Tibbits**, DSC, *Campbeltown*

Private E. **Tomblin**, 1 Commando

Corporal R. M. **Tomsett**, 2 Commando

Sub-Lieutenant (E) A. J. **Toy**, ML 177

Lieutenant J. E. **Vanderwerve**, 2 Commando

Sub-Lieutenant P. H. D. **Vardon-Patten**, ML 298

Stoker D. M. **Vyall**, *Campbeltown*

Guardsman G. W. **Walton**, 2 Commando

Lieutenant Philip **Walton**, 2 Commando

Stoker Petty Officer A. T. **Wade**, *Campbeltown*

Able Seaman J. D. **Walker**, ML 262

Motor Mechanic L. F. **Wallace**, ML 268
Petty Officer R. R. **Ward**, MTB 74
Chief Petty Officer A. P. **Wellstead**, *Campbeltown*
Ordinary Seaman Harold **Westcott**, ML 267
Ordinary Signalman A. **Westwell**, *Campbeltown*
Surgeon-Lieutenant W. J. W. **Winthrop**, *Campbeltown*
Lieutenant Mark **Woodcock**, 3 Commando
Fusilier R. S. **Woodman**, 2 Commando

B. The Awards

The Victoria Cross

Lieutenant-Commander S. H. **Beattie**, Royal Navy*
Sergeant T. F. **Durrant**, Royal Engineers and 1 Commando (*posthumous*)
Lieutenant-Colonel A. C. **Newman**, Essex Regiment and 2 Commando
Commander R. E. D. **Ryder**, Royal Navy
Able Seaman W. A. **Savage**, Royal Naval Volunteer Reserve† (*posthumous*)

The Distinguished Service Order

Lieutenant T. W. **Boyd**, RNVR, ML 160
Major W. O. **Copland**, South Lancashire Regiment and 2 Commando
Lieutenant T. D. L. **Platt**, RNR, ML 447
Captain D. W. **Roy**, Camerons and 2 Commando

The Distinguished Service Cross

Sub-Lieutenant W. H. **Arnold**, ML 446
Lieutenant E. A. **Burt**, ML 262
Sub-Lieutenant L. A. **Clegg**, ML 307
Lieutenant D. M. C. **Curtis**, MGB 314
Lieutenant L. **Fenton**, ML 156
Lieutenant A. R. **Green**, MGB 314
Lieutenant C. S. B. **Irwin**, ML 270
Warrant Engineer W. H. **Locke**, *Campbeltown*
Sub-Lieutenant N. G. **Machin**, ML 156
Lieutenant N. R. **Nock**, ML 258
Lieutenant-Commander W. L. **Stephens**, ML 192
Sub-Lieutenant J. A. **Tait**, ML 160
Lieutenant N. T. B. **Tibbits**, *Campbeltown*

---

* Awarded 'in recognition not only of his own valour but also of that of the unnamed officers and men of a very gallant ship's company'.
† Awarded not only for his own gallantry 'but also for the valour shown by many others' of Coastal Forces.

Lieutenant C. W. **Wallach**, ML 270
Lieutenant N. B. H. **Wallis**, ML 307
Sub-Lieutenant R. T. C. **Worsley**, MGB 314
Sub-Lieutenant R. C. M. V. **Wynn**, MTB 74

The Military Cross

Lieutenant Gerard **Brett**, RUR and 12 Commando
Captain Michael **Burn**, KRRC and 2 Commando
Lieutenant S. W. **Chant**, Gordons and 5 Commando
Captain S. A. **Day**, Royal Signals and 2 Commando
Lieutenant W. W. **Etches**, Royal Warwick and 3 Commando
Captain R. K. **Montgomery**, RE, attached SS Brigade
Lieutenant C. W. B. **Purdon**, RUR and 12 Commando
Lieutenant J. M. **Roderick**, Essex Regiment and 2 Commando
Lieutenant R. O. C. **Swayne**, Herefordshire Regiment and 1 Commando
Captain A. F. A. J. **Terry**, attached 2 Commando
Lieutenant W. H. **Watson**, Black Watch and 2 Commando

The Conspicuous Gallantry Medal

Petty Officer L. S. **Lamb**, ML 160
Able Seaman D. N. **Lambert**, ML 447
Chief Motor Mechanic W. H. **Lovegrove**, MTB 74
Ordinary Seaman A. W. **Tew**, ML 446

The Distinguished Conduct Medal

Sergeant F. A. **Carr**, RE and 5 Commando
Sergeant W. A. **Challington**, Camerons and 2 Commando
Sergeant A. H. **Dockerill**, RA and 1 Commando
Troop Sergeant-Major G. E. **Haines**, East Surreys and 2 Commando
Sergeant D. C. **Randall**, Camerons and 2 Commando

The Distinguished Service Medal

Stoker L. H. **Ball**, ML 262
Motor Mechanic H. **Bracewell**, ML 443
Leading Seaman P. **Brady**, ML 443
Leading Seaman F. H. C. **Catton**, ML 270
Ordinary Telegraphist G. C. **Davidson**, ML 192
Able Seaman J. L. **Elliott**, ML 270
Petty Officer R. **Hambley**, ML 298
Petty Officer Motor Mechanic F. S. **Hemming**, MGB 314
Stoker L. A. **Holloway**, ML 270
Chief Engine-Room Artificer H. **Howard**, *Campbeltown*
Leading Seaman F. **McKee**, MGB 314

Able Seaman C. H. **Miller**, ML 177
Leading Motor Mechanic F. **Morris**, ML 160
Able Seaman T. A. D. **Moyes**, ML 156
Petty Officer W. J. **Newman**, *Campbeltown*
Able Seaman F. **Ormiston**, ML 446
Leading Seaman F. **Overton**, ML 447
Leading Signalman F. C. **Pike**, MGB 314
Able Seaman P. **Reeves**, ML 156
Ordinary Seaman J. S. **Roberts**, ML 307
Able Seaman F. A. **Smith**, MGB 314
Stoker Petty Officer R. F. **Underhill**, *Campbeltown*
Petty Officer Motor Mechanic C. D. **Walker**, ML 160
Ordinary Seaman F. J. W. **Woodward**, ML 307

The Military Medal

Sergeant R. **Bradley**, Royal Berkshire and 2 Commando
Private J. **Brown**, Argyll & Sutherland and 5 Commando
Sergeant R. H. **Butler**, Royal Norfolk and 1 Commando
Sergeant Stewart **Deery**, Royal Inniskilling Fusiliers and 12 Commando
Corporal E. **Douglas**, Camerons and 2 Commando
Private V. **Harding**, Gloucesters and 2 Commando
Lance-Corporal J. L. **Harrington**, RUR and 2 Commando
Private Peter **Honey**, Camerons and 2 Commando
Sergeant James **Johnson**, Gordons and 12 Commando
Sergeant Colin **Jones**, Camerons and 2 Commando
Sergeant A. C. **Searson**, Royal Sussex and 2 Commando
Lance-Corporal R. **Sims**, Somerset Light Infantry and 2 Commando
Corporal G. R. **Wheeler**, Royal Sussex and 2 Commando
Sergeant L. C. **Wickson**, Bedfordshire and Hertfordshire Regiment
and 2 Commando
Corporal A. F. **Woodiwiss**, The Queen's and 2 Commando

Mentioned in Dispatches

(*Those in italics were mentioned posthumously*)

*Sub-Lieutenant G. McNaughton **Baker**, ML 447*
*Stoker E. C. **Barber**, ML 457*
Stoker Petty Officer C. W. H. **Baxter**, *Campbeltown*
Able Seaman E. W. **Bennett**, *Campbeltown*
*Able Seaman H. E. **Bott**, Campbeltown*
Mr. J. **Bourne**, NAAFI, *Campbeltown*
*Lieutenant R. J. G. **Burtenshaw**, Cheshire Regiment and 5 Commando*
*Lieutenant H. S. **Chambers**, ML 447*
*Ordinary Seaman Douglas **Clear**, ML 298*
*Lieutenant T. A. M. **Collier**, ML 457*

Lieutenant M. C. **Denison,** Royal Fusiliers and 2 Commando
Private A. J. **Elliott,** The King's and 2 Commando
Lieutenant H. G. R. **Falconar,** ML 446
*Lieutenant C. H. C. **Gough,** Campbeltown*
*Private J. E. H. **Gwynne,** Camerons and 2 Commando*
*Ordinary Seaman G. H. **Hallett,** ML 192*
*Mr H. **Hargreaves,** Torpedo Gunner, Campbeltown*
*Lieutenant I. B. H. **Henderson,** ML 306*
Private W. A. **Holland,** Border Regiment and 2 Commando
Mr J. N. G. **Holman,** Press
(also awarded the French Croix de Guerre)
Lieutenant H. G. L. **Hopwood,** Essex Regiment and 2 Commando
Lance-Corporal A. **Howarth,** Grenadier Guards and 2 Commando
(also awarded the French Croix de Guerre)
*Ordinary Telegraphist A. H. **Jones,** Campbeltown*
Sergeant A. W. **King,** Royal Norfolk and 1 Commando
Leading Seaman W. E. F. **Leaney,** ML 262
*Leading Seaman Stafford **McKeown,** ML 262*
Gunner R. **Milne,** RA and 2 Commando
Able Seaman R. S. **Mitchell,** ML 177
Lieutenant R. F. **Morgan,** South Lancashire Regiment and 2 Commando
*Regimental Sergeant-Major A. **Moss,** Camerons and 2 Commando*
Leading Seaman L. J. **Newbold,** *Campbeltown*
*Captain W. H. **Pritchard,** MC, RE and SS Brigade*
Stoker Petty Officer D. C. **Pyke,** *Campbeltown*
(also awarded the French Croix de Guerre)
Engine-Room Artificer H. J. **Reay,** *Campbeltown*
(also awarded the French Croix de Guerre)
Leading Seaman S. W. **Rivett,** DSM, ML 268
*Lieutenant M. F. **Rodier,** ML 177*
Sub-Lieutenant Peter **Royal,** ML 443
Able Seaman Reginald **Rushworth,** ML 177
*Leading Seaman W. G. **Sargent,** ML 306*
Lieutenant E. M. M. **Shields,** ML 443
Lance-Corporal H. L. **Simpson,** Gordons and 2 Commando
*Lieutenant C. J. **Smalley,** Manchester Regiment and 2 Commando*
*Chief Motor Mechanic George **Snowball,** ML 192*
*Able Seaman A. R. C. **Stephens,** MGB 314*
Stoker H. A. **Stevens,** *Campbeltown*
Lieutenant J. F. **Stutchbury,** Gordons and 2 Commando
Private R. **Thompson,** Essex Regiment and 2 Commando
Lieutenant A. B. K. **Tillie,** ML 268
Sub-Lieutenant J. A. G. **Williamson,** ML 307
*Surgeon-Lieutenant W. J. W. **Winthrop,** Campbeltown*
Lance-Corporal A. **Young,** Gordons and 2 Commando

C. The Commandos' Targets in Detail

These are set out here in short form in their groups and sub-groups for reference purposes and as a matter of record. For identification of targets, see Figures 5, 6 and 7.

GROUP ONE. Under command of Captain E. S. Hodgson. In port ML column, to land at the Old Mole.

1*a* (ML 14). Demolition (Lieutenant R. O. C. Swayne and eight other ranks). The two most southerly lock gates and the swing bridge in the Southern Entrance (marked *B* on plan). Protection: Lieutenant J. Vanderwerve and four other ranks.

1*b* (ML 12). Demolition (Captain E. W. Bradley and six other ranks). Central lock gate in the Southern Entrance (*C*).

1*c* (ML 11). Demolition (Lieutenant P. Walton and four other ranks). Northern lock gate and lifting bridge of Southern Entrance (*D*). Protection: Second Lieutenant W. H. Watson and four other ranks.

1*d* (ML 13). Demolition (Lieutenant A. D. Wilson, Second Lieutenant P. Basset-Wilson and Lieutenant J. A. Bonvin and twelve other ranks). Boilerhouse, impounding station and hydraulic power station in Old Town (*Z*). Protection: Lieutenant J. B. Houghton (in ML 12).

1*e* (ML 10). Assault (Captain Hodgson, Lieutenant N. Oughtred and twelve other ranks). Destroy gun positions on East Jetty and form protective post at landward end.

1*f* (ML 9). Assault (Captain D. Birney, Lieutenant W. C. Clibborn and twelve other ranks). Destroy two gun positions on the Old Mole and form bridgehead at landward end.

1*g* (ML 11). Captain W. H. Pritchard, MC, and demolition control party for this Group.

GROUP TWO. Under command of Captain M. Burn. In starboard ML column, to land in the Old Entrance.

2*a* (ML 2). Demolition (Lieutenant M. Woodcock and eight other ranks). Two lock gates and the swing bridge in the Old Entrance (*G*) after withdrawal of parties to the northward. Protection: Lieutenant R. F. Morgan and four other ranks.

2*b*. Lieutenant-Colonel Newman's headquarters party.

2*c* (ML 4). Demolition (Lieutenant H. Pennington and four other ranks). Destroy swing bridge at northern end of Submarine Basin (*M*). Protection: Lieutenant M. Jenkins and four other ranks.

2*d* (ML 1). Assault (Captain M. Burn, Lieutenant T. G. Peyton and twelve other ranks). Destroy gun positions on towers adjacent to bridge *M* and form protective block. A further emergency task also detailed.

2*e* (MLs 5 and 6). Assault (Captain R. H. Hooper with Troop Sergeant-Major Haines and twenty-six other ranks). Special task party to destroy two gun positions north of Old Mole if occupied (*F*), silence any ships in the dry dock and come into HQ reserve.

GROUP THREE. Under command of Major W. O. Copland, with Captain R. K. Montgomery for demolition control. In HMS *Campbeltown*.

3*a*. Demolition. Lieutenant R. J. G. Burtenshaw and six other ranks to destroy the outer caisson should *Campbeltown* not succeed; Lieutenant S. W. Chant and four other ranks to destroy the pumping station (*H*); and Lieutenant C. J. Smalley and four other ranks to destroy the adjacent winding-hut. Protection: Lieutenant H. G. L. Hopwood.

3*b*. Demolition. Lieutenant Gerard Brett and six other ranks to destroy the inner caisson (*L*); and Lieutenant C. W. B. Purdon and four other ranks to destroy its adjacent winding-hut. These related tasks under Lieutenant W. W. Etches. Protection: Lieutenant M. C. Denison.

3*c*. Assault (Lieutenant J. Roderick, Lieutenant J. Stutchbury and twelve other ranks). Destroy four gun positions immediately east of outer caisson, destroy any guards in the area of the underground oil tanks and form protective block; drop incendiaries down ventilators of oil tanks if opportunity offers.

3*d*. Assault (Captain D. Roy, Lieutenant J. D. Proctor and twelve other ranks). Destroy gun positions on roof of pumping-house, form bridgehead at bridge *G* to cover withdrawal of parties to the northward and engage any hostile vessels in Submarine Basin.

Bomber Support Programme

First phase. Ten Whitleys from 4 Group to attack Target A (area of the Normandie Dock) from 11.30 pm to 12.30 am.

Second phase. Twenty-five Whitleys from 4 Group to attack Target A from 12.30 am to 1.20 am.

Third phase. Twenty-five Wellingtons from 1 Group to attack Target B (northern end of Penhouet Basin and the adjacent shipbuilding slips, 1800 yards north of the Old Entrance) from 1.20 am to 4 am.

PAN GRAND STRATEGY SERIES

COCKLESHELL HEROES

C. E. Lucas Phillips

PAN BOOKS £6.99

In October 1942, chief of Combined Operations Vice-Admiral Lord Louis Mountbatten unveiled the outline plan for Operation Frankton – destined to become one of the bravest, most courageous and imaginative raids of the entire war.

In December 1942 the plan was put into action. Ten Royal Marines launched a daring attack by canoe on enemy shipping lying in the docks of Bordeaux – a hazardous and successful offensive which only two survived . . .

'A legendary wartime exploit . . . the outstanding Commando raid of the war. You can't stop reading'
Observer

'As a story of human courage, the story of the Cockleshell Heroes will live for generations'
Manchester Evening News

PAN GRAND STRATEGY SERIES

TRENCH WARFARE 1914–1918

The Live and Let Live System

Tony Ashworth

PAN BOOKS £7.99

The story of the great battles of the First World War has been told by historians, journalists and others. The shock and slaughter of the Somme, Verdun and Passchendaele, where soldiers endured unimaginable casualties with amazing courage, is a major theme of most books. Large-scale battles, however, comprised the smaller part of soldiers' total time in combat. For 90 per cent of that time soldiers fought small-scale battles which took place between and throughout large battles. These small conflicts were violent, continual and involved complex weaponry and specialized tactics. Yet, during small battles, soldiers could and often did make choices not possible during large ones. From these choices, there evolved between enemies a curious culture of live and let live which constrained the war culture of kill or be killed in fundamental ways. It was a culture that was spontaneous, unplanned yet ongoing throughout the war, and it gave soldiers some control over conditions of their existence.

The trench warfare culture emerged from a context of mistrust between enemies, dug in within yards of each other and armed to the teeth, where both were rewarded for aggression and punished for the lack of it. It is a story which has not hitherto been told.

All Pan Books are available at your local bookshop or newsagent, or can be ordered direct from the publisher. Indicate the number of copies required and fill in the form below.

Send to: Macmillan General Books C.S.
               Book Service By Post
               PO Box 29, Douglas I-O-M
               IM99 1BQ

or phone: 01624 675137, quoting title, author and credit card number.

or fax: 01624 670923, quoting title, author, and credit card number.

or Internet: http:www.bookpost.co.uk

Please enclose a remittance* to the value of the cover price plus 75 pence per book for post and packing. Overseas customers please allow £1.00 per copy for post and packing.

*Payment may be made in sterling by UK personal cheque, Eurocheque, postal order, sterling draft or international money order, made payable to Book Service By Post.

Alternatively by Access/Visa/MasterCard.

Card No.

Expiry Date

Signature _____

Applicable only in the UK and BFPO addresses.

While every effort is made to keep prices low, it is sometimes necessary to increase prices at short notice. Pan Books reserve the right to show on covers and charge new retail prices which may differ from those advertised in the text or elsewhere.

NAME AND ADDRESS IN BLOCK CAPITAL LETTERS PLEASE

Name _____

Address _____

_____

_____

_____

8/95

Please allow 28 days for delivery.
Please tick box if you do not wish to receive any additional information. ☐